**THE PARK
LEARNING CENTRE**
The Park, Cheltenham
Gloucestershire GL50 2RH
Telephone: 01242 714333

UNIVERSITY OF
GLOUCESTERSHIRE
at Cheltenham and Gloucester

NORMAL LOAN

654 4/2011

*En*Gendering AIDS

Deconstructing Sex, Text and Epidemic

Tamsin Wilton

SAGE Publications
London • Thousand Oaks • New Delhi

SAGE Publications Ltd
6 Bonhill Street
London EC2A 4PU

SAGE Publications Inc.
2455 Teller Road
Thousand Oaks, California 91320

SAGE Publications India Pvt Ltd
32, M-Block Market
Greater Kailash – I
New Delhi 110 048

British Library Cataloguing in Publication data

A catalogue record for this book is available from the British Library.

ISBN 0 7619 5382 5
ISBN 0 7619 5383 3 (pbk)

Library of Congress catalog card number 96–071790

Typeset by Mayhew Typesetting, Rhayader, Powys
Printed in Great Britain by The Cromwell Press Ltd,
Broughton Gifford, Melksham, Wiltshire

For Lesley Doyal, teacher and friend

Contents

The most important work for saving lives must take place in the minefield of representation

Tessa Boffin

the language you speak is made up of words that are killing you

Monique Wittig *Les guérillères*

Acknowledgements

A book like this cannot be produced in isolation. Questions concerning the social aspects of AIDS, pornography, representation, gender and sexuality are (rightly) subject to lively debate, and my own ideas have developed in energetic discussion over many years with many people. I could not have written this book without that kind of interchange, and I am grateful to Diane Richardson, Lisa Adkins, Lesley Doyal, Dede Liss, Frankie Lynch, Jeffrey Weeks, Liz Frost, Norma Daykin, Sue O'Sullivan, Cécile Vélu, Ian Warwick and Cindy Patton as well as students on my 1994 Master's option, 'Representing Women', all of whom have influenced my thinking over the years. Thanks are due to Fiona Stewart of the Institute for the Study of Sexually Transmissible Diseases at La Trobe University, Melbourne, and to Nicola Gavey of the Department of Psychology at the University of Auckland, for being so generous in sharing their own important research with me. I am also very grateful to Professor Susan Kippax of Macquarie University, Sydney, for sharing her work with me and for making it possible for me to attend the third annual 'HIV, AIDS and Society' Conference and to Professor Doreen Rosenthal, Dr Anthony Smith and everyone at the Institute for the Study of Sexually Transmitted Diseases at La Trobe for their hospitality and their generosity in talking with me about their research. Special thanks to La Trobe's Marg Hay, to many students on my 'Social Aspects of HIV/AIDS' module at the University of the West of England, and to the Leicester Lesbian, Gay and Bisexual Community Resource Centre for adding to my collection of safer sex materials. Although every effort has been made to identify the copyright owners of images reproduced here, this has not always been possible. If copyright owners contact us, we will be glad to remedy our omissions.

My son, Tom Coveney, was forthright in his assessment of AIDS educational materials intended for young people, and Stuart Williams taught me much about the life-enhancing properties of gay porn before his death with AIDS. It saddens me that my thanks to Benny Henriksson of RFSL in Stockholm, whose work in organizing the first Scandinavian Conference on Safer Sex was an important early stimulus to my thinking in this area, must also be recorded posthumously, since Benny died with AIDS as I finished writing this.

I would like to acknowledge practical support from the Faculty of Health and Community Studies (now the Faculty of Health and Social

Care) at the University of the West of England, Bristol, for buying me out of my teaching obligations for fifteen days to enable me to finish work on this book, and for supporting my travels in search of knowledge!

Introduction: A Note on Terminology

The central argument of this book is that representational and discursive practices are important in the context of the epidemic of HIV infection because they shape our response to this new health threat very directly, and in ways which are not always easy to recognize or amenable to change. It behoves me then to be punctilious about my own practices as a writer, to make explicit the political nature of the choices that I make about language, and to write reflexively and self-critically. I hope I have done this, and would hope that critical readers will alert me to instances of language use in this book which they find problematic or offensive. Some of my key decisions warrant explanation here.

In referring to the epidemic I use varied terminology, 'the epidemic of HIV infection', 'HIV/AIDS' or 'AIDS epidemic', all with specific meanings. HIV (Human Immunodeficiency Virus) is the virus which damages the immune system to such an extent that infected individuals eventually go on to develop AIDS (Acquired Immune Deficiency Syndrome). AIDS itself is not a disease, nor can it be transmitted from person to person. Rather, it describes a condition of chronic immune system depletion which leaves the body vulnerable to a host of opportunistic infections, including cancers, fungal infections, viruses, protozoa, etc. The clinical diagnosis of AIDS is subject to continual redefinition (for example, the Centers for Disease Control definition of AIDS was expanded in response to complaints that the original definition excluded several conditions specific to women with HIV infection), and many clinicians tend to speak of 'HIV disease' or 'HIV-related diseases/conditions' rather than of AIDS.

Additionally, infection with HIV can cause clinical problems quite apart from damage to the immune system. In some individuals it may give rise to drenching night sweats or a brief 'flu'-like episode (generally around the time of infection). The virus may cross the blood–brain barrier and cause encephalitises (brain inflammations) leading to disturbances of emotion/mood or dementia. It may cause neurological damage, with difficulty in coordination, balance, etc. It is preventing infection with HIV which represents the initial health emergency, and has become the focus of health education campaigns worldwide. The second health emergency is to prevent the development of severe immune system deterioration in people with HIV infection, and the third is to develop therapies to prevent, control or eradicate the many opportunistic infections in immune-compromised individuals.

AIDS may be a relatively incoherent clinical term, but its *cultural* significance is enormous. The word 'AIDS' is overburdened with proliferating and always contingent meanings, encompassing notions of clinical disease, social dis/ease, contamination, exclusion, discrimination, hostility, economic/material inequalities, religious doctrine, political expediency, moralism/morality, sexuality, deviance, criminality, risk, blame, disfigurement and death. This is a far from exhaustive list because the full list could fill a book by itself, and it is this complex of social, cultural, political and clinical meanings which I take to be encompassed in the word 'AIDS'. The *social construction* of the epidemic, in other words. In this book, I use 'HIV infection/disease' to refer to the clinical entity, 'AIDS' to refer to the epidemic as socially constructed, and 'HIV/AIDS' when I want to refer to both.

Sexual identity is a protean, shifting set of meanings and is always contingent on social, cultural, material and geographic location. When I refer to 'lesbians' or to 'gay men' I am referring only to those groups of people who have access to a self-consciously lesbian or gay identity and choose to adopt/perform such an identity. Even within this group there are profound dissimilarities, and I have tried to be as specific as possible, differentiating between, for example, men on the urban gay scene in Western industrial nations and isolated gay men who, because of age, disability, poverty, geographical, ethnic or class location, do not partake in that scene. 'Homosexual' is a term coined by the (pseudo)science of sexology and, as such, is deeply implicated in the pathologization of lesbian and gay people. I generally avoid using it, except where context specifies its use. 'Homosex' and 'heterosex', on the other hand seem to me to be unambiguous and useful shorthand ways of denoting 'sexual activity between persons of the same sex' or 'sexual activity between persons of different sexes' respectively, and I use them accordingly.

The transmission of HIV related to drug use is, again, not as straightforward as some would have us believe. It is only the sharing of uncleaned injecting equipment between already-infected and uninfected user which poses a risk, and this takes place in highly specific circumstances. Many recreational drugs are not illegal (alcohol, nicotine, caffeine), and many illegal drugs are not commonly injected (marijuana, ecstasy, LSD), whilst many substances which are injected are legitimate medical treatments (insulin, Factor 8). It is vital to distinguish between the drug user who is at risk of HIV and the drug user who isn't. Additionally, the phrase 'intravenous drug (ab)user' is problematic, both because the notion of 'abuse' carries pejorative moralistic overtones and because it refers so specifically to the practice of injecting into a vein. Much drug injecting, whether clinical or recreational, is intramuscular or into the subcutaneous tissue ('skin-popping'), activities which, in the appropriate circumstances, are as risky for HIV transmission as injecting into a vein. In order to be as clear as possible I use the phrase 'injecting street drug user' to describe those users whose drug use may expose them to HIV infection.

The question of how to describe the so-called 'Third World' and 'First World' countries, always problematic, has become more so with the disintegration of the Soviet bloc. Phrases which adhere to a progress-narrative paradigm, such as 'developed' and 'underdeveloped' or 'developing' imply that the 'underdeveloped' nations should hurry up and catch up with the 'developed' nations, and fail to recognize that the 'developed' nations are only as wealthy and technologically advanced as they are *because* they have pillaged and continue to pillage the resources of countries exploited during colonialism. Such language also fails to question the costs of technological development, costs which include pollution, smoking and obesity and possible global environmental catastrophe and which suggest that industrialization may not unproblematically be held up as worthy of international emulation. It is also increasingly the case that the so-called 'industrialized' nations may more fittingly be thought of as 'post-industrial', since the growth of international capitalism, with its global markets and multinational corporations, has resulted in mass unemployment and the development of post-Fordist labour conditions in the West and the so-called 'greening of labour', the dispersal by multi-national manufacturers of manufacturing processes to poorer countries where wage bills, health and safety legislation and pollution controls are below the standards achieved in the West.

I have found this probably the most difficult problem to resolve, partly due to the dramatic shifts taking place as I write in the status of many central European countries, the former Soviet Union, etc. I have (somewhat arbitrarily) chosen to refer to 'the West' as shorthand for the former colonial powers and other advanced European countries plus those massive former colonies where white colonists succeeded in all but exterminating the indigent people (the United States, Canada, New Zealand and Australia) and whose economic and political power is considerable. Where so-called Third World countries are mentioned, I usually refer to them geographically (sub-Saharan Africa, the Far East, etc.), since lumping them together erases important economic, demographic, geographical, cultural and religious differences which are generally significant in the context of HIV/AIDS.

Finally, I do not use the term 'risk group'. This is because categorizing certain groups of people as 'at risk' implies that those outside such groups are somehow *not* at risk. It is also because the accepted taxonomic conventions whereby individuals are assigned to such 'risk groups' are misleading. Injecting street drug users, for example, will be presumed 'at risk' from their drug use, rather than from sexual transmission, and, if HIV positive, will go on record as infected through drug use *not* through sex. Similarly, HIV positive gay men will be assumed to have acquired HIV from male partners, even if they have had sex with female partners as well.

1
Sex, Texts, Power

Those of us involved in the struggle against HIV/AIDS are an odd lot. Inclined to respond with enthusiasm to the sight of a used condom, carefully knotted, lying on the ground (a much-prized indicator that someone, somewhere, is practising safer sex) and to spend our leisure time encouraging our friends to talk about sex and drugs, we view the world from a peculiar (in both senses of the word) perspective. I spend much of my time wondering, not why the advent of AIDS gave rise to panic, but why there is so *little* panic. In my more pessimistic moments I am inclined to entertain friends and colleagues with scenarios of global economic catastrophe, the collapse of health care infrastructures – the problem of AIDS is, according to Dr Donald McDonald, 'bigger than the Public Health Service' (Brandt, 1985: 188) – and unimaginable consequences for human rights, civil liberties and women's rights (in particular women's reproductive rights).[1]

The single aspect of AIDS which I find most disturbing is that the overdeveloped nations of the West have managed to develop a colossal and expensive AIDS industry, comprising governmental and non-governmental agencies, academics, health educators, scientists, social scientists, medical professionals, writers, publishers, journals, newsletters, conferences and symposia, which has almost entirely failed to intervene effectively in the social, economic and political infrastructures which we know to be instrumental in the continuing rapid growth of the pandemic. 'AIDS', as Allan Brandt puts it, 'makes explicit, as few diseases could, the complex interaction of social, cultural and biological forces' and 'demonstrates how economics and politics cannot be separated from disease' (Brandt, 1985: 199–204). Yet, rather than developing appropriate and wide-ranging interventions informed by this awareness, Western governments have tended to cling obdurately to health policies which stress individual (rather than collective) responsibility for health, and to kowtow to self-appointed guardians of public morality such as fundamentalists of various religions. The reactionary and outmoded emphasis on individual responsibility for health is expedient as a cost-cutting exercise in the face of ever-increasing health care costs,[2] but also appeases (and is ultimately rooted in) a moralistic and victim-blaming model of disease:

> There remain those who believe fear of disease will lead to a higher morality . . .
> To those who subscribe to this belief, the message is clear: the way to control sexually transmitted disease is not through medical means but rather through moral rectitude. A disease such as AIDS is controlled by controlling individual conduct . . . The current trend in health policy is to accept this model of disease

and to apply it to a myriad of other diseases, to reduce the emphasis on social or external determinants of disease and health, and to stress individual responsibility. (Brandt, 1985: 203)

Although at first sight the notion of making changes in sexual and street drug injecting behaviours appears exemplary of the model of individual responsibility, this assumes a naively asocial model of individual psychology. Rather, both the *initial adoption* and the *continued practice* of safer sexual and injecting behaviours is intimately bound up with social factors such as gender, 'race', socio-economic class, geographical location and kin/peer relations, and with related socio-psychological factors such as self-esteem and sexual identity, and it is with some of these factors that this book is concerned.

Who are the women in AIDS?

It is becoming common to read that women's needs are not being properly identified or met in the context of HIV/AIDS (Berer with Ray, 1993; Squire, 1993; Richardson, 1989; Panos Institute, 1990a; Patton, 1994). This assertion of failure to meet women's health care needs is present more generally in feminist literature on health (Miles, 1991; Graham, 1993; Doyal, 1995). It is, of course, the very existence of feminist writers, and of a specifically oppositional feminist discourse which prioritizes women, that makes such assertions possible, just as it is the existence of gay liberation movements and of a queer discourse in resistance to homophobia that makes it possible to identify the widespread failure to meet the needs of gay men (King, 1993; Kayal, 1993).

It is undoubtedly the case that the HIV/AIDS-related needs of women are marginalized, ignored and denied, and that women's subjugation to men is both reflected in and reinforced by the ways in which the pandemic has been gendered. In this, however, women are not unique. The social group whose HIV/AIDS-related needs *are* adequately met *does not exist*. Whether in the field of health education, health promotion, health care, social care or the provision of resources, questions of morality, political expediency, religious dogma or ideological hegemony are generally given precedence over preventing the transmission of HIV or improving the survival time and well-being of people living with HIV or AIDS.

In the context of HIV/AIDS (very much a *heterosexually* transmitted condition), deconstructing the gendering of the pandemic is important for two reasons. Firstly, because large numbers of women have been and continue to be needlessly infected with HIV, become ill with HIV-related conditions faster than comparable men, and die more quickly than men once diagnosed with AIDS (Califia, 1995; Bury, 1994; ACT UP/NY Women and AIDS Book Group, 1990). Secondly, because the gendering of AIDS has profound implications for the ability of *all* people – men as well as women, straight as well as gay – to protect themselves from infection and to live well with HIV or AIDS if already infected. The discursive construction of AIDS intersects with and nuances a range of pre-existing discursive 'packages' of gender and the erotic, as well as of 'race', class and disease. In so doing, it is instrumental in the socio-cultural constitution of 'women', but also of 'men', 'heterosexual' and 'homosexual'.

> Discourse on AIDS – medical and social policy writing, political rhetoric, media representations and public talk about HIV and AIDS – tends to ignore, sideline or pathologize women. The discourse is both under- and over-gendered. The categories of 'women' often seem like screens onto which other social conflicts – around for instance 'race', sexuality and poverty – are being projected in disguised forms. (Squire, 1993: 5)

It is important to deconstruct not only the 'woman' of gendered AIDS discourse, but the co-constitution of 'not-woman' so produced. It is also important to identify the manipulation of gender polarity in the constitution of other presumptive polarities – 'race', class, sexuality, etc. For example, some commentators have suggested that the discursive gendering of AIDS incorporates into the textual/ideological 'feminine' any and every 'other' according to an internal logic whereby the *subject* of AIDS discursive production – the producer of discourse, the owner of the discursive 'gaze' – is masculinized and the *object* feminized. Thus not only are gay men, lesbians, people of colour, poor people, haemophiliacs and 'junkies' all feminized, so too are those living with HIV and AIDS (Juhasz, 1993).

Cindy Patton suggests that AIDS discourse is organized within and has given rise to what she terms the 'queer paradigm' (Patton, 1985; 1994: 19), whereby people living with HIV/AIDS or *vulnerable* to HIV infection ('risk groups', in the invidious and unhelpful parlance of establishment statisticians) are constituted as queer. Although there is, as Treichler (1988a: 261) comments, 'evidence that in some respects [gay men] do fill the role (of contaminated other) that women, especially prostitutes, have played in the past', it is clear from what we know of the history of the sexually transmitted diseases (STDs) (Llewellyn-Jones, 1985; Brandt, 1985) that the queering of the other identified by Patton derives from (and clearly intersects with) the feminizing of the other which is so marked a feature both of the project of imperial colonialism (McClintock, 1995) and of the social construction of STDs. I suggest that it is more helpful to interrogate the 'queer paradigm' as a specific manifestation of a more general gendered paradigm and to identify the probable consequences of that gendering.

One glaringly obvious characteristic of AIDS discourse is its erasure of heterosexual men from the discursive field. This is inevitable within the intellectual matrix of a model of 'gender' organized quite precisely around the invisible and unproblematized *norm* of heteromasculinity (see below pp. 95–100), but has very negative consequences for health promotion. In particular, the negative consequences of masculine socialization and of the imperative to demonstrate competence in a restrictively narrow range of male-performativity behaviours, go largely unrecognized. Swedish sex educator Erik Centerwall has warned that boys and young men experience emotional isolation and that the process of developing a heterosexual male identity is a problematic one:

> The message has often been that male sexuality is wicked and that men are dirty and inconsiderate. This message may also be a male self-experience. It is a negative sexuality which makes me a man in the eyes of other men. The wicked urge becomes something that creates identity. (in Berer with Ray, 1993: 203)

In the context of gendered relations of power, a gender/sexual identity which achieves coherence around a 'wicked urge' is clearly troubling; in the context of preventing the further spread of an invariably fatal sexually transmitted disease it becomes profoundly disturbing.

Is HIV a sexually transmitted disease?

This book focuses on the sexual transmission of HIV and draws comparisons between the social construction of AIDS and historical shifts in the social construction of syphilis and gonorrhoea. But to what extent is it accurate to present HIV as an STD? While HIV is capable of being transmitted through specific kinds of sexual contact, it may also be transmitted 'vertically' (from HIV positive mother to infant during pregnancy or delivery), or by direct blood/blood contact (by receiving infected blood or blood products during medical procedures or by the sharing of street drug injecting equipment between HIV-infected and HIV-uninfected users without proper cleaning procedures).

It is probably more useful and accurate to think of it primarily as a blood-borne infection, similar in transmission routes to hepatitis. 'To include in the category [of STD] those diseases which "can be [sexually] transmitted" makes the category so large as to be meaningless' (Wellings, 1983). Moreover, to present HIV as an STD is to disregard other potential transmission scenarios, with possibly fatal consequences, and to locate HIV in an already stigmatized category of diseases. Since HIV/AIDS is in any case profoundly stigmatized and stigmatizing, to inflexibly categorize it as an STD would compound an already grave problem. Nevertheless, although HIV should not be presented simply as a sexually transmitted disease, the principal mode of transmission remains (hetero)sexual (WHO, cited in Panos Institute, 1990a). Indeed, with increasing use of procedures to protect the blood supply, with wider use of needle exchange schemes for injecting street drug users and better dissemination of information on cleaning injection equipment, other modes of transmission can be expected to decrease. Inevitably the proportion of cases of infection due to sexual transmission is growing and will continue to do so. The only category other than sexual transmission which can confidently be expected to increase is vertical transmission to infants, since increasing numbers of infected women will inevitably result in increasing numbers of infected infants (Panos Institute, 1989; 1992; WHO, 1994).

In order to understand the nature of the pandemic, and to get an accurate idea of the extent and rate of growth, AIDS must be seen at a *global* level. However, local social and economic factors have a sharp impact on the *initial* epidemiology of HIV infection over quite small geographical areas. Thus, for many reasons, it was possible for heterosexuals in the West to believe, for a few years at least, that HIV was in some way associated with sexual contact between men, or with the urban gay male lifestyle (Davies et al., 1993; Panos Institute, 1990b). A lethal combination of denial, racism and homophobia ensured that this foolish misunderstanding became widespread and long-lived, *even though* it was very soon clear that, in most countries around the world, heterosex was overwhelmingly the commonest means of transmission. The white racist imaginary simply (and familiarly) constituted the epidemiological trend in the United States (where the majority infected with HIV were and still are gay men) as the global norm and declared that the (putatively *abnormal*) high rate of heterosexual transmission in the so-called Third World – especially sub-Saharan Africa – was due to pre-existing abnormalities, failures or pathologies among the (black) indigenous populations. Thus it was suggested that black African men refused to admit to homosexual practices, engaged in abnormally violent heterosex, were uncontrollably promiscuous, frequently used prostitutes and had multiple wives (Wilton 1992a; Panos Institute, 1990a). Thus, just as heterosexual scientists had argued that it was something about *being gay* which resulted in large numbers of gay men becoming infected, white scientists argued that it was something about *being black* which resulted in the high rate of heterosexual transmission in some African countries.

Current estimates suggest that over 75 per cent of HIV infections occur through heterosex, with the sharing of street drug equipment, vertical transmission, sex between men and receipt of infected blood/blood products *together* accounting for another 25 per cent (WHO, cited in Panos Institute, 1990b).

The extremely long asymptomatic period of HIV infection means that its epidemiology is very slow to reflect change. In the industrialized West, therefore, it remains the case that the groups hardest hit by HIV/AIDS are gay communities, and that the socio-political ramifications of homophobia continue to deny those communities the resources they need, especially in terms of health education (King, 1993). Nor should it be supposed that AIDS-associated homophobia is a problem solely for lesbians and gay men. The ideological intersections of gender and sexuality which are so directly expressed in homophobic discourse impact on the lives of *all* members of societies organized around the heterosexual imperative.

It would be both arrogant and foolish of me to write about the intersections of sex and gender as though they were universal or even directly comparable across cultures. Such intersections, and the meanings which accrue to them, are culturally and historically specific to a fine degree. For example I know, from my own experience, that there is not one 'lesbian community' in Bristol, England, but several, and that language, behaviours and dress which would be appropriate in one might be quite unacceptable in another. In other words, the intersections of sex and gender as they coalesce around the performance 'lesbian' produce (and are in turn produced by) very different sets of meanings among different groups of women in one middle-sized city. For this reason I have chosen to focus most closely on HIV/AIDS health education in those countries whose culture is most familiar to me, the Anglophone nation states which trace their roots back to British imperialist expansion.

It could be argued that to do this is to risk colluding with or reinforcing an already endemic cultural ethnocentrism/Anglocentrism, a risk which I suspect is unavoidable. However, by critiquing and problematizing the representational practices of health educators in this privileged group of nations, I hope also to subvert the status as unquestioned global 'norm' – or worse, as developmental role-model – which those nations generally appropriate for themselves. In the last few years of the twentieth century it is surely timely to question the progress made by these most privileged nations towards achieving the health-promotional goals laid down by the World Health Organization in its *Health for All by the Year 2,000* agenda (Abel-Smith, 1994).

Why look at pictures in a crisis?

In the midst of a terrible global pandemic which shows no signs of slowing, and which threatens to cause economic and social chaos as well as the suffering and untimely death of millions, it might seem self-indulgent to devote an entire book to deconstructing representational practices. What have the work of Francophone lesbian feminist writer Monique Wittig or the Holocaust got to do with saving lives in the time of AIDS? Why waste time tracing the historical attitude to female prostitutes in the great European epidemics of syphilis in the late Middle Ages? Why problematize the obviously successful gay community campaigns to promote safer sex? Surely this is fiddling while not just Rome but the entire planet burns?

If I did not believe that questions of representation are of crucial importance in the struggle against AIDS I would have written a different book. But representational practices both reflect and *construct* social and psychological 'reality', and the representation of AIDS has profound consequences for the impact of the epidemic.

The epidemic of HIV infection does not move through the human population of our planet as through a neutral biological field in the way that a purely biomedical model of disease might suggest. It has long been recognized that social factors such as socio-economic class, geographical location or occupation exert a significant influence on who becomes ill, why, how and at what age, and on their chances of recovery (Townsend et al., 1988; Hart, 1985; Abel-Smith, 1994). It would indeed be surprising if the human immunodeficiency virus were an exception to this, and clearly it is not. AIDS is rapidly becoming a disease of poverty both globally, in its observable impact on countries impoverished by colonialist exploitation, and locally, in its tendency to affect disproportionate numbers of the poorest people even in the rich nations of the industrialized West (Panos Institute 1992).

It has always been the case that gender is among the most significant of social factors in its impact on health and life chances (Doyal, 1995; Graham, 1993), and that the oppression of women results in their being numbered disproportionately among the poor. Feminist writers have also identified a tendency to intransigent sexism in biomedical discourse (and in health care practice) whereby the biomedical 'norm' is characteristically male and the female is constructed as an inadequate, faulty or *inherently pathological* departure from the male norm (Homans, 1985; Ehrenreich and English, 1979). Such discursive constitutions can have very direct effects on the provision of health care, and on the abilities of women (in particular) to protect and maintain their health. As the newly emerging market in men's health magazines demonstrates, the impact of gender on the health of men themselves is also now being recognized (see, for example, East Midlands Men's Health Network, 1994).

In the time of AIDS it is already abundantly clear that the cultural and social implications of gendered relations of power have alarming implications for our ability to prevent the sexual transmission of HIV (Mann, 1993; Berer with Ray, 1993; Patton, 1994; Doyal et al., 1994).

Sex and (con)text

Integral to the maintenance and reproduction of gender – as a set of social roles, as a socio-political institution and as an ideology – are those practices of cultural production which re/present male, female, lesbian, gay, heterosexual.[3] Texts are instrumental in the constitution of subjectivity (we decide what kind of woman or man we are in response to information about masculinity or femininity available in our culture, and most of that information is in the form of texts), and of social norms and institutions. A text, in this context, is any artefact which carries meanings. Thus a body may be a text; meanings may be written onto it by means of garments, cosmetics, perfumes, scars, surgery (liposuction, breast augmentation/ reduction, face lifts, etc.), shaving, plucking, cutting and styling the hair, colouring the nails, lips, hair or skin, dieting, overeating, piercing (of ears, nipples, navel, labia, nose, etc.), exercising, moving in a particular way. Since we locate both gender and the erotic primarily and precisely in the body, what we say with this body-text largely concerns our gender identity and our sexual identity. As Judith Butler (1990, 1994) suggests, we *perform* our gender and sexuality. This performance is both a performing *on* and a performing *with* bodies. In the context of the sexual transmission of HIV the body-as-text has particular significance, as does the representation of bodies. As I hope to make clear, the way in which gender and sexuality are represented has important implications for individuals' ability to prevent the sexual transmission of HIV by practising safer sex. Additionally, the way bodies-with-AIDS are represented impacts directly on the ability of people with HIV infection or with AIDS to sustain rich and satisfying sexual lives.

Text and epidemic

It cannot be stated too often or too clearly that health education and promotion are *all we have* in the struggle against the HIV pandemic. It is unlikely that a vaccine will be developed in the foreseeable future, since HIV mutates so rapidly (as much as a thousand times more rapidly than the influenza virus) that it presents medical researchers with a 'moving target' (Brandt, 1985; British Broadcasting Corporation, 1995). Even if such a vaccine were to be developed in the near future it is important to recognize that the pharmaceuticals industry and medical industry are dominated by the profit motive. A vaccine against HIV would be a licence to print money, so it is unlikely that it would be cheap enough and widely enough available to make much impact on the rate of spread of HIV. Furthermore, although researchers are continually developing more sophisticated treatments for the opportunistic infections associated with AIDS, such treatments are beyond the reach of all but the privileged inhabitants of the very wealthiest nations (and, with current changes in health care policies, may not be affordable even within the wealthiest nations for very much longer). The *only* strategy available to us is to instigate and maintain a worldwide shift in sexual behaviour. Such a shift demands health-promoting transformations in the social and cultural infrastructure of each nation (see below pp. 39–52), the magnitude of which seems daunting.

Effective health *education*, a key instrument in the HIV/AIDS health promotional enterprise, presents a less daunting prospect than total social transformation. There are health educational organizations in most countries, whether located in the statutory, voluntary or commercial sector, and a substantial body of experience has been amassed concerning good and effective health educational practice. That experience has not always been put to good use in the struggle against HIV/AIDS, all too often being superseded by a reactionary political agenda. It was depressing, for example, to witness the British government resorting to techniques *known to be ineffective* in its early AIDS education campaigns. Television adverts showing monumental masonry crashing to the ground amid wreaths of dry ice, followed by a wordy and extremely negative leaflet sent out to every household, were (expensive) examples of what was already known to be poor health educational practice (Naidoo and Wills, 1994).

For the foreseeable future, then, health education will remain our primary tool in the struggle against AIDS. As a body of *texts*, the representational practices of health education are instrumental in the discursive constitution of gender and sexuality and, as such, should be subject to informed and vigorous critical deconstruction. That is my aim here.

On Catch 22

It is an inevitable consequence of interrogating systematic oppressions such as gender or 'race' that the resultant critique partakes (in however oppositional a way) of the very discourse which it was intended to disrupt. In particular, political activist initiatives directed at disrupting gender and sexuality – initiatives such as feminism, gay liberation, queer activism – tend to reify and reproduce, by their very opposition, the taxonomic categories they seek to disturb (Wilton, 1994a; Butler, 1990). Judith Butler has been especially concerned to highlight the theoretical and political problems this unintended reification may lead to:

> Foucault points out that juridical systems of power *produce* the subjects they subsequently come to represent . . . And the feminist subject turns out to be discursively constituted by the very political system that is supposed to facilitate its emancipation. (Butler, 1990: 2; emphasis in original)

Within feminist discourse this tendency has led to a specific construction of woman-as-victim-of-patriarchy which is deeply problematic in the context of a wider project of empowerment. It is, after all, difficult to identify the specifics of women's oppression without thereby contributing to the discursive constitution of femininity as frail, weak, vulnerable – precisely the attributes traditionally assigned to femininity in heteropatriarchal discourse. The risk I run in this book is of producing that which I wish to eradicate – a discursively constituted 'woman' (and this includes gay men, for reasons explained below) who is powerless and intrinsically a victim, and a hegemonic regime of gender and sexuality (a regime which I term *heteropolarity*) which is monolithic and invulnerable.

I recognize that reading is an active process and that there are very real limits to the degree to which the author of any text may guarantee (or even direct) the intended readings of that text. However, I would ask that this book be read from a position of specific awareness. Awareness that the hegemonic ideology which I am describing is everywhere subject to discredit, to subversion, to disobedience, to attempted transformation. Women (and men) are not merely the objects of hegemonic discourse (nor, of course, are its supposed subjects ever only its subjects), nor do they respond with passive obedience to its ideological, social or political constraints. It is in the nature of hegemony that it is produced in contestation, that its always precarious status is maintained as much in opposition as in collusion, that it may never be guaranteed nor static.

At this point it is instructive to consider the ironies which attend the
history of this book. Originally commissioned by British academic publishers Taylor and Francis, it ran into difficulties when they refused to
publish any of the illustrations depicting sex acts or nudity.[4] Given that the
need for explicitness in safer sex educational materials is one of the key
arguments of the book, the irony struck me as fairly acute. The fact that a
few remarkably bland images safely tucked away between the pages of an
academic book give rise to such anxiety is a timely reminder of the social,
cultural and institutional forces which so powerfully militate against the
promotion of sexual safety.

Conclusion

It is as true to say that those oppressed/objectified by hegemonic AIDS
discourse have demonstrated resilience, revolutionary energy and survival
skills as that they have been oppressed. By engaging with aspects of
oppression here, my intention is not to reproduce the victim/ization of
women (and gay men) but to suggest that some of that resilient trans-
formatory energy needs to be directed towards the sexualized representational practices of health education. Although there has been a fairly
consistent critique of AIDS representational practice which has engaged
with press and broadcast media representations and with medical discourse
(Armitage et al., 1987; Lupton, 1994; Watney, 1987; Zita Grover, 1988),
surprisingly little attention has been paid to HIV/AIDS health educational
materials. It is, moreover, easier for AIDS activists and health educators to
influence health educational materials than to change the agenda of the
newspaper barons, the television networks, Hollywood or the medical
profession – as the urban gay men's AIDS activist communities have so
amply demonstrated. My aim here is to suggest ways in which health
educational materials (and practices) may be developed which transcend
the heteropolar paradigm and which, in consequence, may be instrumental
in the continuing struggle against intersecting oppressions which is so
fundamental a part of the struggle against AIDS.

Notes

1. Dr McDonald was Acting Assistant Secretary of the United States Department of
Health and Human Services at the time, and well placed to make this assessment.
    2. One may only imagine what the implications of an individual model of, say, defence
would be. Each citizen individually responsible for defending themselves against attack and
invasion? Back to rifles and half-bricks rather than nuclear missiles, submarines and tanks?
This is far from being a flippant comparison, since the United States spends more on defence
in *five hours* than it does on health care in *five years* (Crimp with Rolston, 1990).
    3. What about bisexuality? I include bisexuality under the general heading of
'heterosexuality' rather than (as is currently fashionable) under the heading 'queer'. This is
for two main reasons: firstly, the hegemonic regime of gender which structures and organizes

the erotic remains untroubled by bisexuality – which is eminently recuperable as 'kinky' straight sex – and secondly because bisexuals, whatever their gender, announce by their self-identification as bisexual their continuing allegiance to the dominant regime of gender (men by continuing to fuck women, women by continuing to position themselves as sexual objects for male pleasure). For a detailed discussion of the straightness of bisexuality see Wilson, 1993.

4. For a full account of this incident, see my article 'Safe Sex, Safer Publishers' in *The Times Higher Educational Supplement*, 23 June 1995: 17–18.

2

A Sexed and Gendered Desire: Obstacles to Sexual Safety

'Every time I have safe sex, I feel like I'm getting back at straight society. I have a lot of sex, and I feel like I'm avenging the deaths of my friends. It's like I can say see, I can still be queer and you can't make me die.'

(gay safe sex activist cited in Patton, 1994: 114)

Unprotected sex has been and continues to be by far the commonest route for the transmission of HIV globally and in Britain (WHO, 1994). Profound changes in the sexual practices of peoples in every region of every country in the world are essential if the epidemic is to be significantly slowed. It is in theory not difficult to minimize the risk of sexual transmission of HIV infection. Long-time AIDS activist and commentator Cindy Patton has summed up her safe sex advice as, 'Don't get semen in your anus or vagina' (cited in Boffin, 1990: 164), a non-gender-specific rule which has much to recommend it. *Safe sex*, that is avoidance of sexual activities involving penetration of either vagina or anus with a penis, will reduce the risk to as near zero as is possible, and *safer sex* – using a condom during anal or vaginal penetration – while not by any means foolproof, significantly reduces the chance of viral transmission. Although evidence concerning the likelihood of HIV transmission during fellatio is inconclusive, it is generally regarded as low risk, while cunnilingus is thought to be still less risky. Indeed if sex were no more than a biological activity there would be few obstacles to prevent the widespread adoption of a successful and straightforward safer sex strategy which would halt the epidemic in its tracks. Yet of course biology is probably the least significant component of human sexual activity, sex being perhaps the paradigmatic social site of overdetermined and multiple social meaning-making.[1]

The set of meanings most ineradicably encoded within and by means of sexual behaviours – and the social prescriptions and proscriptions which cohere around such behaviours – are those to do with gender. It is not possible to disengage gender and the erotic or to consider the politics of the sexual in isolation from sexual politics. Some writers have suggested that one (conceptually? chronologically? epistemologically?) precedes the other. Judith Butler, for example, discusses the relationship between gender and (homo)sexuality in a way that implicitly accords precedence to gender:

Precisely because homophobia often operates through the attribution of a damaged, failed, or otherwise abjected gender to homosexuals, that is, calling gay men 'feminine' or calling lesbians 'masculine', and because the homophobic terror over performing homosexual acts, where it exists, is often also a terror over losing proper gender ('no longer being a real or proper man' or 'no longer being a real or proper woman'), it seems crucial to retain a theoretical apparatus that will account for how sexuality is regulated through the policing and shaming of gender. (Butler, 1994: 27)

In fact, gender and the erotic are co-dependent, mutually inflective and co-constitutive. We also therefore need a theoretical apparatus that will account for the regulation of gender through the 'policing and shaming' of sexuality, and such an apparatus was, of course, developed long ago by radical feminists working on issues such as the sexual harassment of young women in schools or adult women in the workplace (Wise and Stanley, 1987; Jones and Mahony, 1989; Lees, 1993). There has been a recent tendency for queer theory (exemplified by writers such as Judith Butler, Eve Kosofsky Sedgwick and Elizabeth Grosz) to assert its theoretical edge over feminism, one result of which has been to privilege an analysis which claims regimes of gender as instrumental in the social control/construction of sexuality, rather than vice versa. Indeed both feminism and queer have tended to reify a binarism of gender and the erotic which is inadequate and misleading. As Frank Mort insists, 'Modern sexuality is . . . a *dispersed field*, not a restricted one, organized around *multiple points of reference*' (Mort, 1994: 212, emphasis in original); points of reference which clearly must include 'race', class, dis/ability, age, nationality and all the other social and cultural fictions which name us and codify our relations.

Class, gender, 'race', age, dis/ability and nationality are all descriptive/expressive of (directional) vectors of power and control and each of them, while hardly *determining* our sexual lives, has a profound impact on how we constitute and present our sexual selves, how we relate sexually to our partners and how the social construction of sexuality develops and shifts (having, therefore, a significant impact on the extent to which we are able to take steps to protect ourselves against HIV infection). Clearly all these social/cultural variables intersect one with another, and all are marked and directed by sexuality in turn. It is a moot point whether the erotic is 'actually' the uniquely privileged site for the coalescence/contestation of this multiplicity of fictions, and the question is probably inappropriate since it depends on the proposition that there exists, somewhere 'outside' culture and discourse, some kind of 'authentic truth' about sexuality. About sexual/erotic *discursive* activity in Western culture, however, we can be clear. Since the seventeenth century, as Foucault suggests (1976: 17), 'around and apropos of sex, one sees a veritable discursive explosion'. Whether the erotic is 'really' some kind of primary junction of signification for all other vectors of power is undecidable and irrelevant. For, in the cacophonic and stentorian speaking about sex which permeates discourse, cultural productivity and social relations/structures, meanings of gender, 'race', etc. are present with particular insistence and particular clarity. The discursive explosion of the erotic is flagrantly and copiously available for reading/

deconstruction, and the nature of this availability (sex begins to seem like the 'loose woman' of discourse!) in itself proclaims much about the social, cultural and subjective significance of sex and sexuality.

In the late modern/postmodern milieu sex is not simply a set of behaviours. Rather, since that (perhaps random) historical moment immortalized by Foucault as the birth of 'the homosexual' as species (Foucault, 1976), sexuality has become instrumental in the constitution of subjectivity. What we do sexually, and what sort of people we prefer to do it with, names us as a particular *kind* of person: a homosexual, a bisexual, a heterosexual, a pederast, a sadomasochist, etc. And this taxonomic project of the self has enormous implications for self-esteem, for sexual behaviours, for the social infrastructures which organize sexuality – all in turn implicated in the daunting task of promoting safer sex in the age of AIDS.

Reframing feminist accounts

The institutions and practices of patriarchy significantly impede women's abilities to avoid or to live well with HIV infection, and this is one of the central themes of this book. It is important, however, to avoid constructing a simplistic model of patriarchy which ignores 'race', class and other oppressions. Such a model merely reinscribes Western cultural imperialism and results in a white Western feminism which behaves as if it were what bell hooks calls the 'authoritative overseer' of feminisms in the so-called Third World (hooks, 1994). Sexuality is as much present as a reference point in 'race', class, gender, age, etc. as they are in it, and the complex interpenetrations of these various constructs nuance and disturb unitary categories such as 'patriarchy'. The white Catholic woman in Belfast whose religion prohibits the use of condoms and the black Zimbabwean woman whose culture encourages her to enhance her male partner's sexual pleasure by inserting herbs into her vagina to tighten and dry it (Pitts et al., 1994), are of course both at increased risk of HIV infection because of the institutional power of patriarchy. But, just as questions of 'race', gender, nationality and sexuality interact to shape their very different subjectivities, so they interact to shape 'patriarchies' that are as distinctive as the allotropes of sulphur.[2] In the context of HIV/AIDS, questions of 'race', class, sexual identity and nationality impact especially strongly upon gender relations and upon sexual relations. As such, they must not be absent from an analysis which privileges gender. '[R]ather than restating binary dualisms,' as Mort put it, 'it is important to grasp the multiple points of construction of modern sexuality *for all of us*' (Mort, 1994: 213; emphasis in original). Any attempt to understand the HIV pandemic which fails to take into consideration feminist accounts of women's oppression will be radically flawed and hopelessly inadequate. On the other hand, feminist accounts which present gender as an unmediated universal binary, or 'patriarchy' as monolithic and ubiquitous, end up by reifying that which they seek to disturb and collude with rather than oppose the relations of power which make women so vulnerable in the context of HIV/AIDS. For example, when Janice Raymond writes: 'If we are lesbian feminists, we feel and act on behalf of women as women . . . We feel and act for all women because we are women' (1996: 227–8), her words reinforce with precision the polarity of gendered power which it is the job of feminism to short-circuit. Such ironies are deeply troubling in relation to AIDS.

Towards the body?

Class, age, 'race', nationality and dis/ability all impact profoundly on the social construction of AIDS, and on the ability of individuals to respond to the epidemic, to protect themselves from HIV infection or to get appropriate care if they become infected, on the policy agenda and, ultimately, on who dies and who survives. They also, of course, impact profoundly one upon another, and upon gender, the central concern of this book. Yet I believe that the social, cultural and theoretical co-dependency of gender (always already 'racialized', located in a context of nationality, age, class and dis/ability) and the erotic (always already similarly located and inflected) is more significant than the relations among age, 'race', dis/ability, class, nationality and either gender or the erotic.

This is partly due to what I can only think of as the remorseless mapping of the sexual onto the always already gendered body, a mapping which, in tandem with Cartesian dualism, has structured Western thinking in the modern era. Thus a body which has a vagina and uterus is understood as *for* penetration (and by implication, impregnation) by a penis, while a body which has a penis is understood as *for* penetrating (and impregnating) a vagina/uterus. The meaning of the body (perceived as 'sexed') is a sexual/erotic one, and, at the level of fleshly topography, meaning is reduced to an unthinkingly naive functionalism. This functionalism (penis is to vagina as plug is to socket) has been reinforced and made manifest by creation myth, religious doctrine, scientific theory or appeals to nature, aesthetic values or commonsense, paradigmatic fictions contingent on time and place (history and culture). The same immediate relation to the body does not exist for, say, 'race' or age, factors whose significance is located more clearly in the wider social arena, at a certain distance from matters of skin and flesh.

So, although I agree with Butler that gender is performative (Butler, 1990), and that the performance of gender can subvert, interrogate or replicate dominant notions of gendered sexuality (and sexed genderality), it is crucial not to lose sight of the body as a site of sexed and erotic meanings that precede (and may take precedence over) any such performances. It is, after all, the fact that the drag queen has a penis,[3] that the drag king does not, that the (male to female) transsexual once had a penis, that the lesbian boy has breasts and a vagina,[4] which gives their disobedient performance its meaning.

If this epidemic, and its love-child, Queer, have taught us anything, it is that sexual and gender *identity* are problematic concepts. In Europe and the US social-scientific research has 'discovered' that many men who have sex with men consider their heterosexual identity to be uncompromised by their behaviour (Humphreys, 1970; Aggleton et al., 1990),[5] psychologists have found that having sex, or even long-term relationships, with men is considered by some lesbians not to compromise a lesbian identity, while heterosexual women appear unwilling to admit to a heterosexual identity (Kitzinger and Wilkinson, 1993). At the same time, queer culture is playing cheerily with gender-fuck and developing the notion of gender transience; the Sisters of Perpetual Indulgence,[6] lesbian boys, a reclaiming and reinscription of lesbian butch and fem, radical fairies and the stylish gender signifiers mix-and-match of Julian Clary or kd lang all indicate a refusal to obey the rules of the gender game and situate gender as, in Bakhtinian terms, a chronotope.[7]

Yet in the midst of this proliferation of sexualized genders and gendered sexualities in the West, health education continues to address safe/safer sex information to discrete sex/gender groups. There are campaigns (not enough) targeted at gay men, an almost-silence directed at lesbians (regarded by too many health educators as not at risk), and entirely distinct campaigns aimed at heterosexuals (which tend to be apparently undifferentiated by gender).

Thus, despite my own unwillingness to allow sexual identities to coalesce from the swirling fluidities of the postmodern erotic, despite the high-visibility disruptions of old certainties about such identities, I am obliged to engage with these health education strategies on their own terms. It is important to do so, because such strategies, whether initiated by governments or by self-identified erotic communities, do not merely address already-existing sexual cohorts; rather they are instrumental in discursively constituting the very sexual identities they purport to have simply responded to (Wilton, 1994a), hence facilitating or impeding the ability of individuals to practise safe(r) sex. It remains strategically and politically important to speak from and to *locations* in the sex/gender/erotic arena, locations inhabited and embodied by gay men, lesbians, heterosexual men and heterosexual women, while acknowledging how contingent, inadequate and oppressive such a taxonomy might be. It is also likely, at the simplest level, that my own understandings of the HIV pandemic are profoundly shaped by my being a lesbian and speaking from that location.

Gay men: deviant, dissident and dispensable

It is by now fairly generally accepted that HIV infection and AIDS, having first come to the notice of the medical profession in the United States as a cluster of previously rare conditions in young gay men, has continued to affect disproportionate numbers of gay men in the developed world.

Although the *proportion* of gay men among newly diagnosed AIDS cases has tended to fall (from 93 per cent in 1986 to 73 per cent in 1991 in the UK, for example), *numbers* continue to rise, and there is substantial evidence to suggest that infection rates among younger gay men are increasing rather than decreasing (King, 1993). Gay communities in the industrialized West have experienced a 'tidal wave of death' (Watney, 1994), especially in the United States, where rates of HIV infection among some cohorts of gay men in urban centres reached 73.1 per cent by 1985 (King, 1993: 11).

The early days of the epidemic in the so-called First World were characterized by administrative and political inaction rooted in homophobia. The hegemony of heterosexism was so total (and, indeed, totalitarian) that the deaths of the first people with AIDS were ignored because they happened to be gay men. Indeed, in some quarters the new sickness was *applauded* precisely because it was killing gay men (Wilton, 1992a; Patton, 1990). Faced with an inexplicable health crisis, and with neglect and hostility from the bodies whose job it normally was to respond to health crises, gay men (and many lesbians) began to organize to provide the services they needed and to construct a political agenda. '[B]ecause PWAs [people with AIDS] were being left to die unfed and uncared for, the community had to respond and create a specific, often militant, gay/AIDS agenda' (Kayal, 1993: 9).

This resulted in the growth of an extraordinary number of AIDS-related services provided by the gay community. Helplines, bereavement counselling, legal and welfare advice, buddying, practical help for people with HIV infection and AIDS, respite care, drop-in centres, advice on complementary and allopathic therapies for HIV infection and the associated opportunistic infections and sometimes even financial help for people living with HIV/AIDS, have all been set up by lesbian and gay communities. Gay Men's Health Crisis (GMHC) in New York, started in 1981, raised $11,000 for the Kaposi Sarcoma Fund at New York University Medical Center by three months' fundraising in gay community venues, and by mid-1982 had raised a further $50,000 for medical research (Kayal, 1993). At this time government funding for medical research into the new medical emergency was zero. GMHC is now the largest AIDS agency and gay organization in the world, with a yearly budget of around $20 million (Kayal, 1993: 2). Significantly the first safe sex advice was developed and circulated by gay men, often in the face of censorship and seizure of materials (Wilton, 1992a), some time before the human immunodeficiency virus was identified as the infectious agent responsible for AIDS. Rodger McFarlane, formerly of Gay Men's Health Crisis New York, summed up the response: 'We were forced to take care of ourselves because we learnt that if you have certain diseases, certain lifestyles, you can't expect the same services as other parts of society' (Rooney, 1991: 4).

Admirable and extraordinary as this outpouring of energy, care and skill has been (and continues to be), it has inevitably led to some complex problems, and gay men (among others) have tended to lose out as a result. The first problem lies in the unwillingness of the heterosexual majority to engage with the presence of gay men. Many non-gay observers – and these of course included those in charge in the medical and policy arenas – assumed that, having succeeded so admirably in developing community strategies to combat HIV infection and to support those already infected, the gay community had met its own needs. Doubtless the willingness to assume this was in part motivated by homophobia. This resulted in a continuing neglect of gay men by public bodies. A British study of local AIDS policies, carried out in 1990 by the Health Education Authority and the King's Fund Institute, found that neither the government nor the local authorities had made adequate efforts to target HIV/AIDS health promotion strategies at gay men:

> Within the four most frequently targeted groups, authorities tended to concentrate their efforts on drug users, young people . . . and schoolchildren. Overall, authorities have not tended to select gay men for a campaign of their own. In part, this mirrors the Government's approach: which has only recently designed a specific campaign for gay and bisexual men. (Beardshaw et al., 1990: 19)

A later survey on behalf of the *National AIDS Manual* concluded that less than 1 per cent of available resources for HIV prevention work in Britain has been directed at gay men (Hobbs, 1992). Ironically, it is the high standard of information produced by and for the gay male community that seems to have led to (or at any rate enabled heterosexual health educators to justify) the neglect of the one group still most at risk of acquiring HIV infection:

> Staff . . . explained that [gay men] had been omitted because the information produced independently by gay groups was considered to be extremely effective in encouraging homosexuals to adopt safer sexual practices . . . Other policy documents reflected the views expressed by one authority which stated 'as a group, gay men probably know more about the disease and how it is spread than any other group in society . . .' (Beardshaw et al., 1990: 9)

While the success of gay men's self-help strategy was enabling heterosexual health educators to justify ignoring their needs, the community initiatives originally established by lesbians and gay men were becoming professionalized into what Cindy Patton (1989) has called the 'AIDS industry'. Most gay-initiated projects had chosen never to exclude non-gay people from their service provision. Groups such as the Terrence Higgins Trust in London had, from the very beginning, offered services to *everyone* affected by HIV/AIDS, and had deemed it politically essential to insist that the virus did not discriminate between gay and straight, and that everyone was at risk. It wasn't long before neither public bodies nor gay-initiated AIDS voluntary organizations were concentrating on gay men, while gay men continued to be the group hardest hit by the epidemic (King, 1993).

The obvious injustice of this led some activists to call for the 're-gaying' of AIDS (King, 1993), a call premised on the belief – ironically in line with radical Right economic policies – that money should follow need and, crucially, on the belief that a gay identity is powerfully supportive of safe sexual behaviours. It is this second belief that interests me here. Given that gay men have never had to consider using condoms as a form of contraception, how has it been possible for so many (though probably never a majority of) gay men to incorporate something so obviously associated with heterosexual sex into their own sexual repertoires?

Up yours! Identity, community, safety

Commentators generally agree that it is not desiring or having sex with another man but rather having a gay *identity* which enables men to practise safe and/or safer sex (Patton, 1989; 1990; King, 1993). The relationship of identity to practice, always a complex one, is especially so when considering gay identity which is perforce negotiated in response/resistance to the homophobic construction of homosexuality as predicated upon execrated sexual behaviours; specifically, receptive anal erotic behaviours such as being fucked in the arse, rimmed or fisted (Simpson, 1994). Gay men, precisely *because* their sexual behaviour is the site of their oppression/ execration, have developed an oppositional discourse around sexual behaviour which constructs man-with-man sexual activity as both healthy (in opposition to dominant discourses of homosexuality as sick, diseased, pathological) and politically radical (in opposition to dominant discourses of gender which asign/ascribe activity and passivity differentially to men and to women). Furthermore, this oppositional discourse has been opportunistically commercialized and the process of commercialization itself characterized as political – gay money for gay businesses (see below pp. 110–13 for further discussion of this).[8] As Dennis Altman describes, this politics of the sexual has reversed the meanings attached to the kinds of sexual encounter available to gay men before decriminalization:

> the growth of both gay assertion and a commercial gay world meant an affirmation of sex outside relationships as a positive good, a means of expressing both sensuality and community . . . it was taking one of the most characteristic features of homosexual life as it had existed before such assertion – promiscuity, often in fleeting and anonymous encounters due to fear of discovery – and making of it a virtue. (Altman, 1986: 142)

One of the most painful – and politically difficult – aspects of the AIDS epidemic for many gay men has been the recognition that the free market sexuality which embodied (though never unchallenged, and never for all gay men) a proud, assertive sexuality of resistance *at the same time* established the precise mechanisms whereby HIV was able to spread with such devastating swiftness through gay urban communities (King, 1993). To many gay men the epidemic seemed to line up with the moral entrepreneurs of the New Right in an onslaught against this new and hardwon playfulness:

> The celebrated gay culture of the late 1960s and 1970s is gone, eclipsed by the so-called moral majority that determinedly acts on its agenda to have gays, who are already oppressed, punished further . . . For once, we were living – dancing as it were – and we were happy. Now we are dying, in part because of this carefree abandon. (Kayal, 1993: 23)

The experience of living in the midst of death, the recognition that community organizing was the only way to survive in the face of official neglect, were powerful spurs to the development of a gay safer sex strategy. But so, too, was a uniquely queer ability to think and talk about things sexual, an ability which springs from the struggle against homophobia. Stigmatized on account of their sexuality, gay men (and lesbians) talk and think about sex and sexual 'identity' far more than heterosexuals.

AIDS provoked in the wider heterosexual culture a crisis of panic around anal eroticism, a panic that has always marked homophobic speaking, and is mapped onto anxieties about gender:

> Homophobia is a holograph of fears: fear of a different subculture, fear of forbidden male–male desires, and fear of anal penetration. Symbolically, AIDS has collapsed gay sexuality and straight sexual anxiety under the sign of anal sex . . . The anus's forbidden status . . . combines with the anus's lack of gender reference. Thus, desires centering on the anus cannot infallibly be stabilized to produce 'heterosexuality' and anal sex becomes a key site of (hetero)sexual danger through loss of gender reference. (Patton, 1990: 118)

It is this which, I suggest, makes possible the relatively widespread use of condoms among gay-identified men. Having represented gay sex as healthy, having reclaimed/reconstructed the anus as a site/sign of pleasure and the erotic and hence having incorporated anal penetration into the cultural matrix of gay identity and (importantly) *community*, gay men had already developed the conceptual framework which enabled them to 'think' safer sex and to 'do' it. Sodomy had become a privileged sign of rebelliousness to homophobic oppression:

> Anal intercourse, as it happens, is not just a risky element in a sexual repertoire. It is a practice that has had major historical significance in the social construction of men's homosexuality. It was specifically targeted by religious and criminal sanctions against 'the abominable crime of buggery' and has remained central to hostile stereotypes of homosexual men . . . It is a practice which carries a heavy load of social meaning. For gay men it is likely to symbolize oppression and freedom even for those who do not find it a significant part of sexual pleasure. (Connell et al., cited in King, 1993: 158)

In addition to the reclamation of anality, there is the familiar disobedience to gender stereotype. Accustomed to resisting the inscription of stigmatizing femininity onto gay male desire/love/sex, it is a relatively small step to resist the stigma attached to the use of condoms. Indeed, for gay men the stigma attached to condoms is inevitably different from the stigma they carry for heterosexual men (see p. 34), having a more distant (indeed, purely symbolic) association with gendered relations of power as they inhere in heterosex.

The use of condoms during anal penetration was constructed within gay male sexual-political discourse as politically radical, resistant to homophobia and protective of the gay brotherhood/community with, as King suggests, 'the ultimate goal of modifying gay identity so that it *means* safer sex' (King, 1993: xii). This correlated with the construction of AIDS as potentially instrumental in the homophobic genocide of gay men by a hostile, moralistic and wilfully negligent polity (Kramer, 1990). In the face of this neglect, it was gay men themselves who coined the term 'safer sex' (Patton, 1989) and who set about disseminating safer sex information using gay community networks. In the US, condoms were in widespread use by gay men long before any health educational interventions by the administration (Davies et al., 1990), while in Britain the Terrence Higgins Trust (THT), set up by a group of gay men in 1982, reprinted safer sex information produced by Gay Men's Health Crisis in New York. The first UK conference on AIDS was organized in 1983 by London Lesbian and Gay Switchboard, while community newspaper *Capital Gay* promoted safer sexual practices to its readers. Such interventions were met with widespread hostility: safer sex material produced in 1983 by the Gay Medical Association was 'impounded by the Metropolitan Police under the 1964 Obscene Publication Laws' (Davies et al., 1990: 72).

Yet the adoption of safer sex by gay men is a complex and far from straightforward issue. In the early days there was much denial among gay men that they were at risk, many viewing reports of what was then known as 'Gay-Related Immune Deficiency' (GRID) as a fiction invented by a homophobic medical industry to prevent men having sex with each other or to bankrupt gay-run businesses which revolved around commercial sex (Kramer, 1990; Shilts, 1987). It is easy to make too much of this initial reaction. In fact, denial is an accepted feature of most people's response to trauma or loss, and this is as true of the epidemic as of any other catastrophe (Spence, 1986). It must not be forgotten that the impact of AIDS on the gay male communities in the West has to date gone far beyond its impact on non-gay communities. Kayal writes: 'it is virtually impossible to live as a gay man in New York City and not be aware of the surrounding specter of death. The city is simply dying. Even when in the best of health, legions of men are simply waiting to be diagnosed' (Kayal, 1993: 17). In the face of such traumatic and terrifying circumstances, Edwards suggests, it is the transformation of initial denial into activism, rather than the denial itself, that is strange:

The impact of such an epidemic is perhaps most simply explained in psychological terms of shock, denial, anger and grief and this is indeed approximately the pattern of impact of AIDS on the gay male community who were initially shocked, denied sexual transmission and were furious at the accusations of causality, until the loss of friends and lovers to AIDS, dying in their tens and dozens, led to widespread grief and intensive activism. This move from a community devastated and shocked to a community consolidated and activated has happened at colossal speed. (Edwards, 1994: 123)

Repeated research studies have indicated that gay men changed their sexual practices to a dramatic extent over a very short period of time (King, 1993). Yet, of course, it is not as simple as that on an individual level. Some research has indicated that the practice of safer sex depends less on allegiance to the gay community or to a gay identity than on the nature of the sexual relationship involved (long-term, short-term, casual or committed), on where you happen to live (in an urban centre or an isolated rural community), on your age or on your own perceptions of the risk attached to any specific sex act, and on the local community norms regarding safer sexual practices (Coxon, 1985; Davies et al., 1990; King, 1993; Kayal, 1993). There is growing evidence in Britain and the US of a 'gay generation gap', with younger gay men just coming out onto the scene believing that AIDS is a problem for the previous generation (Glanz, 1991; King, 1993).

An additional complication arises when recognizing that communities and identities do not and cannot remain static over time. It is not possible to speak of 'the' gay community response to AIDS; rather there are many responses, shifting across time and between geographically and/or culturally distinct communities. During a recent visit to Australia,[9] for example, I was startled to learn of a tendency among some HIV positive gay men to eroticize *unsafe* sex. On reflection, this seems inevitable. It is one thing to use condoms and non-penetrative techniques as a *temporary measure*, as a stopgap until medical science has developed a cure or vaccine for HIV; it is quite another to face a lifetime of safe or safer sex, especially between already infected men. Over the last decade it has become clear that vaccines and cures are still a very long way off, and recognizing this unpleasant truth is bound to engender quite radical shifts in perceptions of the epidemic and of safer sex as an infection-control strategy. Moreover, the experience of living through this time of AIDS, of losing so many friends, ex-lovers, colleagues and community figures, will in itself inevitably give rise to unpredictable social and psychological consequences. It is perhaps unsurprising that one response might be to eroticize the flesh/flesh contact of unprotected intercourse, or even the ultimate intimacy of sharing with someone else *your* virus, *your* sickness and ultimate death.

In terms of safer sex education, it remains the case that gay men trust and give credence to safer sex advice and HIV/AIDS reporting generally in the gay press rather than in the straight press, broadcast media or official health education campaigns (Davies et al., 1990), but it is only a minority of gay men who have access to such resources. In Britain, the high street newsagent chain W.H. Smith refused until 1994 to stock *Gay Times*, and then only on the top shelf along with heterosexual porn magazines, *Capital Gay* is only available within London, and the recent rash of British lesbian and gay 'lifestyle' magazines (*Boyz*, *Shebang*, *Lip*, etc.) are hard to come by outside the capital and impossible to find outside major cities.

Moreover, the positioning of safe sex within gay men's communities is complex, and shifts in sometimes subtle ways over time. Research is ongoing to chart the changes in negotiating sexual safety which take place at various times in the life course of individual gay men (e.g. Kippax et al., 1995), the ways in which other social variables such as ethnicity interact with a gay identity to influence sexual practices (e.g. Te Puni Kokiri, 1994) or the ways in which different gay communities respond to the sexual needs of their HIV positive members (e.g. Green, 1994).

Complex though the relationship between a positive gay identity and the practice of safer sex is, it is still more complex for men who have sex with men without identifying as gay. 'The extent to which sexual identity and behaviour vary between groups of homosexually active men across and between the boundaries of race, age, class, locale, relationship status and so on remains under-researched' (King, 1993: 6), and one result of this has been the need to create a 'new' label – men who have sex with men – in order to be able to speak and write about a range of sexual experiences and identities much wider than Western sociology/epidemiology is accustomed to assuming. One of the things which the epidemic has hammered home is the inadequacy and fundamental meaninglessness of the hegemonic and paranoid model of sexuality-as-polarity (male and female as opposites, gay and straight as opposites). Davies et al. in their final report to the Department of Health (1990: 143) comment that:

> there remains an abiding assumption, often obscurely implicit though sometimes brashly explicit, that homosexual men and heterosexual men form two hermetic communities . . . despite the fact that there are women and men who will affirm the identity 'bisexual', there are many more who, terming themselves gay or straight will engage, regularly or infrequently in sex with partners of either gender.

British government bodies such as the Health Education Authority have developed a positive approach to safer sex promotion targeted at gay men. However, such gay-targeted campaigns have been almost exclusively restricted to the gay press (one telling exception is the recent introduction of press ads addressed to young gay men just coming out, which are placed in student magazines distributed on university campuses). Many men who have sex with men continue to perceive themselves as *heterosexual*, do not frequent the gay 'scene' or read the gay press, and are consequently unlikely to have access to the information about safer sex which they need. For such men, the gay-associated fear and stigma which the heterosexual majority has mapped onto AIDS serves to impede their ability to protect themselves and their partners from HIV infection. Tony Coxon writes:

> Homosexuality, then, is like an iceberg; the 'tip', the visible gay people, contains those known to be homosexual, who . . . are happier with their identity, more likely to be in a relationship, more likely to be 'on the scene' and be active in gay politics and self-help groups, and also be more responsive to health education and work out the implications of AIDS for their own life. The mass of homosexuals, by contrast, are only known to be such to a very limited section of their acquaintances . . . if to any. [They] are more likely to involve themselves in impersonal and 'quickie' sex. They are not likely to be at ease with their identity and are more likely to live a life in fear of being exposed . . . [I]t is important to

realise that the effect of increasing public intolerance and prejudice resulting from
the AIDS scare is driving gays *back* into the closet. (Coxon, 1985: 5)

So, although it may not be said that a gay identity *per se* enables the
adoption of safer sexual behaviours, *not* having a gay identity certainly
militates against the adoption of such behaviours. This is something which
has been supported by research findings thoughout the various gay
communities of the developed Western world. Research into sexual
behaviours among gay men in Australia found, for example, that: 'Men
who are isolated from others like themselves and are unattached to gay
community in any form are those least likely to change' (Kippax et al.,
1990).

In addition to the significance of self-identifying as gay are the consequences of the ascriptive label 'gay' or (more usually) 'homosexual'. In the
context of the epidemic in the West a vast amount of time and energy has
been devoted to interventions in gay male sexuality; interventions which,
while many have been problematic, oppressive or offensive, have foregrounded 'homosexuality' and constructed gay men *as* first and foremost
sexual, something which has conspicuously not happened with other groups
(Wilton, 1994a). There have been copious studies of gay male sexual
behaviour (Davies et al., 1990; 1993; Fitzpatrick et al., 1990), imaginative
outreach work in public sites where men have sex with men (Lerro, 1989),
condom promotion at gay bars and clubs (King, 1993), even the design and
promotion of a 'gay-identified' condom, the Hot Rubber, suitable for anal
sex (Staub, 1991).[10] Nothing like this has been directed at lesbians, at
heterosexual men or heterosexual women.

That shifting, contingent and reactive fiction 'gay identity' turns out,
then, to be of enormous significance in preventing sickness and saving lives.
What of that related fiction, 'lesbian identity'?

A good licking? Questions of lesbian sexual safety

Lesbians and lesbian sexuality figure largely as a set of absences in AIDS
discourse, both mainstream and activist/oppositional. The epidemic has
catalysed an unprecedented explosion of speech acts about sex and the
erotic in Western societies, unprecedented because the statutory agencies
which traditionally repress or restrain speech about sex (or, at least – *pace*
Foucault – *appear* to do so) have been obliged to facilitate or to join in the
speaking:

> There is a funny side to it; never before have so many 'four-letter' words – fuck,
> blow, lick, cock et cetera as it is bluntly put in many of these safer sex pamphlets
> and comics – been printed with the help of (Conservative) government money
> and made available to the general public. (Schmidt, 1990: 45)

Yet at the heart of this unaccustomed Babel lies a familiar silence about the
kinds of sex women have with each other. It is a silence which is quite
extraordinarily omnipresent in the literature about safer sex (see below pp.

92–5). Safer sex handbooks on sale in mainstream bookshops, while they deal in some detail with heterosex and in adequate (albeit embarrassed) fashion with sex between men, refuse to mention sex between women (e.g. Breitman et al., 1987; Gordon and Mitchell, 1988; Haddon and Prentice, 1989),[11] while material about young people and safe sex either ignores lesbians entirely (e.g. DiClemente, 1992) or skims over what lesbians actually *do* in bed: 'The answer is: much the same as straights', at least according to one author (Cousins-Mills, 1988: 39). Key publications on women and HIV/AIDS all too often devote nothing more than a token paragraph or two to lesbian issues (e.g. Berer with Ray, 1993; Panos Institute, 1990a), although some among those written from an activist or feminist standpoint have been notably better at including material on lesbians (e.g. Rieder and Ruppelt, 1988; ACT UP/NY Women and AIDS Book Group, 1990; Richardson, 1989; 1990; Wilton, 1992a; Doyal et al., 1994).

Almost no research has been done into lesbian sexual behaviours, their beliefs about HIV/AIDS or about the degree to which they believe themselves to be at risk. This is compounded by the failure of scientific research to adequately investigate the mechanics of HIV transmission between women, so that risk-reduction guidelines given to lesbians is conflicting (Wilton, 1994b; Richardson, 1992; 1994; Bury, 1994). Typical of safer sex advice (in this case aimed at adolescents) is the *Streetwize UK AIDS Issue* comic produced by Nottingham Health Authority and the Department of Community Medicine and Epidemiology at the University of Nottingham (no date). In a section entitled 'Are You Streetwize about What Is Risky?' the risk of sexual transmission is briefly discussed. It is worth citing this section in full, as it is fairly typical of such materials, which are popular with health educators targeting 'youth':

MEN AND WOMEN HAVING SEX (heterosexuality). AIDS can be caught through heterosexual sex. The numbers of AIDS cases among heterosexuals will continue to rise.

HAVING SEX WITH BOTH MEN AND WOMEN (bisexuality). Having sex puts people at risk from HIV. Bisexuals are more likely to have sex with homosexual men. If they then have sex with heterosexual women it could spread HIV in the heterosexual community.

MEN HAVING SEX TOGETHER (homosexuality). *Receptive* rather than penetrative anal intercourse (i.e. being entered in the back passage rather than doing the penetrating) puts you at higher risk of catching HIV. Homosexual (gay) men have the greatest incidence of AIDS *at the moment* BUT, other groups' figures are rising. Gay men have proved that changes in sexual behaviour (safer sex) slows the spread of HIV.

WOMEN HAVING SEX TOGETHER (lesbianism). These women are at low risk of catching or transmitting AIDS through sexual activity. (all *sic* Gillies and O'Sullivan, n.d.: 38–9)

This profoundly misleading text is paradigmatic of the construction of discrete sexual constituencies within and by AIDS health education discourse, and is especially revealing in its construction of lesbian sexuality. Note that the only sexual act described is anal penetration, and that it is associated *exclusively* (and definitively) with gay men. Heterosex remains undescribed: it is (presumably) assumed that what is meant by 'men and women having sex' is vaginal intercourse.[12] Not only are 'bisexuals' offensively characterized as a threat to the 'heterosexual community' (the 'it' referred to as spreading HIV is the *act* of bisexual sex with a heterosexual woman) rather than as vulnerable to infection themselves, but they are assumed to be *male*. It is nonsense to suggest that bisexual *women* are 'likely to have sex with homosexual men', or that they will then 'spread HIV into the heterosexual community' by having sex with a heterosexual woman. Bisexuality, then, is *male* sexuality, although again it is left unclear what bisexual behaviours consist of. Lesbianism is merely dismissed; lesbians are 'these women' (heterosexuals, bisexuals and homosexuals have notably *not* been referred to as 'these people' or 'these men') and are simply and mystifyingly 'at low risk'.

What is especially invidious is the distinction drawn between gay men's safer sexual behaviours, which has something to teach non-gay people: 'Gay men have proved that changes in sexual behaviour . . . slows the spread of HIV' and lesbian low risk sexual behaviours. Why, we might be forgiven for asking, if 'these women are at low risk' are readers not encouraged to learn from them? *Why* exactly are they at low risk? What do they do that protects them? It is hugely significant that, rather than ask these questions, 'these women' are dismissed as unimportant. They are at 'low risk' and hence *not of concern* to an educational strategy attempting to encourage low-risk behaviour.

For lesbians, this is an all too familiar scenario, since one of the most ubiquitous instruments of lesbian oppression is the erasure of 'lesbian' from discourse, the invisibility of lesbians (Rich, 1981; Smyth, 1990; Smith, 1992; Wilton, 1995b). This is true even within lesbian and gay or queer discourse, as exemplified by the tendency on the part of many gay male writers to say 'gay people' when they mean 'gay men' (e.g. Bronski, 1989; Kayal, 1993). As Kleinberg notes, 'Lesbians are usually dismissed as unimportant, as nuisances. It is the lowest rung on the ladder of social contempt' (Kleinberg, 1987: 36).

In terms of factors instrumental in facilitating or impeding the practice of safer sex between/among lesbians, it is the stubborn erasure of the lesbian presence and specifically of a lesbian erotic from the social and from the cultural that is most significant. As lesbians we are, simply and inevitably, confused and uncertain about whether we are at risk of transmitting HIV during sex, what sexual behaviours put us at risk, how we may reduce that risk, and how important it is that we should be doing so (Califia, 1995; Richardson, 1994; Adams, 1988).

This profound lack of knowledge is startling in the context of AIDS, certainly the most intensively researched infectious medical condition in history. Given that HIV is still, in epidemiological terms, a relatively new pathogen, the amount of scientific information that has been gathered about the virus and its interactions with its human host is quite extraordinary. 'Never before has so much been learned about a new disease in so short a span of time' (WHO, 1994). That funding for essential medical research in the post-industrial West had first to be donated by the gay community says much about the social position of gay men in these countries. That the scientific community should remain so ignorant about something as basic as the sexual transmission of HIV between women says much about the social position of lesbians worldwide, and about attitudes to female sexuality more generally. As Pat Califia suggests, a certain carelessness exists with regard to HIV epidemiological statistics for women, which is attributable to simple sexism:

> The fact is that the CDC [Centers for Disease Control] don't know whether lesbians are at risk for AIDS or not because they don't bother to ask . . . Despite the absence of any official statistics on lesbians, we've still been able to determine that at least 100 women with AIDS in the CDC's files have reported having sex with other women. Nearly 700 out of 5,000 women's sexual preferences couldn't be categorized because there wasn't enough information on the report forms. The CDC are unable to determine how 23 per cent of the women with AIDS became infected. Wouldn't we be a lot more upset if one fourth of the men who had AIDS became ill for an unknown reason? (Califia, 1995: 219)

What *is* becoming clear in the midst of this bizarre ignorance is that sexual transmission between women seems to be possible, although very rare (Bury, 1994). Lesbians have become HIV infected and continue to do so, lesbians have died, are dying and will die with AIDS (Brown, 1988; Patton and Kelly, 1987). Yet safer sex information available to lesbians continues to be difficult to obtain and often contradictory (Califia, 1988; 1995).

As sodomy has been constituted as the definitive and paradigmatic gay male act, so has cunnilingus for lesbians.[13] I am unaware of any research into the development of this construct, but it leaves a clear trace in safer sex discourse in the West. Emblematic of that trace is the dental dam. Dams are small squares of latex designed for use during dental work, and have been adopted by lesbians for use as a barrier method of prophylaxis during cunnilingus (Califia, 1988; Patton and Kelly, 1987; Leonard, 1990; Acevedo, 1990). It is probable that this requisitioning of dental latex was enabled by the social positioning of lesbians *vis-à-vis* gay men. Certainly I can find no evidence that statutory or scientific bodies instigated the use of barrier methods during cunnilingus as part of their safer sex propaganda campaigns; this inventive advice came from within the queer/lesbian and gay communities that were engaging with the meanings and implications of the epidemic and of safer sex long before anyone else (Patton, 1989). Dental dams should then be seen as an intrinsic part of the socio-political response of lesbian communities to the social and political threat of the epidemic as much as its health risk. If eating pussy is constituted by homophobic discourse as the definitional lesbian act then lesbian stigma is closely bound up with that act; it follows, according to the dynamic of

Foucault's notion of the reverse discourse, that lesbian resistance is likely to involve a recuperation of the stigmatized act and an assertion of pride in its practice.[14] The use of dental dams is an assertion of the determination to keep this practice 'safe', although studies have shown that dislike of dams is widespread among lesbians (Hunter et al., cited in Patton, 1994), and information about woman-to-woman transmission of HIV has not been widely enough disseminated within lesbian communities (and is, in any case, not clear enough) to make the need for such technologies of protection obvious (Patton, 1994).

It is important to understand that lesbian resistance to homophobia is significantly different from gay men's resistance in many ways. Lesbians are subject to at least a double jeopardy – sexism and homophobia (black lesbians are additionally subject to racism, Jewish lesbians to anti-Semitism, etc.) – and one result of this strange brew is that lesbian sexuality *per se* is subject to a uniquely powerful attempt at discursive erasure. The disavowal and repression of women's autonomous sexuality – of female desire, sexual agency and sexual pleasure – is instrumental in the patriarchal project, and lesbian desire, negating as it does the phallocentrism/androcentrism of patriarchal constructs of sexuality, is literally unspeakable within the lexica of patriarchies.[15]

Within hegemonic discourse, 'sex' carries meanings which are elided with social/cultural constructs of masculinity. Sex is something done *by* men *to* women (Jackson, 1988), and the profoundly gendered language of the erotic makes this power differential plain, even for queers. Gay men *are* men (the feminization of the gay man in homophobic discourse is shaming precisely because it is a *man* that is so characterized); what is more, they are men uniquely distant from contact with women's sexuality. Additionally, gay men are defined and abjected by reason of their sexual behaviour. Gay male sex is, therefore, made *more* visible, *more* spoken about than the sex of non-gay men. Lesbians, on the other hand, not only *are* women, but desire and have sex with other women. It is not simply the need to silence the possibility of lesbianism in order to control female sexual behaviour, nor the vigorous repression of a kind of sex that denies the primacy of the penis, that results in lesbian erasure (although both are contributory). It is simply that to speak about sex is to speak about what men *do* and what women *are*. Which is why the 'lesbian' most easily recognized in the West is the 'lesbian' of heterosexual men's porn (Wilton, 1994b), the 'lesbian' who is a lesbian *for* men. 'Gay male sex', as Marilyn Frye has written, 'is *articulate*. It is articulate to a degree that, in my world, lesbian "sex" does not remotely approach . . . I have, in effect, no linguistic community, no language, and therefore, in one important sense, no knowledge' (Frye, 1990: 310–11). To be a lesbian within lesbian feminist discourse has long been to be constructed in resistance to erasure, to invisibility – although, ironically, some feminist discourse constructs lesbians in resistance to the erotic (Raymond, 1996; Jeffreys, 1990; essays in Lucia-Hoagland and

Penelope, 1988). To be a lesbian in this epidemic has become almost to be defined by lack of knowledge about sex, and about sexual safety in particular.

Women who have sex with men – her master's voice?

As many feminist commentators have said, heterosex has never been safe for women (Doyal, 1995; Richardson, 1989; Wilton, 1994a). Biologically, the act of penile penetration puts women at risk of pregnancy, cervical cancer and many sexually transmitted infections, including HIV (Doyal, 1995). Socially, women tend to have relatively little power within hetero-sexual relationships, whatever the nature of those relationships. The majority of the world's women are economically dependent on their male family members, and this usually means, either directly or indirectly, on their male sexual partners. In many parts of the world sex work remains the only or primary source of income for women who lack the support of a male breadwinner (WHO, 1994). Although this pattern of inequality is most overt in the so-called Third World, it still exists (to a less absolute extent) in those countries in the post-industrial West where some form of welfare state combined with women's freer participation in the workforce make starvation less likely for women who lack access to a male wage (Doyal, 1995). In consequence it is only a tiny minority of women who may be said to have any choice over whether or not to engage in heterosex, let alone to determine the nature of their sexual encounters with men. Ironically it may be that women who sell sex are better able than those who do not to successfully incorporate condom use in their sexual encounters; although this is less likely when the woman is selling sex to finance her drug addiction, and there is evidence to suggest that use of condoms by sex workers may be restricted to commercial encounters and may not extend to their intimate relationships (Misha, 1993; Butcher, 1994).

Women's relative powerlessness in heterosex is largely determined by the material inequalities that obtain between women and men in every country in the world (Morgan, 1984; Seager and Olson, 1986), material inequalities that give rise to and are in turn supported by powerful cultural and ideological constructs of gender. Thus a regime of gender in which women are dependent on men has been profoundly *naturalized* within and by whichever paradigm is hegemonic in the various cultures of the world. Whether a culture does its 'truth-telling' through religious doctrine, traditional myths, the arts or the sciences, conspicuous among the 'truths' told are those concerning women's 'natural' and *rightful* inferiority/ subordination to men. In the post-industrial West after more than a century of feminist struggle there is an active and self-conscious oppositional discourse in challenge to this ideology; despite which men still make use of religious doctrine, medical mythology, and simple physical coercion to maintain their superordination over women. A relatively recent (and still undertheorized) cultural phenomenon that has been instrumental in women's oppression is the commercialization of sexualized gender relations within and by capitalism; both institutionally in the production/ reproduction division of labour so central to Marxist feminism (Adkins, 1995), and individually in the manipulation of intimate and erotic relations by advertisers seeking to stimulate consumption.

Women's oppression, then, is characterized by complexity and by an interpenetration of the material and the ideological that defies simple deconstruction. It is this vast and complex set of relations that impacts on women's ability to adopt safer sexual practices in their encounters and relationships with men. Cindy Patton (1994: 113), suggests that 'Perhaps the most deadly erasure of women's needs has been in the area of HIV infection prevention.' However, this in itself erases the complex and multiple dangers which sex holds for the majority of the world's women (Doyal, 1995).

The HIV-related danger to women is twofold. Biologically, women are more likely – studies suggest anywhere between two and three times more likely – than men to acquire HIV infection through heterosex (Bury, 1994; Patton, 1994; Doyal, 1995). Yet the social consequences of patriarchal power relations and their various means of enforcement mean that women are also at risk *from the very need to negotiate safer sex*. In contrast to the very public and affirmative incorporation of safer sex into (urban, politicized) gay male identities, 'Women[16] . . . in the absence of a strong women's movement, must fight their battle for safer sex on the carefully guarded and privatized domain of relationships with individual men' (Patton, 1989: 242), and it is that privatized domain, the arena of the 'domestic', of the family, which has been identified by much feminist research as the most dangerous place for women (Coote and Campbell, 1987; French, 1992; Hague and Malos, 1993).

The difficulty women have in negotiating safer heterosex is inextricably bound up with the supposedly unproblematic nature of heterosexuality. As the unquestioned (and unquestionable) norm, heterosexual (meaning penis-in-vagina) sex, although a vociferous presence in the datasphere of contemporary electronic cultural production, tends to remain unspecific and undeconstructed. Few non-queers question their desires or sexual activities, puzzle over why they are 'that way inclined' or what they should actually *do* in the pursuit of sexual pleasure. There is little in non-queer culture that parallels the vocal debate about specific sexual practices (sadomasochism, use of sex toys, cruising, etc.) that take place in some sections of lesbian communities, or the politicizing of other sexual/relationship practices (condom use, promiscuity, non-monogamy) that has occurred among some urban gay men. 'Heterosexuals . . . may initially experience fewer opportunities for exposure to HIV but also have fewer experiences of sexual community that can provide the locus for transformation to safer sex values' (Patton, 1989: 242). For black or minority ethnic women, simply accessing adequate and appropriate information about safer sex may be especially problematic either because such materials are not produced in their first language or appropriately distributed or because their access to any written materials is restricted by traditional patriarchal custom (Black HIV/AIDS Network, 1991).

The relatively private and inarticulate nature of heterosex – within whatever community – is, for women, only one factor acting to impede their ability to protect themselves from the heterosexual transmission of HIV. The principal factor is the gender of their sexual partners; the thing that makes safer heterosex so difficult for women to achieve is the fact that they are having sex – and hence negotiating safer sex – with men. Even in a social and cultural context which allows for the possibility of women expressing their needs around sex (and such are in a minority, globally speaking), women fear embarrassment, ridicule, loss of status, stigma, desertion, emotional or economic sanctions and outright physical violence in response to their attempts to negotiate safer heterosex (Gavey, 1993; Doyal, 1995; Doud, 1990; Wilton and Aggleton, 1991; Holland et al., 1991; 1994a; Patton, 1994; Stewart, 1991). For many women the potential risks of broaching the subject of safer sex with their male partners are more immediate and more pressing than the potential risk of illness and death from HIV infection. Cindy Patton writes of 'a depth of resistance to change [in sexual behaviour] among members of the [non-gay] "general public", a resistance to change that is far more hazardous to women than to men', and asks: 'Why, at the very core of heterosexual identity, is there an incapacity to understand what is being said about safer sex' (Patton, 1994: 114). In AIDS discourse it all too often goes without saying that the distinguishing characteristic of heterosex is that it takes place between people positioned at opposite (and conflictual) ends of the polarized binary that is the structure of gender in pre-millennial Western culture. Heterosex is more immediately structured by gendered power inequalities than homosex (whether between women or between men).[17] I suggest that the resistance identified by Patton is not a heterosexual resistance *per se*, but a resistance on the part of heterosexual *men*, and that 'at the heart of heterosexual identity'[18] lies that most totemized of notions, heterosexual ('real') masculinity.

See Dick pretend nothing's happening!

Outwith the queer and/or activist arenas, AIDS discourse is not distinguished by its radical nature. Indeed, much is overweeningly reactionary, specifically in terms of its construction of gender/sex. It tends to be positively docile to the unwritten pro-forma of hegemonic heteropatriarchal discursive practice in its collusion with the invisibility, the un-gazed-at and unproblematized status of (heterosexual) masculinity. I put 'heterosexual' in brackets, because heteropatriarchal discourse admits of no other

– 'masculinity' *means* that-which-fucks-women (into submission), and sex between men is stigmatized precisely because of its escape from the discursive limits of 'authentic' masculinity (Simpson, 1994).

Masculinity and men are, paradoxically, largely absent from discourses of sexuality or, indeed, of gender, '[I]n all the voluminous literature on sex and sexuality, there is very little on male sexuality as such' (Metcalf, 1985: 1). This invisibility of masculinity and of men is very different from the invisibility of lesbians. Lesbians are made invisible by and within heteropatriarchal discourse because they constitute an 'alarming subject' (Pratt, cited in Hoogland, 1994: 21):

> the persistence with which the [lesbian] is erased from the phallocentric con-
> ceptual universe is not so much incidental as overdetermined, and thus
> motivated. As such it can and should be read 'symptomatically', as a discursive
> knot or 'nodal point' in the text of phallocentric culture as a whole. (Hoogland,
> 1994: 21)

The invisibility of masculinity, I suggest, springs from its status as 'alarmed subject', and is qualitatively different from lesbian invisibility in that the master of discursive production, the paradigmatic speaker, the owner of the 'gaze' that reflexively constructs culture is the (white, heterosexual, middle-class) 'man'. This speaking man is the one who silences the lesbian. It is also he who vanishes masculinity, since it constitutes the position *from which he speaks* and from which he wields and reproduces his power over the (troublesomely proliferating) 'others' (see below, pp. 95–103). The motivation for the continuing production of white-initiated heteropatriarchal discourse is to reflect and reproduce through time the dominant construct of the other-as-subordinate and to reflect and reproduce through time the dominant construct of the speaking man as (rightfully, inevitably) superordinate. Phallic masculinity, the sign and instrument of hetero-patriarchal dominance, is in fact vulnerable and must be shielded from the problematizing gaze (this often works quite literally: to represent the penis in its always disappointing engorged state is a criminal act in Britain and many other Western countries). This hiding (like the hiding of lesbians) is a hiding to preserve male power, and its success may be measured, according to Foucault, by the invisibility of the act of hiding itself. For Foucault, the success of power 'is proportional to its ability to hide its own mechanisms . . . its secrecy . . . is indispensable to its operation' (cited in Simpson, 1994: 14).

It is unsurprising, then, that nominally heterosexual men are the group most characterized by their absence from the AIDS literature. The populations of concern, judging by the literature, are: gay men, prostitutes (primarily, though not exclusively women), 'adolescents' (sex usually undetermined), injecting drug users (constructed by their substance ab/use rather than their gender), women, Third World populations (again, tending to focus on women-as-mothers or women-as-prostitutes), bisexuals and 'the hard to reach' (see, e.g. Aggleton et al., 1990; Paalman, 1990; WHO, 1994).

Where men's sexual activity with women is recognized it is with reluctance, and the 'men' tend to be defined by something *other* than their masculinity: they are haemophiliacs, homeless people, injecting drug users, street youth or users of prostitutes.

Research shows that it is men who have sex with women who are most unable/reluctant to practise safer sex. For health educators, 'success' in reaching such men is measured in increases in condom use that appear pathetically slight when compared to the massive increase reported in gay communities (Health Education Authority, 1988; King, 1993), and young women (the most thoroughly researched group of putative heterosexuals is 'youth') consistently report difficulty in negotiating condom use with young men (Holland et al., 1991; Stewart, 1991; 1992). Yet this reluctance is barely acknowledged in the literature, with most writers (even those with a feminist approach) concentrating on the need to encourage assertiveness in women, rather than responsibility or compliance among men. As I have written elsewhere:

> As the monolithic norm around which patriarchal culture is constructed, masculinity is un-selfconscious, unquestioned and undefined. Its nature is that of the hole in the mint – an organising absence. Male power, organized around such evanescence, is consequently displaced onto that visible and given symbol of innate maleness, the penis, and onto practices which label and disempower those who are *other*, practices which range from queer-bashing and rape to the construction of the rigid gender demarcations which structure all our social relations. (Wilton and Aggleton, 1991: 154)

The practice of unsafe sex is, I suggest, of a piece with 'queer-bashing . . . rape [and] . . . rigid gender demarcations' in that it is fundamental to the project of masculinity. For masculinity, as many writers have recognized, is not a property of the body or of the psyche, but rather an acting out of a (paranoid) social script, a performance, an endless striving after the unattainable goal of phallicism (Giddens, 1992; Butler, 1990; 1994; Wilton, 1995b). It is important to recognize that masculinity is a relative rather than an absolute identity. To 'be' masculine is to be *not* feminine. '[M]asculinity, having no definition imposed upon it by a more powerful other (as is the case with femininity) achieves its own identity by a continual process of negative reference to *less* powerful others, specifically to women and to gay men' (Wilton and Aggleton, 1991: 154). This is the disavowed fragility at the heart of hegemony. In much the same way whiteness is *not-blackness*, to be white is to have power, including the power of naming over 'black' others; but it is also, perilously, to draw that power *from* its distinctiveness from 'black' otherness.

To enact and embody masculinity, then, means to continually prove one's difference from stigmatized and disempowered femininity. This impacts in clear and direct ways on the practice of safer sex. If we consider condoms, it becomes obvious that for a man to use a condom while having sex with a woman is ideologically risky. He is putting his masculinity at risk by so doing, because condom use is feminizing. It is feminizing because one or more of the following is taking place:

- He is agreeing to a request from a woman that he change his sexual behaviour, thus allowing her to define the terms of the sexual engagement. This is feminizing because the hegemonic construct of masculinity constitutes sexual knowledge and control as *male* (Holland et al., 1994b; Davidson, 1990).
- He is deprioritizing his own sexual *pleasure* (or a culturally agreed pleasure, unmediated penis/vagina contact) in the interests of sexual *safety*. This is feminizing because male sexual pleasure is *the* defining principle of heterosex to the extent that, unless male ejaculation takes place inside the vagina, the sex is not 'real sex' (Wilton and Aggleton, 1991; Richardson, 1990; 1993).
- He is demonstrating a degree of control over his sexual behaviour which is feminizing in that it is in direct contradiction of the dominant social scripting of male sexuality, namely that it is an uncontrollable or barely controllable force (Richardson, 1993). This assumption, which Weeks (1986) refers to as the 'hydraulic model' of male sexuality, obliges women to assume responsibility for their own safety in heterosex, since the man, subject to these uncontrollable urges, 'cannot be held responsible' once aroused (Wilton, 1992b).
- Thus, it is also feminizing that he accepts or takes responsibility for his partner's and his own sexual safety. Risk-taking is generally constructed as masculine and hence masculinizing, while to be concerned for/about safety especially during heterosex is constructed as feminine (Wilton, 1992b; Holland et al., 1994b; Richardson, 1993).

If condom use threatens the security of masculine identity, non-penetrative sex risks abandoning it altogether. Culturally and socially an adult male is defined by and expresses/maintains his social status by the act of sexually penetrating his social inferiors – usually (though not exclusively) women (Wilton, 1992b). Vaginal penetration is totemized as real, adult sex. Anything else tends to be dismissively labelled 'foreplay', meaning preparation, the sexual equivalent of filling the cracks in the wall before you can get on with the 'real' job of painting it. It is by engaging in penis-in-vagina ejaculation that men as well as women lose their virginity;[19] a status change that marks the only rite of passage to adulthood (apart from passing one's driving test) that remains in late modern Western cultures. Having achieved adult male status by gaining access to women's vaginas in this way, to choose to 'go back' to activities such as masturbation, inter-crural intercourse, frottage, oral sex, etc. is seen as retrogressive. Not only would such a choice mark a return to the less powerful status of youth, it would involve the voluntary surrender of the right of vaginal access that pre-eminently signifies masculinity. Safe or safer heterosex is ideologically intolerable within the terms of masculinity.

Instrumentality vs intimacy? The lonely male and the cruel feminist

Most of the (few) writers on masculinity agree that masculine sexuality is instrumental, often violent, and alienated (Stoltenberg, 1989; Davidson, 1990; Kayal, 1993; Bly, 1992; Giddens, 1992). This is a theme familiar in the feminist writings of the early years of both the first and the second wave of the women's liberation movement (Ryan, 1992; Millett, 1977; Firestone, 1979; Brownmiller, 1975), but its takeup by the (male) writers of the men's movement has been marked by a change in meaning. While feminism problematized the instrumentality and violence of men's sexuality and tended to see this as intrinsic to the social construction of masculinity and the socialization of male children (Formani, 1991), male writers have tended to identify feminism itself as responsible. In other words, feminists are to blame for those aspects of men's sexuality which they have critiqued!

Robert Bly's bestseller, *Iron John* (1992), is typical of this trend. While insisting on his sympathy with feminism, Bly manipulates myth, story and legend to protest the feminization of men and to reinstate the biological determinism that feminism challenges:

> In the seventies I began to see all over the country a phenomenon that we might call the 'soft male' . . . many of these men are not happy. You quickly notice the lack of energy in them. They are life-preserving but not exactly life-giving . . . The strong or life-giving women who graduated from the sixties, so to speak, or who have inherited an older spirit, played an important part in producing this life-preserving, but not life-giving, man . . . Some energetic women . . . chose and still choose soft men to be their lovers and, in a way, perhaps, to be their sons . . . Young men for various reasons wanted their harder women, and women began to desire softer men. It seemed like a nice arrangement for a while, but we've lived with it long enough now to see that it isn't working out. (Bly, 1992: 2–3)

In this mythography of gender, women mysteriously (it has to be mysterious, since to transfer this model into the material world would be to expose it as the fantasy it is) acquire the power to change men, to make them *soft*. Given the elision of masculinity and (tumescent) phallic power, the effeminization and destruction of masculinity in that word 'soft' should not be underestimated. Meanwhile, the women themselves have become 'hard' (men do not in any way contribute to this hardness in women; some of them simply choose it), i.e. phallic. And this change has, according to Bly, been extensive enough and lasted long enough for 'us' to see that it 'isn't working out'. In other words, disrupting gender roles is not a good idea. Turning from Bly, who represents the woolly fringe of the men's movement, how does a cool-headed social scientist view this change in masculinity?

Anthony Giddens, in *The Transformation of Intimacy* (1992), suggests that men's withdrawal from the (historically recent) business of intimacy was consequent upon the separation of domestic and public spheres that followed capitalism, while their current anxieties concern the (again, recent) separation of sex from reproduction that contraceptive and reproductive technologies allow:

> The claims to power of maleness depend upon a dangling piece of flesh that has now lost its distinctive connection to reproduction. This is a new castration indeed; women can now see men, at least on a cognitive level, as just as much a functionless appendage as the male sexual organ itself. (Giddens, 1992: 153)

The phallus is now not only 'soft', but 'dangling', and the modern man 'castrated' by technology. Yet the third characteristic of modern male sexuality, violence, Giddens suggests is due not to economic or technological change, but to women's refusal to play the gender game any more. Whereas, in the past, men's violence expressed patriarchal power, now it expresses a response to *women's* refusal of that power:

> a large amount of male sexual violence now stems from insecurity and inadequacy rather than from a seamless continuation of patriarchal dominance. Violence is a destructive reaction to the waning of female complicity. (ibid.)

Women, whichever way you look at it, cannot win. Either submit to patriarchal gender roles and the violence that goes along with them, or resist, and suffer the violence that your resistance 'provokes'.

Phallic masculinity, then, is a social and cultural construct that makes it extremely difficult to begin the widespread and fundamental changes in sexual behaviour which this epidemic demands. As Diane Richardson puts it:

> The belief that men have strong sexual desires which women are responsible for controlling or 'provoking', coupled with the expectation that women have an obligation to meet men's sexual 'needs', helps to explain why women can find it difficult to refuse unwanted sex and/or insist on the kind of sex they would like. They may also find it difficult to refuse men because they fear the consequences; for instance, the threat of, or actual, violence or their partner rejecting them. (Richardson, 1993: 87)

The promotion of sexual safety is now, as it always has been, obstructed by the social construction of gender, specifically the social construction of masculinity. How, then, to devise policies that enable populations to remain uninfected during the HIV pandemic? It is unimaginable that any government, however totalitarian, would be technologically and politically able to impose the specific sexual behaviours needed to prevent transmission. Even where unacceptable sexual behaviours are or have been subject to the death penalty, people don't stop engaging in them, as trial records and other documents indicate (see, e.g. Katz, 1983; Brown, 1989; Haeberle, 1989). In a democratic society, the only means available to slow the spread of HIV infection is health promotion/education. In order to assess how effective health education may be in transforming the social relations of sexuality, we need to consider how such education works. This is the subject of the next chapter.

Notes

1. Sex is not, of course, the only biological activity to be overloaded with social meaning; both eating and defecating spring to mind. However, it does appear to be the primary and principal significant act in most human societies.

2. For those whose school chemistry didn't cover sulphur . . . sulphur is an element that exists in three basic forms, as a crystal, a powder and a kind of gooey mess. All three extraordinarily different forms remain pure sulphur, much as coal and diamonds remain carbon.

3. And I am sure there is an issue here when considering the current reigning queen of drag queens in the West, RuPaul. As a *very* tall black gay man, RuPaul's queerly overstated drag resonates with the promise of what s/he has to hide under those clinging dresses – the mythical gargantuan penis of the black male.

4. What has not yet, as far as I know, been explored by cultural practitioners or theorists is the set of meanings which coalesce around – or perhaps I should say, which *resist* coalescing around – the idea of the lesbian uterus. The reproductive potential of the 'female' body takes on a complex and undertheorized set of meanings when the sexual pleasures of that body are lesbian.

5. This is not new and not a consequence of AIDS research. Land Humphreys' research, for example, was carried out in the late 1960s. What is new is that these findings now have an easily recognised significance, whereas before (being intrinsically threatening to comfortable categories of hetero- and homosexuality) they were of interest mainly to academics.

6. An order of gay male nuns, currently with chapters (convents?) in the US, Britain and France who take very seriously their calling to fight against sexual guilt and who canonized queer filmmaker Derek Jarman (St Derek of Dungeness). The sisters regularly turn up to bless the marchers on annual lesbian and Gay Pride parades, demonstrations, etc. I am proud to count myself among the faithful who have been blessed in this way!

7. The notion of the chronotope describes a 'thing' which is of both time and place. Of course, whether such performances can ever write new rules, or throw away the rule book altogether, is another question. It is, I think, enough for now that they disobey.

8. There are regular letters in the gay press complaining about non-gay businesses (such as straight pubs and clubs which have a regular gay night) exploiting their gay clientele. The commercial gay scene in Britain, although supported by groups such as the Gay Business Association, has inevitably been less profitable and less gay-owned than in the US.

9. This was in July 1995, when I attended the 'Sexuality and Medicine' conference at the University of Melbourne, and the third annual 'HIV, AIDS and Society' conference at Macquarie University, Sydney. I should emphasize that this is *not* an indication of widespread sexual irresponsibility among Australian gay men. On the contrary, unprotected sex usually takes place between seropositive partners. As Gary Prestage, Sue Kippax and Jason Noble comment in their paper on this question, 'Overwhelmingly positive men restrict their unprotected anal intercourse to encounters with other positive men' (Prestage et al., 1995: 12).

10. This happened in Switzerland, not England, where the British Standards Institution is still refusing to set a standard for condoms designed for anal use, and where manufacturers continue to market their condoms for vaginal use only, in order to pre-empt possible legal action should a condom break during anal intercourse (see King, 1993 for a full discussion of this problem).

11. The work of Diane Richardson is the one important exception to this rule. It is no accident that Richardson is herself a lesbian and writes from a feminist perspective.

12. Of course, AIDS cannot be 'caught', as is suggested here. It is more than a little peculiar that this text describes AIDS as 'caught through heterosexual sex', while gay men are described as 'at higher risk of catching HIV' during passive anal penetration (active penetration being irresponsibly dismissed as of no potential risk) while the kind of sex bisexuals have with heterosexual women 'could spread HIV in the heterosexual community' and lesbians are 'at low risk of catching or transmitting AIDS'. There seems to be an

association between men and HIV and women and AIDS. Material such as this is positively dangerous.

13. For example, a special 'lesbian' issue of the British soft porn mag *For Men* contains 17 pictorial scenarios featuring two women, *all* of which incorporate a written paragraph describing cunnilingus as the *reason why* women have sex with other women: 'Kelly and I like guys but we regularly go to bed with other girls . . . Let's be honest. All women love oral, and no man can suck a clit as well as a woman' (*For Men*, 2(6) March 1995: 122).

14. That this is the case is indicated, for example, in John Sayles' 1983 film *Lianna*, in which the ex-heterosexual housewife recognizes her newly found lesbian identity by confronting her reflection in a bathroom mirror and announcing that she 'eats pussy'. The scene (powerfully in such a meek little film) encapsulated the notion of a reverse discourse: Lianna is trying on for size the street insults which now apply to her, and is pleased rather than horrified to find that the cap fits.

15. I use 'patriarchies' in the plural here to indicate the multiple, heterogeneous and specific nature of patriarchal hegemony in different cultures and at different historical moments.

16. For 'women' here, read 'women who have sex with men'. Of course, it is not exclusively heterosexual women who have sex with men; some lesbians sell sex to men or have occasional sexual encounters with gay or non-gay men. However, by failing here to distinguish between exclusively lesbian 'women' and women who have sex with men, Patton is erasing lesbian sexuality in a disturbing way.

17. Queer relationships may not be understood as existing outside the sphere of influence of gendered power relations, nor of having eradicated (or even necessarily become aware of) the playing out of such relations in man/man or woman/woman sexual behaviour and relationships. By definition, however, gender polarity is referential and tangential, a force acting upon the relationship from 'outside', from the social/cultural matrix within which queer sex is embedded, rather than being a taken-for-granted project of the relationship, as it is for woman/man sexual behaviour and relationships.

18. Although the very concept of heterosexual identity is a dubious one. If there were such a thing (and the mind refuses to grasp images such as Straight Pride marches and T-shirt slogans such as 'What a heterosexual looks like') then the adoption of safer sexual practices would not be, as it is now, a near impossibility.

19. I remember earnest debate in the girls' cloakroom at my school as to whether you could be said to have lost your virginity if the boy didn't ejaculate inside you. Opinion was fairly evenly divided: the important thing is, of course, that none of us ever questioned whether or not our own orgasms were as significant.

3

Look after Yourself: HIV/AIDS Health Education and Promotion

We take health education very much for granted as a response to this epidemic, and have quickly become accustomed to the novel idea of health educators telling us how to have sex. Yet statutory health education and health promotion are historically recent ideas, and we know relatively little about how (or if) they work. As with any other large-scale social initiative, health education and health promotion comprise discourses which inevitably reproduce or rupture hegemonic regimes of gender. In the context of an epidemic whose epidemiology and consequences are so profoundly shaped by gender and by sexuality, it is of crucial importance to deconstruct the textual and discursive practices within health education/promotion which coalesce around sex, gender and the erotic.

The development of health education

Health education in Britain has its roots in the nineteenth century, as the health hazards consequent on industrialization and urbanization became a national priority. Epidemic disease was rife in the overcrowded and poverty-stricken cities, and this led to a particular association in the middle-class mind between poverty, immorality and disease. Victorian Britain represents the zenith of bourgeois morality, a narrow and puritanical doctrine which constructed poverty as a personality disorder and made little distinction between physical and moral 'dirt' or between physiological and moral 'sickness'. The consequences of this medico-moral paradigm for the treatment of sexually transmitted diseases, the venereal diseases (VD) as they were then still known, were lethal.

Many hospitals refused to admit patients with VD, charitable dispensaries would not supply them with medication and even the workhouse infirmaries would not admit VD-infected paupers. On the extremist fringe of the medical profession were those who opposed research into venereal diseases, believing that the discovery of a cure would be against the will of God: 'syphilis had been created as a punishment for fornication and if it could be cured "fornication would be universal"' (Smith, 1979: 295).[1] As with so much health and welfare policy in the nineteenth and early twentieth centuries, war was the spur to activity. Health education directed at preventing the spread of VD became seen as a matter of urgency during the First World War (1914–18), when between 10 per cent and 20 per cent of soldiers were found to be infected. At this point the first 'shock horror' campaigns were initiated, attempting to encourage sexual abstinence among the troops by showing them 'lurid pictures of diseased genitals' (Naidoo and Wills, 1994: 63).

Health education was, from its origins, an attempt by professionals, experts and middle-class people to educate poor and working-class people about health, nutrition and hygiene for their own good. The public health reforms of the nineteenth century, which resulted in a dramatic reduction in mortality and morbidity from infectious diseases, were accompanied by the belief that the poor should be educated in ways to prevent ill-health. Such 'top-down' intervention ranged from the formal and officially sanctioned activities of the medical officers of health (appointed to each town by law from 1848) to the informal and philanthropic. A good example of the latter is Charles Elme Francatelli's *A Plain Cookery Book for the Working Classes* (1861; modern facsimile, 1993). Francatelli was chief cook to Queen Victoria, and his *Plain Cookery Book* contains household remedies for minor ailments and a recipe for 'economical and substantial soup for distribution to the poor'. It also contains Francatelli's advice on how to prepare the cuts of cold meat which, although out of the economic reach of the poor, might be donated to them:

> Besides, some of you who are living close to noblemen and gentlemen's mansions in the country, or otherwise, may perhaps stand a chance of now and then receiving a donation of this kind. (Francatelli, 1861/1993: 44)

In this socio-economic climate, where the means to pay for a healthy diet and healthy accommodation were clearly limited to the privileged, *knowledge* and *information* about how to promote health and well-being were seen as the property of the economic and social elite. Additionally, the medical profession and allopathic medicine were rising to a position of intellectual and social dominance. The medical model of health, which constructs health *negatively*, as the absence of disease or injury, was starting to structure lay understandings of health and illness, and so the 'scientific' knowledge and skills needed to prevent disease were seen as residing in medical experts (Hart, 1985; Oakley, 1976).

Gender, power and health education

As a 'top-down' approach, based on an authority model, health education operates along familiar axes of power. Structural inequalities founded upon gender traditionally kept women out of both public life and the professions and effectively prevented their becoming 'experts' in anything. Indeed, the model of authority itself is patriarchal. It is in the nature of authority to exercise its juridical and disciplinary regimen on the powerless, thereby both justifying and maintaining the superordination of the powerful. Health education, as an institutional activity, follows pre-existing unidirectional circuits of power, rather as an electrical charge flows round a circuit board. In so doing it both conforms to and reasserts the hegemony of the structural and institutional networks whereby power is differentially assigned and enacted.

Because of their already subordinate position on the axis of gender power, women tend to be the object of health education discourse and men the subject. It is difficult for health education to be anything other than a set of masculinist texts, informed by and giving voice to heteropatriarchal ideology and constructing (in common with all heteropatriarchal texts) woman-as-problematic-other. Clearly social power does not operate in discrete binaries/polarities. Rather, multiple axes intersect to form a constantly mutable network in which different kinds of power inhere, a kind of internet of discourses which compete and collude in struggles over ordination. Thus issues such as class, 'race', sexuality, age and dis/ability both have significance in their own right and multiply interpolate with gender in the arena of health education (as everywhere else).

Gender and sexuality have an additional specific significance in the field of health and welfare. Women have always been constructed and addressed by the welfare state and the medical profession in terms of their primary function to the nation state: the care and reproduction of the workforce. This is most overt during times of conflict, when the workforce is required to fight and die to defend the state, or during times of economic crisis (such as the post-Second World War years) when the workforce is inadequate to the demands of economic recovery (Pateman, 1992). The founding of the welfare state in Britain was quite explicitly allied to the need to produce fitter sons of empire, and to support women in their job of ensuring a steady stream of such sons. Moreover, the eugenics movement was enthusiatically supported in Britain and the United States until Hitler's adoption of eugenicist ideals to fuel the Holocaust brought it into disrepute, but traces of the stock-breeding approach of eugenics may be detected in much public sector discourse up until the early 1960s.

The health care available to women, together with the education of girls generally and health education in particular, aimed to produce women who were capable and effective wives and mothers. The 'woman' constructed in public sector discourse *means* 'wife-and-mother'. There is no recognition that women may have needs which do not relate to this heterosexual production role; there are no services provided which aim to meet such needs. Health education aimed to create a world of clean (in both the literal and metaphoric sense), hygienic homes, and mothers were the primary instrument in this project. In 1906, a medical officer of health wrote:

> First, concentrate on the mother. What the mother is the children are. The stream is no purer than the source. Let us glorify, dignify and purify motherhood by every means in our power . . . We have got to have better and cleaner homes, more sober homes . . . we have got to have cleanliness wherever we can get it. (cited in Oakley, 1976: 41)

Women are, in the terms of this model of health education, no more than instruments of infection control. Any notion of the position of women's own health needs, or of the potential costs to their health of ensuring 'better and cleaner homes', remains unrecognized.

It is a characteristic of health education (as opposed to health promotion) that it focuses on the individual. Even where the preferred approach is community based or participatory (Naidoo and Wills, 1994), the emphasis is on individuals taking whatever action is open to them (and this may include action within a community context), to prevent disease or improve their health. This individualism is problematic on two counts, firstly because it easily slides into victim-blaming and secondly because it is open to manipulation by the New Right in its renovation of classic free market liberalism. New Right ideology mandates minimal or non-existent state intervention, 'rolling back the state', in an economy driven by uncontrolled market forces. The presumptive aim of health education within this paradigm is to transform people into informed consumers both of health care and of other products – foods, household utensils, clothing, etc. – which may be health promoting or health compromising. The Department of Health (DoH) publication, *Health of the Nation* (DoH, 1992: 4) states clearly its strategy that the aim of health education is 'to ensure that individuals are able to exercise informed choice when selecting the lifestyles which they adopt'.

The New Right goal of reducing public spending and increasing reliance on the mixed economy of welfare[2] also means that it is politically convenient to insist that health is primarily the responsibility of the individual. The Department of Health and Social Security (DHSS), as it then was,[3] published a white paper, *Prevention and Health: Everybody's Business* in 1976, which set out quite overtly the position that the individual was responsible for his own (the male pronoun is used throughout) health:

> To a large extent though, it is clear that the weight of responsibility for his own health lies on the shoulders of the individual himself. The smoking-related diseases, alcoholism and other drug dependencies, obesity and its consequences, and the sexually transmitted diseases are among the preventable problems of our time and, in relation to all of these, the individual must decide for himself. (cited in Naidoo and Wills, 1994: 67)

With this focus on the choices of the individual as its foundational assumption, the practice of health education includes both the giving of *information* about health and the encouragement of *behaviour change* in the direction of health-promoting behaviours. Early in the development of health education it was thought that information alone could lead to behaviour change, but clearly this is not the case. If it were, nobody would smoke, eat junk food or drink too much alcohol, let alone practise unsafe sex. Health education has developed more sophisticated techniques and approaches in recognition of this fact, but it remains true that:

The rationale of health education has been to inform people about the prevention of disease and to motivate them to change their behaviour, through persuasion and mass communication techniques, and to equip them through education with the skills for a healthy lifestyle. (Naidoo and Wills, 1994: 68)

Unfortunately neither skills nor information is enough to enable individuals to make healthy choices in the face of systematic and structural inequalities. Social variables such as gender, sexuality, socio-economic class and 'race' have a demonstrable impact on the health of individuals and groups (Ewles and Simnett, 1985). Of these, material inequality is widely recognized (by almost everyone except government ministers) as being the single most significant factor influencing the health and life chances of individuals on both a local and an international level (Townsend et al., 1988), and such inequalities have a disproportionate effect on women (Seager and Olson, 1986; Graham, 1993; Doyal, 1995). Women generally tend to have far less control over their lives than do men, and far fewer choices are open to women in respect of diet, leisure activities, housing, sexual behaviour, etc. Health and illness are not discrete biological experiences confined to the body of the individual but are located at the interface between the individual and the social:

a person's health is inextricably related to everything surrounding that person and it is impossible to be healthy in a 'sick' society which does not provide the resources for basic physical and emotional needs. (Ewles and Simnett, 1985: 6)

Individual health cannot be detached from societal health, and there are many economic and political structures in any society, beyond the control of the individual or even the 'community', which tend to determine health status across groups of people similarly sited relative to such structures. Growing recognition of the importance of structural influences on health led to the development of the idea of health *promotion*.

Promoting health: a structural approach

It was the Canadian Minister of National Health and Welfare, Marc Lalonde, who first used the term 'health promotion', in a major report published in 1974, *A New Perspective on the Health of Canadians*, which foregrounded social determinants of health (Naidoo and Wills, 1994: 74). During the decades that followed, the WHO encouraged a shift in emphasis from medical care (the treatment of disease and injury) to primary *health* care (the prevention of disease and injury and the positive enhancement of health). In 1977 the World Health Assembly at Alma Ata agreed that 'there should be the attainment by all the people of the world by the year 2000 of a level of health that will permit them to lead a socially and economically productive life' (Naidoo and Wills, 1994: 74). In international efforts to reach this goal, the WHO developed a model of health promotion which was far-reaching, and which took into account the structural, political and cultural determinants of health. This model involves the population as a whole (rather than focusing on groups perceived to be 'at risk' from specific hazards), is directed towards action on the determinants of health, combines diverse approaches ranging from education to fiscal policy change and lays particular emphasis on public participation. Importantly, while recognizing that health professionals have an important role to play, health promotion is located in the socio-political sphere rather than the clinical (Scriven and Orme, 1996; Abel-Smith, 1994; Naidoo and Wills, 1994; Homans and Aggleton, 1988).

Although health education is seen as an intrinsic part of health promotion, health promotion in this paradigm potentially offers more to women than health education alone. The WHO identifies fundamental conditions which need to be met as the baseline for improving health, and these are extremely wide-ranging. They include peace and freedom from the fear of war (including the fear of global nuclear holocaust experienced in developed nations during the Cold War), the satisfaction of basic needs, political commitment and public support for health-promoting public policy, and social justice/equality of opportunity for all.

This strongly supports the position of feminist health activists around the world who have long argued that women's social and political inequality directly compromises their health and life chances (Doyal, 1995; Smyke, 1991; Seager and Olson, 1986). The assumption that adequate information and training in skills such as assertiveness will enable individuals to make healthy choices fails to take account of the wide range of material, institutional, political, ideological and cultural factors which structure the lives of people and communities. As Abel-Smith tersely puts it, 'To a large extent people are prisoners of their values and the values of the society they live in, and are limited by their economic and social environment, *quite apart from any health knowledge they may possess*' (Abel-Smith, 1994: 33; emphasis added). The concept of health promotion mandates action where needed in all social arenas, so 'making the healthier choice the easier choice' has come to be regarded by many as its definitional objective (Milio, cited in Naidoo and Wills, 1994: 77).

The socio-political institution of gender operates on all levels: material, institutional, political, psychological, ideological and cultural, and as such exercises a profound and general influence on both women's and men's health, including their vulnerability to HIV infection and their life chances once infected. Globally, women's subordination to men places them at risk of acquiring HIV infection and reduces their quality of life and survival time once diagnosed with AIDS (Doyal, 1994; Bury, 1994; Panos Institute, 1990; Berer with Ray, 1993). The official response to the epidemic has largely relied on traditional health education strategies, resorting to mass information campaigns, shock-horror tactics and the targeting of specific social groups assumed to be at risk (and assumed to be discrete). How appropriate has health education been in the context of this epidemic, and what would a health promotion strategy for HIV/AIDS consist of?

Sexual communities, sexual choices: the limits to health education

Whether or not health education alone is sufficient to prevent people becoming infected with HIV, it is undoubtedly true that disseminating straightforward factual information about the virus, its effects and routes of transmission, as well as the means of avoiding transmission, was and continues to be a first requirement of the public health response to AIDS. Modern technologies of transportation have ensured that HIV has spread to every country in the world faster than any other infectious disease in the history of humanity, and the long asymptomatic period characteristic of the virus meant that this global spread had largely occurred *before* the new medical emergency was recognized. This presents the world community with a unique challenge: how to ensure that each and every individual has the information they need to prevent transmission and protect the health of those already infected (Wilton, 1992a). Such information must be accessible and easily understood by those who need it, it must be appropriately located in the context of local cultures and traditions and it must avoid giving rise to either panic or despair and fatalism.

Even so apparently simple a matter as the dissemination of effective *information* about HIV is fraught with difficulty. Lay beliefs about health and illness vary widely between cultures and, even in industrialized Western cultures, seldom conform to allopathic medical understandings (Abel-Smith, 1994; Homans and Aggleton, 1988; Warwick et al., 1988). Information about health is not passively consumed but actively *processed* in the context of pre-existing health beliefs. Any information which appears to diverge greatly from already held beliefs is likely to be rejected or profoundly modified by the individual, and this has been shown to result in sometimes extraordinary lay beliefs about HIV/AIDS (Warwick et al., 1988). Additionally, 'health' is not compartmentalized in isolation from more general beliefs about life, so the social, political, religious and moral attitudes which an individual holds will all nuance their understandings about HIV.

This process of 'meaning-making' has emerged as profoundly significant in this epidemic. Alongside minority conviction that AIDS was 'caused by' the CIA, the KGB, spores from a passing comet or scientific experiments by extra-terrestrial aliens lie more disturbing and destructive convictions. In the industrialized West the decimation of gay communities by the virus has led to a stubborn heterosexual 'illusion of invulnerability' (Phillips, 1993), while the long-standing historical construction of women's sexuality as dangerous to men's health (see next chapter) has had a profound impact on both women's and men's ability to practise safer heterosex. Such lay beliefs are not eradicated in any straightforward sense by medical training: some are likely to influence the practice of medical professionals and health educators (Aggleton, 1990).

It is not simply lay health beliefs which influence the effective incorporation of HIV/AIDS health education into people's lives. The political and moral agenda of different societies and of different interest groups within societies may have a powerful impact not only on the reception and interpretation of health education texts but also on which health education advice may be made publicly available in the first place. In the context of HIV/AIDS, the impact of factors such as these has been quite overt, with a dramatic contrast between the health education carried out within statutory bodies and that originating in deviant subcultures.

Statutory bodies are, by definition, generally dependent on public funds and hence are inextricably bound to the political process. In democratic countries this means that moneys are unlikely to be made available for interventions which politicians perceive as unpopular with the electorate. It is notoriously hard to gauge public opinion; those who wish to retain their political position depend on opinion polls, media presentations, letters from constituents, statements from lobbyists and interest groups and other such straws in the wind. The result of this is that 'public opinion' as received by those in power is in fact the opinions of those with the financial, social and personal means to make their opinion heard: the well-educated, the confident, the wealthy, the articulate and those with access to the machinery of representation (in both the political and textual sense). It is still the case that the vast majority of those with such resources are men. This means that the health education produced in the public/statutory sector is likely to be largely in the continued interests of men as a class. 'Whatever is not male, preferably white, hierarchical and patriarchal, is other than and less than – that is, women, women not wanting men, and men perceived as acting otherwise than within the prerogatives of male power' (Gordon, cited in Kayal, 1993: 24).

The AIDS agenda has also been quite cynically manipulated by those whom Philip Kayal (1993: 25) calls 'moral entrepreneurs'; the religious fundamentalists, New Right politicians and representatives of the self-styled 'moral majority'. This has resulted in a policing of information exchange whose consequences have been no less than lethal. Information about safer street drug injecting practices has been suppressed in case it was interpreted as demonstrating a 'permissive attitude towards drug use' (Institute of Medicine, 1986). Safer sex information targeted at gay men has been impounded by customs officials (Wilton, 1992a), suppressed by local and national government officials (Institute of Medicine, 1986) or, in one incredible scenario, smuggled across national borders by government ministers in order to avoid customs seizure (Homans and Aggleton, 1988).

Faced with the homophobic negligence of statutory bodies and free from the constraints imposed by public accountability, many deviant subcultural groups have taken it upon themselves to mount proactive and urgent HIV/ AIDS health education campaigns. The vast AIDS industry now established in most countries in the industrialized West owes more to the energy of the lesbian and gay community than to official administrations. Local communities of gay men and of sex workers have mounted vigorous and imaginative community-based educational initiatives, using language and methods rooted in and accessible to their communities (Patton, 1994; Kramer, 1990; Kayal, 1993). Indeed, some gay communities have made it their goal to incorporate the practice of safer sex into gay identity, as a sign of men's choice to love and care for other men (Kayal, 1993).

The relationship between this spontaneous, politically driven activism and elected administrations has been difficult. Governments have in some cases been only too grateful to offload their responsibility for educating gay men about HIV/AIDS onto the lesbian and gay community (Wilton, 1994a; Whitehead, 1989; Stoddard, 1989), grant-aiding many such organizations rather than locating the work firmly in the more secure, well-funded statutory sector. In such cases funding may be withdrawn without warning or may be dependent on imposed criteria being met, and is always on an insecure, temporary basis. AIDS service organizations (ASOs) in the voluntary sector are therefore obliged to devote much of their time and energy to fundraising. There are critics who suggest that 'all these [voluntary] groups have perhaps enabled the government both to starve AIDS funding and to distance itself from education work, research, and the care of people with AIDS' (Whitehead, 1989: 108).

There has also been a tendency for statutory bodies to attempt to locate their own health education interventions directed at the gay community within the community/activist paradigm. The central paradigm of HIV/ AIDS health education has been, as Cindy Patton (1994: 50) observes, to target 'education at *practices* through *identity*' (emphasis added), something evidenced by the plethora of badly written, poorly drawn 'comic book' style educational materials aimed at young people. To attempt to exploit subcultural genres or mores in order to promote top-down health education messages is both patronizing and ineffective. '[P]rofessionally imposed notions of cultural community may be experienced by clients as coercive rather than enabling' (Naidoo and Wills, 1994: 162). For women there is the additional problem that most subcultural groups are as male dominated as mainstream society, and may be even more riddled with sexist assumptions and misogyny.

Health education for women: more of the same?

HIV/AIDS health education seems unlikely to be able to offer much to women. Statutory health education is controlled by the patriarchal state, and as such has demonstrably reinforced the traditional discursive construction of women's sexuality as of interest only insofar as it represents a risk to heterosexual men (see p. 55). Health education within the voluntary sector takes place within intersecting micro-cultural locations, few of which are controlled by or involve women, and most of which coalesce around political and ideological positions which at best marginalize and at worst actively oppress women.

There is, even for gay men, a contradiction at the heart of AIDS activist health education, which has its roots in the need to defend gay men simultaneously against homophobia and HIV infection:

> gay men asserted the primacy of their 'community' and 'identity' while disputing the association of identity with practices. They argued that epidemiologists should focus on risk practices, even if changes to safe sex norms seemed easier to accomplish if gay men took on a positive identity that associated risk reduction with pride in self and community. (Patton, 1994: 48)

For injecting drug users the criminality and stigmatized nature of their drug use results in secrecy, isolation and a high degree of suspicion and para-noia. Street drug injecting 'communities' are characterized by extremely loose, friable connections and by cynicism towards mainstream social institutions. There may be a fatalism engendered by addiction (although it is important to recognize that only a minority of street drugs are addictive), which makes it hard to focus on health risks that will not appear until months or years into the future. Indeed, Abel-Smith suggests that such fatalism is widespread outside the middle-class culture of deferred gratifi-cation:

> If people have never absorbed middle class aspiring values, it is useless to direct health education messages at them as if they had. If life is a matter of luck and the future can take care of itself, it is of little interest to be told what activities which give pleasure today run risks of major health damage in the future. (Abel-Smith, 1994: 36–7)

Additionally, those who inject drugs may have good reason to be cynical about the motives of health educators. Health education has traditionally presented drugs such as heroin in a baroque and dramatic light, suggesting that they are immediately addictive, profoundly damaging to health, and have far-reaching destructive effects on individuals' lives. Although this is sometimes the case, it is often not, and those who witness at first hand the contrast between the Gothic tendencies of official drugs propaganda and the more manageable drug use of their daily lives are bound to question the content and hidden agenda of health education. It is hard to see how a sense of 'community' might be positively exploited by health educators in this context.

If the notion of community- or identity-based health education is inappropriate for many 'at risk' groups, and problematic even in the context of gay men, it is fundamentally inadequate where women are concerned. There are many women whose gender identity is profoundly shaped by their lesbianism, their work in the sex industry or their use of injected drugs, but their relationship to their sexuality or their drug use is equally profoundly shaped by their gender, and as such it may be quite inappropriate to target them straightforwardly as drug users or as 'gay'.

Within the AIDS crisis, lesbians have been marginalized both by establishment interventions which assume that women having sex with women are not at risk of HIV infection and by the gay/queer community norms which became established around safer sex. Some gay men expressed resentment towards those lesbians who pointed out that their need for safer sex information was not recognized, going so far as to accuse them of 'virus envy' (Richardson, 1994). Moreover, some lesbians, assuming that woman-to-woman sexual transmission was impossible, cast doubts on the sexual identity of lesbians who were concerned and represented HIV as something associated with dirty, unpleasant practices which lesbians were unlikely to get up to:

> In order to become infected [with HIV], I would need to be in contact with an infected person, and to do something to cause the virus to enter my bloodstream. I don't fancy the scenario, but a penis or penises, semen, infected blood and dirty needles would usually have to come into the picture somewhere. I'm not A.I.D.S. prone merely by being a lesbian, mixing with other lesbians . . . or socializing among gay men (if, indeed, I did have gay male friends). (Hart, 1985: 91)

Cindy Patton observed similar reactions among lesbians in the United States, and strongly suggests that this response was unhelpful (to say the least) to those women who wanted to explore safer sexual options:

> women who became associated with calls to safe sex, or who publicly claimed to use dental dams, were thought to have some suspect aspect to their sexual practices, and individual lesbians who raised the question of safe sex and practised it were immediately cast as the 'risky' partner . . . lesbians who pursued technical innovations were greeted as paranoid, ludicrous, envious of the attention gay men's sexuality had attracted, or masochistically willing to submit to practices which would shackle their sexuality. (Patton, 1994: 69)

For lesbians, then, identity and a sense of community have not supported the development of a confident safer sex discourse as has been the case with gay men. Neither statutory nor voluntary/activist health education interventions have succeeded in identifying and meeting the needs of lesbians for appropriate HIV/AIDS information.

Women in the sex industry, particularly those who sell sex, represent the one group of heterosexually active women who have been able to organize around the provision of safer sex information at a community level. In geopolitical locations as different as New Zealand, Holland, Britain, the United States and many countries in sub-Saharan Africa, women who sell sex have organized to produce and disseminate information about safe sex (Butcher, 1994; Patton, 1994; Berer with Ray, 1993). In other countries, however, women sex workers have been targeted by discriminatory practices which, while offering the simulacrum of safety to the clients/johns, leave the women themselves open to risk. In Thailand, for example, a system was introduced in 1990 whereby sex workers testing negative for HIV antibody were issued with a green card, so that johns did not have to use a condom. In the Philippines, where the main source of income is the presence of US army bases, the law until recently insisted that all long-term visitors be tested for HIV antibodies, *except US military personnel* (Butcher, 1994), thus putting local sex workers at increased risk of contracting HIV infection from US servicemen.

Prostitution is generally presented as extreme and deviant female behaviour, although there is a strong case for regarding it as existing on a much wider continuum of gendered economic relations. As an execrated (and often criminal) behaviour, however, prostitution can (although it does not always) offer the foundation for an oppositional identity, for a sense of community and for resistance to oppression which is, ironically, not so easily available to non-prostitute heterosexually active women.

While AIDS community activist discourse has marginalized lesbian women there is at least a lively debate about HIV and safer sex in lesbian/ queer circles. This is not the case for heterosexual women. While women who have sex with men for money have been able, in some cultures, to develop a resistance to stigma, and community support for the practice of safer sex, this is not the case for women who don't charge. As we have seen, not charging is a significant marker for sex workers themselves inasmuch as using a condom may mark the division between their working lives and intimate relationships, with condomless intercourse retained as a mark of intimacy with lovers and partners (Day and Ward, 1990). The act of *unprotected* penile penetration appears to be taking on a new symbolic significance in the light of this epidemic, a disturbing unintended consequence of the widespread promotion of condom use. Not only do sex workers signify the intimacy of their love relationships by not using condoms; research into male clients of sex workers suggests that this system of signification holds true for them too:

> A recent study among German sex tourists in Thailand . . . revealed that some of the men romanticize their relationships with Thai sex workers, staying with them for a number of days and regarding them as lovers rather than prostitutes. This seems to encourage them to forget that commercial sex is involved and they consequently do not see a need for safer sex. (WHO, 1991: 1)

The romanticization of unprotected intercourse should, perhaps, have been predicted. It was surely inevitable that, in response to safer sex advice based on the familiar (and irrelevant) moralism which constructed AIDS as the consequence or even punishment for deviance – homosexuality, promiscuity, sex outside marriage, prostitution – and which prioritized the promotion of condom use over the (far more problematic) promotion of alternatives to penetration, condoms should become associated with dangerous (i.e. deviant) sexual behaviours. The ridiculous but culturally unavoidable mapping of safer sex promotion onto anachronistic moralism could have no other consequence. The message, in Britain, the US and many other countries (notable exceptions have been Holland and Scandinavian countries such as Denmark and Sweden), has been that HIV infection is a consequence of morally unacceptable behaviour (what Cindy Patton calls the 'queer paradigm') and that *if* you put yourself at risk by choosing to indulge in such behaviour, *then* you should wear a condom. Condom use itself, by this paradigm, becomes a mark not of safety but of deviance.

This paradigm makes the non-use of condoms inevitable on two counts. Firstly, those who do not believe their intimate relationships to be deviant (heterosexual lovers), or who know them to be deviant but celebrate that deviance as an act of resistance to oppression (some gay men, some sex workers), will be unlikely to introduce such a marker of disapprobation into their sexual repertoire. Secondly, those who *do* use condoms for encounters which they regard as avowedly deviant (sex work, casual sex between men, using prostitutes) are unlikely to use them in encounters which must be somehow distinguished from the deviant. This parallels the unintended consequences of health education aimed at injecting drug users. In situations where the behaviour targeted as risky is injecting drug use, both health educators and drug users themselves are likely to regard the risk as having been (ritualistically?) averted by safer injecting practices, and may be less likely to consider the need for safer sex. It is the deviant behaviour, the drug injecting, which is identified as the source of risk, so 'normal' heterosexual behaviour need not be modified.

Health education has not only failed to meet the needs of women (and hence, by implication, of men who have sex with women) but has in many ways promoted behaviours which put women and men at risk. In terms of health *promotion*, making the healthier choice the easier choice, what needs to happen?

Promoting sexual safety

In order for the sexual transmission of HIV to be significantly slowed (something which shows no signs of happening) and eventually stopped, we need to change the world. At least the following conditions must be met:

- Men and women, whatever their sexual preference, should have adequate information about safer sex techniques to enable them to enjoy satisfying sexual relationships with however many sexual partners they choose.
- Both women and men should be able to assume that safer sex will be the norm in *all* their sexual encounters.
- Non-penetrative sex should be universally accepted and valued as enjoyable, normal and morally right.
- Where penetrative sex is chosen, high-quality condoms and lubricant should be freely and easily available to whoever wants them.
- Both men and women should take responsibility for decisions around sexual safety, including decisions that relate to conception and childbirth, in heterosexual and non-heterosexual contexts.
- People living with HIV infection and with AIDS should be confident that their sexual partners, current or prospective, will have the knowledge and skills to engage in sex with them lovingly and carefully, in ways which protect the health of both.

These may seem to be, indeed they are, basic human rights. The right to bodily integrity is fundamental to human dignity. Yet only a minority of people around the world have the ability to choose how they use their bodies sexually. In order for the above conditions to be met, global and local cultures would have to undergo unimaginable changes.

There would, in the first place, have to be universal peace. The business of warfare is the paradigmatic exemplar of machismo, and the rape of women (and sometimes men) is rarely absent from military conflict. There would also have to be a global redistribution of wealth, from the rich nations to the poor, from rich to poor within nations and from men to women. Only this would ensure the adequate availability of condoms and offer alternatives to prostitution for the many women trying to make a living for themselves and their children outside relationships with men in paid employment. There would have to be massive ideological shifts; religious leaders would have to support both non-penetrative sex (which is by definition sex for pleasure, not for reproduction) and the use of condoms, and the question of sexual choice (how many partners, of which gender, within or outwith marriage) would have to be removed from the agenda of the state, social stigma, religious dogma or moral disapprobation. Sex education aimed at young people in schools and out would need to be explicit, sex-positive and informative, rather than (as is too often the case at present) being exploited to promote a narrowly moralistic doctrine (Aggleton et al., 1990).

Health *promotion* in the context of safer sex is a monumental task, and one which is clearly unattainable in the urgent timescale dictated by the remorseless growth of this global pandemic. Gender is one of the two most significant social factors contributing to continued epidemic growth, the other (inseparable from gender) being material inequality. To make the healthier choice the easier choice demands no less than the absolute eradication of the institution of male supremacy.

Notes

1. There are unhappy parallels here with the well-publicized attitude of too many medical professionals who similarly regard HIV/AIDS as an instrument of divine will (Wilton, 1992a).

2. The 'mixed economy of welfare' refers to the fact that health and social care are provided by and within four 'sectors': the statutory (for example, the National Health Service), the private or commercial (private health insurance, complementary practitioners), the voluntary (health charities, self-help groups) and the informal or domestic (in the home/family).

3. The British Departments of Health and Social Security are now two separate government departments.

4

Queen of the Fountain of Love: Gender, Disease and Death

Prostitutes have been blamed for breaches of national security, the fall of principalities and mighty men, the desecration of hearth and home. Now they are being blamed in many quarters for the 'spread' of AIDS. (Treichler, 1988b: 25)

Gendered constructs of sexuality

As a socio-cultural institution/set of institutions, gender clearly has an intimate relationship with biology but is neither caused by nor simply a human response to biological difference. One of the key projects of radical feminists (and recently of feminist-identified men) has been the continuing deconstruction of both femininity and masculinity, and the identification of the social and cultural mechanisms which have constructed and maintained the hegemony of what might best be thought of as the 'narratives' of sexual difference/heteropolarity.

The narratives of sexual difference are present in all discursive arenas from the courtly love tradition of mediaeval troubadours (where they are somewhat transparently encoded) to the supposed gender-neutral territories of chemistry (with its mother and daughter elements) and engineering (with its female gauges and threads), where they are encoded so opaquely as to bespeak a general social construct that is utterly taken for granted. The presence of such narratives within the various discursive spheres does not merely reflect a 'reality' – whether social, biological or psychological – which predates discourse. It is not the case that there is human society and *then* there is language with which to describe it. Rather, gender *is* discursively constituted. For it is by texts that social meanings are made – and 'texts' here includes all mark-making and sound-making which encodes human meanings and which is capable of being 'read', from books and films to 'fashion statements', body piercing and the Internet. The ideas 'woman' and 'man' acquire meaning at the active interface between the social and the psychological, between a culture and the individual (both of which are, of course, mutually co-constitutive). This meaning-making activity takes place by and in the production/writing and consumption/reading of texts. Each individual in postmodern post-industrial cultures, cultures characterized by information saturation, is continually exposed to encoded statements about sex/gender (and 'race' and class and age and size and dis/ability) which must be processed and which become part of that individual's own subjectivity (a sense of a 'self' as properly or improperly male or female). In turn, each individual performs (whether obediently or disobediently) their own sex/gender (Butler, 1990), which performance in turn becomes part of the cacophonic socio-cultural textuality within which and by means of which 'male' and 'female', 'queer' and 'straight' have meaning.

To speak of the 'social construction' of genders or of sexualities is not to posit either as unreal or open to casual transformation (Butler, 1993), for there is nothing *more* real, nothing 'authentic' which is somehow positioned outside of social construction. HIV, micro-particle of living tissue, is as far as we know utterly indifferent to the human response to its presence on the planet. But human beings experience HIV and AIDS through language, through discourse. The early construction of AIDS in the West as a 'gay plague', and its parallel construction as 'African', have had profound and complex consequences for the spread of the epidemic, for the abilities of various populations to adopt safer practices and avoid infection and for the treatment of those infected and sick. As Allan Brandt tersely puts it, 'These 'social constructions are more than merely metaphors. They have very real socio-political implications' (Brandt, 1988: 148).

The production and consumption of sex/gender narratives, because such narratives are implicit in the continued reflexive narrative project which is identity (Mellor and Shilling, 1993), and because they structure social and cultural life, are crucial both to HIV prevention and to the proper treatment of people living with HIV. A critique of the representational practices which codify sex/gender is not a luxury to be tacked onto the 'real' medical/scientific work, it is absolutely central to developing a successful strategy for slowing the spread of HIV/AIDS.

> People have been stigmatized (and destroyed) as much by the 'idea' of AIDS as by its reality. Since . . . the construction of images of disease is a dynamic process to which the sufferers, real and imagined, constantly respond, it is in our best interests to recognize the process. (Gilman, 1988: 88)

As we have seen, health promotion in the context of HIV (as in any other context) involves catalysing change on a social, material and ideological level. The ubiquitous global fiction of sex/gender is instrumental in subordinating women to men and this, in turn, makes it very difficult for either women or men to protect themselves and their sexual partners from infection. Jonathan Mann, former director-general of the WHO, recognizes that 'Again and again we have seen that discrimination creates an environment of increased risk for women – linked directly with their unequal role, rights and status' (Mann, 1993: 3). In order to combat such discrimination, it is necessary to engage with the texts which maintain the heteropolar narrative of sex/gender.

Bodies, diseases, doctors and words

Among discourses that construct sex/gender narratives, those which deal with bodies may be expected to be especially powerful, since the bodily differences between women and men play a key part in heterobinarism. Medical, religious and political discourse have all engaged with the body, and in particular with the problem of disease. In so doing, they have produced specific intersections of significance among gender, sexuality and disease which, together with all such practices of signification, form and maintain relations of power between women and men, black and white, poor and rich, etc. Notions of 'sickness' and 'health' are always already political notions, deployed in the interests of the powerful against the powerless. My interest in this chapter is to explore the deployment of the idea of sickness as it relates to sexuality, taking the historical response to sexually transmitted diseases in the West as my starting point.

The problem of sickness has been approached in the West through two, often competing, paradigms: the religious and the medico-scientific. Both have traditionally been (and continue to be) dominated by men. Religious and scientific texts have, with a few notable exceptions, been produced by men and intended for consumption by other men. Women have by and large been the textual/discursive *object*, not the subject. As Treichler points out (1988a: 191), 'With respect to the medical construction of women's bodies . . . men are the constructors, women the constructed'. There is, of course, a parallel masculinist construction of men's bodies, and it should be borne in mind that the sexist construction of the masculine body, as well as that of the feminine, is likely to have its own unhelpful impact on men's and women's health, something which is of particular significance in the context of STDs generally and HIV in particular.

Triumph of Dame Syphilis

The recorded history of attempts to control the spread of STDs goes back to biblical times. When Moses led the Israelites in war against the Midianites the victorious Israelites captured and raped the Midianite women, resulting in a 'plague amongst the congregation of the Lord' which modern commentators identify as gonorrhoea (Llewellyn-Jones, 1985). Moses' response was to quarantine the men involved for seven days outside the Israelite camp. The Midianite women were put to death. In this episode, from around 3,000 BC, the women are seen as representing a source of contamination and disease, a possible *risk* to men. It is the risk represented by women which must be eradicated, in this case by exterminating the women.

This construction of gender, whereby women exist as the property of men and their health or otherwise is only of concern insofar as it affects the men who make use of them, is both expressed in and gives rise to the phenomenon of prostitution and social responses to prostitution. If gender were not structured around a dynamic of power then both women and men would have equal access to sex in exchange for money.[1] As it is, there are large numbers of women for whom the only alternative to starvation for themselves and any children they may have is to sell sex. The absolute social and economic dependence on men which was until recently the norm for most of the world's women both reflected and maintained the social construction of man-as-actor/subject and woman-as-object which is so powerful in the medical construction of gendered bodies. It is a construct which has profound consequences for the health of both women and men, although the consequences for women are often the most dramatically visible:

> Men believed that intercourse with a virgin child would cure VD. In 1884 a man with 'bad syphilitis ulcers' raped a girl of 14. His defence was that he had not intended to harm her, but only to cure himself . . . 'Quack doctresses' had kept special brothels in Liverpool, since 1827 at least, to provide this cure. The children used were often imbeciles. Three who became infected and were placed in the Liverpool Lock Hospital were 9, 7 and 5½ respectively. (Smith, 1979: 303)

The intersection of three oppressions – of women, of children and of the disabled – here makes clear that social power inheres in (and is expressed by) the ability of the powerful to make what use he pleases of the powerless. The rape of virgin children to 'cure' venereal disease has disturbing contemporary parallels in the reported tendency of men to take younger and younger girls as sexual 'partners' in an attempt to protect themselves from HIV infection (Berer with Ray, 1993; Panos Institute, 1990a).

In the twelfth century in England, 'London brothel-keepers were forbidden to supply clients with women who suffered from "the perilous infirmity of burning" [gonorrhoea]' (Llewellyn-Jones, 1985: 132). No steps were taken to protect the women who worked in the brothels. Indeed, so culturally ingrained is the construct of the diseased and dangerous whore that the idea of forbidding *men* who were diseased from visiting brothels and putting the women there at risk seems outlandish.

But it was the great European epidemic of syphilis which gave rise to the most overtly gendered (and xenophobic) victim-blaming. Syphilis appeared in Europe in the late fifteenth century, brought, it is generally thought, by sailors returning from the Americas.[2] Mercenary soldiers fighting in European wars, such as Charles VIII of France's 1494 siege of Naples or Perkin Warbeck's ill-fated attempt in 1497 to invade England from Scotland, spread the new disease rapidly across Europe, whilst by 1506 merchant travellers and explorers had carried it as far afield as India, China and Japan.

A common theme which marks the response of almost all nations to the syphilis epidemic is the desire to attribute *blame* for 'importing' the disease into previously healthy communities. Gilman sees this as a universal human tendency to disavow guilt: 'The desire to locate the origin of a disease is the desire to be assured that we are not at fault, that we have been invaded from without, polluted by some external agent' (Gilman, 1988: 100). This is especially true of diseases which are spread through sexual contact. The medico-moral conflation of physiological sickness with notions of moral contamination or sinfulness has a long history, and sexuality has always been the pre-eminent site of meanings (often vehemently contested) around pollution, contamination, sin and subversion. This conflation is perhaps most clearly seen in the 'Social Purity' movement of Victorian England or the 'social hygiene' of early twentieth-century US campaigners. The desire to ab/ject the guilt of sickness onto a body already seen as in some way guilty (because already infidel, polluted or dangerous) is doubly imperative in the case of sexually transmitted diseases. Thus, in the terms of whichever group is hegemonic in any place at any time (and therefore has control of the machinery of representation), syphilis was named as the property of *the other*. Otherness was largely ascribed along nationalist lines:

> As the people of each country became infected, each tried to put the blame for the new and terrifying disease on its neighbour. The Italians called it the Spanish disease. The French, who were first infected in 1495, called it the Italian or Neapolitan disease . . . It reached England in 1497, where it was called the French disease . . . It reached China in 1505 and Japan a year later where it was called 'manka bassam' or the Portuguese disease. (Llewellyn-Jones, 1985: 136)

The deadly new plague was always attributed to an enemy, taking on associations of invasion, treachery, the destruction of a nation's defensive strength. In the nineteenth century, with the need to justify the rapidly expanding slave trade and the colonialist exploitation of Africa, a new theory asserted that syphilis, far from being the penalty for Columbus' colonial endeavours, had originated in Africa (Gilman, 1988).

It was not only foreigners who were cast as 'other' and constructed as the source of syphilis. Sexually active women, especially those who exchanged sex for money or goods, have been cast as 'reservoirs of infection' for STDs since at least the fifteenth century. As Gilman puts it:

> We find . . . a continuity in the representation of the sufferer of a sexually transmitted disease as an outsider . . . by the Enlightenment the image of the outsider, the other, the deviant, is that of woman as source of pollution. (Gilman, 1988: 98)

The development of this shift (which Gilman suggests took 200 years to complete) began much earlier than the Enlightenment. For example, in 1498 the Aberdeen authorities published a regulation for the control of the syphilis epidemic which ordered '"all light women to desist from their vice and sin of venery" on pain of being branded', while a popular French print of 1539 depicted 'the high and mighty Dame Syphilis, Queen of the Fountain of Love' as 'le bagage' or camp-follower/army prostitute (Llewellyn-Jones, 1985: 135–6). Thus syphilis itself was gendered, becoming a woman in the popular imagination. This gendered construct depended upon the gendering of sex itself as female. In contrast to the proper manly business of warfare and killing, sex was seen as women's business:

Although heroes have always been perceived as eminently manly, the proof of their virility has been not in love-making but in war-making . . . Contact with women is perceived as debilitating, enervating and ultimately destructive of virility, whereas battles can apparently indefinitely regenerate the strength of males. (Huston, 1985: 121)

Feminist writers have suggested that the paradigmatic occupations for men and women are, respectively, soldier and mother. These, it has been suggested, are the ways by which they achieve citizenship of the modern nation state, by dying for their country or by breeding soldiers to die for their country (Pateman, 1992). The 'good father' is one who is prepared to leave his family and go to war to defend the homeland when called upon, while the 'good mother' keeps the home fires burning and smiles through her tears as she sends her sons off to be killed. But the heteropatriarchal construct of woman is organized around men's conflictual feelings about women, and for every Mother Mary there is a Mary Magdalene. There are, I suggest, *two* paradigmatic and ideologically divergent roles for women: mother and whore. When the men go off to war, the good women stay at home but the bad women follow the men. The soldier is maintained in his masculine gender by the presence of two kinds of women: the faithful wife, mother or sweetheart waiting for him far away at home whose safety he is fighting for, and who knows nothing of the realities of war (or, by implication, of the realities of sex either) and the prostitute or casual pick-up who is prepared to meet his sexual needs while he is away fighting. It is this woman who has taken on the complex burden of signification which has coalesced around the sexually transmitted diseases, and which interweaves notions of masculinity versus femininity, patriotism versus treachery, 'clean', safe familial sexuality versus 'dirty', dangerous commercial sexuality.

The traitorous syphilitic woman

Sander Gilman points out that the gendered encoding of syphilis in the iconography of the sexually transmitted diseases reflects a shift of attention away from the syphilitic as victim to the syphilitic as *dangerous*. Pointing to the many European engravings which depict sympathetically the sufferings of male syphilitics, Gilman notes: 'Only during the Enlightenment does the image of the syphilitic shift from male to female, and with this shift comes another: from victim to source of infection.'[3] It is a moot point whether the epidemic of syphilis shaped the changing cultural construction of female sexuality, or whether the cultural construction of syphilis as intrinsic property of female sexuality was shaped by and incorporated into an already-present construct of female sexuality as rotten at the core.

There is no doubt that the disease model of female sexuality and of the female genitals predates the Enlightenment. Although there is little overt fear and loathing of women's sexuality present in Chaucer, the rottenness of women is a thread which runs clearly through the plays of Shakespeare (although Shakespeare never lets it stand unchallenged). Lear's mad speeches contain one especially vivid passage:

> Down from the waist they are Centaurs,
> Though women all above;
> But to the girdle do the Gods inherit,
> Beneath is all the fiend's; there's hell, there's darkness,
> There is the sulphurous pit – burning, scalding,
> Stench, consumption; fie, fie fie! pah, pah! (*King Lear*, IV.vi, 126–31)

Whatever the precise relationship between the cultural construction of syphilis and that of women, there is no doubt that the feminization of the veneral diseases intersected historically with a general pathologization of the sexual woman to mark 'woman' as hazardous to men.

> Already in the high Middle Ages, woman was shown as both seductive and physically corrupt . . . Female beauty only serves as a mask for corruption and death . . . By the eighteenth century, the corrupt female is associated with the signs of a specific disease, syphilis . . . The change here is also from the innate corruption of the female to her potential for corrupting the male. (Gilman, 1988: 95–6)

This construction of syphilis as *residing in* the always already corrupt bodies of women marked the desirable female body as both fraudulent – apparent beauty/health masking a diseased and ugly reality – and hazardous. To be female was to be diseased; femaleness was itself increasingly coming to be seen as a diseased state hazardous by contact to men's health, a construct powerfully reinforced by medical discourse and paralleling the Judaeo-Christian discursive constitution of femaleness as a sinful state hazardous by contact to men's souls. In the nineteenth century, with the growth in coercive public health measures, attempts to control venereal disease focused not on sexually active men but on prostitutes:

> The Contagious Diseases acts (1864, 1866, 1869) attempted to counter venereal disease by enforcing the compulsory medical inspection of streetwalkers in specified garrison towns and ports. Women suspected of common prostitution could be taken into police custody, subjected to medical examination, and if found venereally infected, detained [in special lock-up hospitals] during the course of treatment. (Porter and Porter, 1988: 105–6)

There was already the beginning of a challenge to the double standard, and the Contagious Diseases Acts were repealed in 1896 in response to feminist activism and popular outcry.

The motherland

There is an additional thread in the knitting together of the narratives of sex, gender and disease: nationalism. Since before the Israelite–Midianite conflict of 3,000 BC, war has always increased the rate of spread of STDs. In keeping with the elision of female sexuality and disease, warmaking has often incorporated a war against women sex workers, labelling their activities as traitorous and marking the women themselves as the enemy.

The First World War

During the First World War, energetic campaigns were mounted in Britain and the United States to combat the menace of venereal diseases. 'Wars,' writes Elizabeth Fee, 'have tended to make venereal diseases visible. The need to mobilize a large and healthy armed force brings venereal disease out of the private sphere and into the center of public policy discussions' (Fee, 1988: 123). Infection control policies during the First World War were discriminatory. Men in the armed forces, demobilized servicemen and merchant seamen were identified as 'reservoirs of infection' (Weindling, 1993: 95), and were offered free, accessible diagnosis and treatment and issued with prophylactic kits – condoms and 'self-disinfection' were both recommended (Fee, 1988; Brandt, 1985; Weindling, 1993). There were some attempts by the British Red Cross and the National Council for Combating Venereal Disease to segregate seamen from indigenous populations, 'enforcing systems of passes, the fencing in of dock areas and the exclusion of visitors to ships', but such measures were motivated by concern for the health and welfare of the men concerned (Weindling, 1993). Lectures, slide shows of diseased genitals and sermons from forces chaplains all urged continence on servicemen. Typifying this approach is General Pershing who, in 1917, set up VD treatment centres in every command in Europe and made it a court-martial offence to fail to seek treatment after possible exposure. His 1917 address makes the call to continence an integral part of the US serviceman's patriotic duty:

> sexual continence is the plain duty of members of the AEF [American Expeditionary Force], both for the vigorous conduct of the war and for the clean health of the American people after the war. Sexual intercourse is not necessary for good health and complete continence is wholly possible. (cited in D'Emilio and Freedman, 1988: 212)

Interwoven in Pershing's address are the traditional belief that sexual contact with women diminishes men's capacity to wage war (sexual continence is necessary 'for the vigorous conduct of the war'), the elision of health, cleanliness and nationalism ('the clean health of the American people') and a dismissal of the construction of male sexuality as *requiring* regular sexual activity.

The provision of services and a degree of individual voluntarism in avoiding infection were the policies directed at men. The treatment accorded women was very different. While men were perceived as being at risk from venereal diseases and attempts were made to offer them some degree of protection and treatment, women were implicitly divided into two groups, the innocent and the guilty. The innocent were those the servicemen were fighting for: the wives, mothers and daughters in the *mother*/land.

The policy towards this group was to *protect* their innocence by *keeping them in ignorance* of facts about VD, a policy with its roots firmly in Victorian constructs of delicate womanhood:

> If a physician were . . . to explain to a lady-patient the doctrines of syphilis, under any circumstance excepting those of the most urgent necessity, he would be guilty . . . of a gross departure from his duty . . . delicacy, that beautiful quality of mind . . . interfered with by obtruded information. (*British Medical Journal*, 1869, cited in Smith, 1979: 297)

Those women not thought to be 'innocent' (in both senses of the word, innocent of sexual desire and of causing syphilis) were generally lumped together under the generic heading 'prostitute', and regarded not as a group especially vulnerable to VD infection but as the group *responsible* for spreading VD. As such, women who had sex for money or, in many cases, simply outside marriage, were on the side of the enemy.

> During World War I, educational materials clearly presented the fighting men as the innocent victims of disease; prostitutes were the guilty spreaders of infection, implicitly working for the enemy against patriotic American soldiers. In many communities prostitutes were the focus, and often the victims and scapegoats, of the new attention to venereal infections. Prostitutes – the women responsible for the defilement of the heroic American soldier – would be regularly rounded up, arrested and jailed in the campaign against vice. (Fee, 1988: 123–4)

At this moment in history, health education materials explicitly constructed prostitutes as both dangerous (as opposed to vulnerable) and unpatriotic, a risk to men and to the nation state. One pamphlet targeting servicemen, entitled *Keep Fit to Fight*, stated that 'Women who solicit soldiers for immoral purposes are usually disease spreaders and friends of the enemy' (D'Emilio and Freedman, 1988: 212). The impact of this official discourse was strengthened by the policy of closing down brothels, and by the forcible detention of suspected prostitutes in internment camps:

> The military suspended writs of habeas corpus, arrested women en masse, and forcibly held more than fifteen thousand in detention centres for periods averaging ten weeks. No men were arrested for patronizing prostitutes. (ibid.)

Feminists and civil rights organizations angrily challenged the double standard implicit in this policy, but the detention of 15,000 women in US internment camps is seldom regarded as worthy of mention in historical accounts of the period, and little had changed by the time of the Second World War.

The Second World War

During the Second World War, anti-VD health education material targeted at troops continued the traditional construction of the prostitute or 'easy' woman as seductive and dangerous. One poster depicts the smiling head of a very ordinary-looking young woman, towering threateningly over three tiny men – a soldier, a sailor and an airman – with the caption 'SHE MAY

LOOK CLEAN BUT pick-ups, "good-time" girls, prostitutes SPREAD SYPHILIS AND GONORRHOEA' (reproduced in Berer with Ray, 1993: 41), while a famous British poster depicted a skull-faced prostitute walking arm in arm with Hirohito and Hitler, with a caption reading 'VD WORST OF THE THREE' (reproduced in Brandt, 1985). Another British poster, published by His Majesty's Stationery Office and aimed at servicemen home on leave, simply shows a skull, wearing a jaunty flowered hat and saying, 'Hello boyfriend, coming my way?' Behind the skull loom the enormous letters 'VD' and the caption reads: 'The "easy" girlfriend spreads Syphilis and Gonorrhoea, which *unless properly treated* may result in blindness, insanity, paralysis, premature death' (reproduced in Baynes, 1972: 75). In this image, woman/sex/disease/death have become almost inseparable, and 'easy' female sexuality *causes* blindness, insanity, paralysis and death. Within the terms of this discursive construct of sex/gender it is simply not possible to imagine the 'easy boyfriend' causing *women* to become blind, mad, paralysed or dead. Sex, disease and death are all *located in* women.

The contrast between the 'easy girlfriend' and the 'heroic mother' in public discourse could not be greater. Another well-known image is from an inter-war Labour Party poster urging 'Mothers – Vote Labour', and showing a monolithic maternal figure, sleeping infant in her arms, silhouetted against the sky and towering above the skyline of an industrial city. Woman under male control in the family is the bearer of life: woman outwith male control and actively sexual is the bearer of death. In this polarity lies the final twist of signification. Uncontrolled female sexuality represents a threat to the imperialist state, threatening to contaminate the national bloodline with the twin evils of STDs and uncertain paternity. A strong thread of pro-natalism and eugenicism runs through nationalist propaganda in both Britain and the US from the late nineteenth to the mid-twentieth centuries, and anything which spilled over the anxious boundaries of heteropolarity was perceived as *nationally* threatening.

Whores, queers and germs: enemies of the people

Fitness to fight and/or to compete effectively in the international market-place is an important consideration for ambitious nations. The effective reproduction of a fit and healthy fighting/labour force is an explicitly expressed concern in public discourse in the industrialized West from the mid-nineteenth century onward, and a thread of eugenicist sentiment runs quite overtly through much popular culture, especially in the British empire. Rudyard Kipling's poem 'The White Man's Burden' famously urged the British people in 1899 to: 'Take up the White Man's burden – / Send forth the best ye breed'. Such sentiments were encouraged and given pseudo-scientific sanction by the medical profession, then at the zenith of its hegemony. Victorian medical discourse explicitly associated healthy mothering with colonial expansion:

> Love of offspring is the healthiest sign of a race, and the natural strength which is its reward stands revealed in connexion with armaments and now more than ever in connexion with colonising power. (Dr W. Ewart, cited in Smith, 1979: 301)

Anything that did not contribute to this reproductive activity, or that thwarted it, was contrary to national or, in the pseudo-scientific jargon of race supremacy, to racial interests. Homosexuality, extra-marital female sexuality, abortion, contraception and the venereal diseases were all anathematized, and all discursively associated with the negative construct of femininity. Moreover, this historical moment has not passed. As Anne McClintock (1995) suggests, purity and motherhood continue to be discursively associated with nationalist struggles in the geopolitical aftermath of colonialism (although at least one recently liberated nation, South Africa, is notable for its rigorous attempts to include lesbian and gay citizenship rights in its political agenda).

In Germany during the 'Third Reich', this discursive package was specifically associated with the Jews, since Jewishness was the paradigmatic 'other' of this most racist of nation-state ideologies:

> In August 1930 the *Völkischer Beobachter*, official paper of the NSDAP [the National Socialist Workers' Party of Germany] informed its readers of what would happen to homosexuals. Since 'all the foul urges of the Jewish soul' come together in homosexuality, 'the law should recognize [them] for what they are – utterly base aberrations of Syrians, extremely serious crimes that should be punished with hanging and deportation. (Grau, 1995: 3)

The resurgence of German nationalism which was embodied in Nazi Fascism offers a startlingly clear instance of the gendering of nationalism, and of the paranoid heterosexualization of that gendered mythos. Masculinity, seamlessly elided with discipline and strength and located at the root of the nation state's struggle for dominance, is perceived as being continually under threat of contamination from the weakening, feminizing (but yet, ironically, all-powerful and ever-present) essence of homosexuality.

> It is not necessary that you and I live, but it is necessary that the German people lives. And it can live only if it has the will to struggle – for to live is to struggle. And it can struggle only if it remains virile (*mannbar*). But it is virile only if it exercises discipline, particularly in sexual matters. Free love is undisciplined and unbridled. That is why we reject it, as we reject everything that is of harm to the people . . . Anyone who aims at male–male or female–female sex is our enemy. We reject everything that emasculates our people and puts it at the mercy of its enemies . . . We therefore reject any sexual deviation (*Unzucht*), particularly between man and man, because it robs us of the last possibility of freeing our people. (Declaration by the National Leadership of the NSDAP, 1928, cited in Grau, 1995: 25)

The Nazi persecution of gay men and lesbians, while still less often acknowledged than the Jewish genocide of Hitler's 'final solution', has been publicly documented (Grau, 1995; Haeberle, 1989; Schoppmann, 1995), although the ideologies of gender, sexuality and nationality which informed it have yet to be adequately theorized. It is perhaps better known that Nazi 'racial hygiene' doctrine during the Third Reich used enforced sterilization and pro-natalist propaganda to promote the interests of the 'Aryan race'. What is less well known is that British, US and New Commonwealth administrations also made use of such policies in the drive to avert 'race suicide'. In Australia in 1904 women who chose not to have children were condemned as 'a menace to social purity and national stability', while US President Roosevelt compared the 'cowardly' childless woman to the man 'who fears to do his duty in battle when the country calls him' (Pateman, 1992: 25–6). It was not only within patriarchal propaganda that motherhood was exalted as woman's patriotic duty. English feminist Maude Royden wrote during the First World War that, 'The state wants children, and to give them is a service both dangerous and honourable. Like the soldier, the mother takes a risk and gives a devotion for which no money can pay' (cited in Pateman, 1992: 26).

The venereal diseases, discursively associated with uncontrolled female sexuality, represented a grave threat to the health of men, children and hence nations. 'Imperial powers,' writes Weindling (1993: 93), 'regarded STDs as a threat to the family, to military and economic power and to the nation's future generations.' Again, medical discourse was overt in its representation of STDs as a threat to racial survival. The American Medical Association held a symposium 'The Duty of the Profession to Womanhood' in 1906, at which one physician spoke out against VD and abortion:

> These vipers of venery which are called clap and pox, lurking as they often do, under the floral tributes of the honeymoon, may so inhibit conception or blight its products that motherhood becomes either an utter impossibility or a veritable curse. The ban placed by venereal disease on fetal life outrivals the criminal interference with the products of conception as a cause of race suicide. (cited in Brandt, 1988: 149)

As soon as the Wasserman test for syphilis was developed (and despite its clinical limitations), several US states instituted compulsory pre-marital screening, and all US soldiers were given the test during the Second World War (Lowy, 1993). Thus the health of fighting men and of future American citizens was protected.

Homosexuality (in men) joined childless women, prostitutes, abortion and STDs as a danger to nation or 'race'. After the conviction of Oscar Wilde in 1895 the *British Medical Journal* published an article deploring 'the growth of "perverted tendencies" which threatened the "basic animal instincts upon which the survival of the race and the Empire depend"' (Smith, 1979: 299). Along with venereal disease, prostitution and sexuality itself, male homosexuality has traditionally been associated with femininity. To be a gay man is to be 'not a proper man', to be like a woman, to forfeit the privileges of masculinity and submit (like a woman) to the desire of other men (Butler, 1993; Edwards, 1994).

Bang up to date – the 'women' of AIDS

STD health education has a long history of feminizing STDs (Brandt, 1985), of discursively constituting a complex coterminosity among 'woman', 'sex', 'disease' and 'death', and of blaming women outwith male control for spreading 'blindness, insanity, paralysis, premature death'. A parallel history of resistance from feminists, civil libertarians and others has problematized these tendencies, but has not succeeded in eradicating them. Thus Llewellyn-Jones, as part of a critique of the historical victim-blaming associated with syphilis, writes quite unselfconsciously that, 'Throughout its recorded history, the main cause of the spread of the disease has been casual fornication, usually with prostitutes . . . street-walkers, who usually refuse or do not seek medical checks, are likely to continue to infect numbers of men' (Llewellyn-Jones, 1985: 139–46). He makes no mention of the johns who are likely to continue to infect numbers of women sex workers. Significantly, the only men whose sexual behaviour Llewellyn-Jones calls into question are gay men. Although he believes that 'as many homosexuals are sexually promiscuous as are heterosexuals' it is homosexual promiscuity, not heterosexual, which he goes on to discuss:

> It is not known whether homosexual promiscuity is due to childhood emotional disturbances which prevent the man from forming any lasting relationship with another person, or whether the contempt shown by society and the penalties it imposes on known homosexuals, are the major factors in homosexual promiscuity. Research in this area is urgently needed. (ibid.: 146)

There is no discussion of the possible causes of heterosexual promiscuity (social contempt, perhaps?), no mention of lesbians, and no call for urgent research into the problem that heterosexual promiscuity poses for the control of STDs. As recently as 1985, the tradition of blaming women sex workers and gay men for the spread of STDs was alive and well. How has HIV/AIDS health educational discourse constructed gender? How are the constructs men, women, queer, straight, sex, disease and death positioned within that discourse?

Sander Gilman traces a historical shift in the iconography of syphilis, from an attentive gaze directed towards the body of the innocent male victim to a turning of that gaze onto the body of the guilty female source (Gilman, 1988). The intersections among gender, sexuality, 'race', class and nationality which inflected this shift lie closer to the surface in the context of AIDS. By epidemiological accident AIDS has come to be associated in the industrialized nations of the West with the male body. As the most powerful and most clamorously vocal nation in the world, the US, in its media reportage of the new medical condition has been disproportionately significant in influencing the international construction of and response to AIDS. '[I]nitial reports of the new syndrome not only set the terms for subsequent policy and planning, but also *gendered as male* the normative body affected by the syndrome, persistently constituting women as exceptions' (Patton, 1994: 8; emphasis added).

But it was not just any male body which became the norm for the media's 'AIDS victim', it was the *gay* male body. This profoundly problematizes the business of encoding or reading gender into the cultural construction of AIDS, as Henry Abelove's comment indicates:

> all of us in the lesbian-gay community are in a sense women. We gay men are socially gendered female, no matter how butch we may look, and lesbians are socially gendered female too, though perhaps less emphatically than the men. (Abelove, 1994: 7)

This social gendering of gay men as female both incorporates and expresses the traditional militaristic/imperialist construct of male homosexuality as threatening 'race suicide' and national disintegration. This is not new:

> Social sanction against the anal penetration of the male body seems to have characterized Western civilization since at least the classical period . . . Because the male body stood as a metaphor for the state, its inviolability was a metaphoric bulwark against invasion. By allowing penetration, the citizen gave up his claim to be a 'real' man and thus . . . should forgo the privileges of citizenship. (Davies et al., 1993: 127)

This classical Greek model of the impenetrable citizen points to what might be thought of as a panoramic construct general to Western thinking, whereby what is ordered, active, effective, expansionistic and politically/ militarily sound is gendered male and represented by/embodied in masculinity. That which is disordered or chaotic, passive or debilitating, ineffectual, non-aggressive or anti-imperialist and politically or militarily suspect or subversive is gendered female. To risk oversimplification, energy is male, entropy female: order is male, chaos female. Biology and the lived experience of bodies bear only a tangential relationship to the always disputed ascription of gender.

Feminist commentators have familiarized us with the pathologization of women's bodies, historians have identified a process whereby VD became feminized. It begins to look as if, in the postmodern millennium, disease itself is female:

> Disease and the woman have something in common – they are both socially devalued or undesirable, marginalized elements which constantly threaten to infiltrate and contaminate that which is more central, health or masculinity. (Doane, 1985: 152)

Doane's description of 'woman' transfers, word for word, to the social position of gay men and to the positioning of gay men within medicomoral discourse. Gilman comments that the feminization of the gay man pre-empts in the context of AIDS the transfer of attention from victim to source which characterized the iconographic history of the European syphilis epidemic: 'Already feminized in the traditional view of his sexuality, the gay man can now also represent the conflation of the images of the male sufferer and the female source of suffering traditionally associated with syphilis' (Gilman, 1988: 99).

To a certain extent, gay men have taken the place of 'the woman' in the epidemic of signification (Treichler, 1988b) which has articulated the Western nations' response to and construction of AIDS. Indeed in the early years of the epidemic, while it was still possible for a heterosexual majority in denial to believe that AIDS was a consequence of male homosexuality, the burden of signifying both victim and perpetrator of this ghastly biological crime was dumped onto the gay male body. The consequences of this for the social and cultural construction of AIDS within and by the Western urban gay male communities were problematic. Firstly, some gay men, in resisting and disavowing the stigma of AIDS-genesis, colluded with the racist blaming of black Africans which was another common feature of mainstream AIDS discourse:

> the most recent evidence strongly suggests that, far from being the 'cause' of Aids, gay men were routinely injected with HIV infected blood products, in the form of gamma globulin used in the treatment of hepatitis-B, which was prepared throughout the 1970s from blood which had been illegally imported from central Africa. (Watney, 1987: 141)[4]

In his (quite reasonable) haste to resist the homophobic representation of gay men as the contaminated wellspring of infection, Watney reinforces the notion of AIDS as 'illegal immigrant', slipping in from *outside* some mythically uncontaminated social space through the agency of *already stigmatized others* to infect the 'naturally' uncontaminated. This construct of AIDS presents the leakage of infection from social outsider to social insider as *unfair*, because it is the natural property of the other (whether gay, black or female) to be diseased and dangerous as it is the natural property of the not-other to be clean, healthy and safe. This model depends for its coherence on identifying a social 'mechanism of leakage', whereby 'natural' social barriers between dangerous other and vulnerable not-other may be breached long enough for infection to occur. In the context of queer sexuality the site of this leakage is supposed to be bisexuals (see above, p. 26), in the context of heterosex it is the prostitute; in the context of 'race' Watney suggests the illegal (and hence uncontrollable) injection of dangerous black blood products into the innocent, white (by inference) male body.

The second troubling implication of the widespread association of AIDS with gay men had more directly lethal consequences. While gay men were declared to be killing each other, while, in the words of President Reagan's assistant Gary Bauer, 'it hadn't spread into the general population yet' (Treichler, 1988a: 23), 'real' women remained largely absent from AIDS discourse, their role as dangerous other taken by gay men. 'A growing literature documents the placement of gay men in AIDS writing as the Contaminated Other,' writes Treichler, 'and there seems evidence that in some respects they do fill the role that women, especially prostitutes, have played in the past.' She goes on to suggest that this gendered scapegoating may have unpredictable effects on the workings of gender among gay men:

> It is not clear what effect AIDS is having on notions of masculinity and
> femininity in the gay community. Gay men's creation of the term 'AIDS widows'
> to designate the men who survive their lovers is a small but positive use by men
> of a 'feminine' linguistic form. On the other hand, sexism remains entrenched.
> (Treichler, 1988a: 261)

Among gay men and among lesbians, where heterosexually gendered sexual
behaviours take place within one gender, the performativity and con-
structedness of gender is relatively transparent and amenable to playful or
political disruption. Among heterosexuals, this has not generally been the
case, and 'real' women soon took their traditional place in AIDS discourse
as the epidemic was (reluctantly) recognized as not specific to gay men.

Once it became apparent that people who were not gay men could and
had become infected with HIV, the familiar heterobinary narratives kicked
in. AIDS discourse depressingly recycled the time-worn clichés. The
complexities of power meant that, while relatively privileged women were
assigned the position of innocent victim or heroic conscript in the war
waged on AIDS, powerless women – prostitutes, injecting street drug users,
women in the developing nations and minority ethnic women – were seen
as the source of infection (Treichler, 1988a).

With docile obedience to the centuries-old script the construct of woman
sex worker as 'reservoir of infection' was recycled – although the belief that
AIDS was a disease of men was so powerful that early accounts from US
servicemen who claimed to have been infected through heterosexual contact
with prostitutes were initially disbelieved. Descriptions of women sex
workers in AIDS discourse tend towards the Gothic and partake of racism
and classism as much as sexism. A dangerous little book aimed at school-
children and called simply *AIDS* (Kirkpatrick and Kirkpatrick, 1987)
claims that 'It seems likely that prostitutes in particular, and promiscuity
more generally, have made central Africa the most AIDS-ridden area in the
world', and even that standard-bearer of English liberalism the *Guardian*
published an article in which 'the Nairobi hooker emerges after dark to
preen and stalk her prey' (3 February 1987). The body of the prostitute has
long been the privileged location for the feminization of STDs, and of a
disgusted/fascinated medico-moral construct of diseased sexuality. In the
context of AIDS this is ironic, since sex workers have been among the
communities most able and willing to educate their peers about safer sex
and to adopt safer sexual practices.[5] Treichler writes:

> Prostitutes – despite their long-standing professional knowledge of STDs and
> continued activism about AIDS – have long been portrayed as so contaminated
> that their bodies are . . . 'always dripping', virtual laboratory cultures for viral
> replication. (1988a: 207)

She cites extraordinarily vivid historical texts which contribute to this
construction of the woman sex worker as wellspring of contamination. 'One
nineteenth-century analogy likened the [presumably male] body to a house
and the prostitute to the house's cesspool; more broadly, her body is the
sewer into which the social body excretes its excess (as a nineteenth-century

physician put it, "the seminal drain")' (ibid.: 262). Images of disgusting liquid waste permeate early twentieth-century writings on prostitution too. Treichler quotes from a nursing manual written by Lavinia Dock in 1910, 'which states that prostitution "is now certainly the abiding place and inexhaustible source of . . . veneral disease, as the marshy swamp is the abode of the malaria-carrying mosquito, or the polluted water supply of the typhoid bacillus"' (ibid.: 251). Water and fluidity in general have long been associated in the anxious male imagination with the female body, and the overdeterminedly waterlogged nature of many descriptions of prostitutes suggests that prostitution is cast within this discourse as an excess of femaleness. There is no difference in *kind* between the knowing, diseased prostitute and the innocent, cleanly familial woman, merely a difference in degree. The foundational assertion is, I suggest, that male control – in the shape of the patriarchal heterosexual family – is necessary in order to contain the amorphous wet stuff of femaleness within the bounds of decency and health. Women outside heteropatriarchal control are excessively female, excessively wet, overflowing the boundaries of health, order and the law.

This suggestion is supported by the clear tendency of medical discourse to construct the female body as unruly, flawed and (because the male body is the paradigm and norm) intrinsically *abnormal*, i.e. pathological. This tendency appears coeval with Western medicine; it was Hippocrates himself who famously asked, 'What is woman? Disease'; and, despite active feminist resistance, it has continued up to the present (Doane, 1985; Ussher, 1991).

Nor has discrimination against prostitutes been simply textual. In the US a convicted HIV positive prostitute in Florida was put under house arrest and made to wear an electronic collar which alerted local police whenever she left her house (Treichler, 1988b; Patton, 1994). In India in 1989, almost 500 women prostitutes were illegally detained in remand centres when they tested positive for HIV, while Sweden, Germany and Australia have all detained HIV positive sex workers (Panos Institute, 1990a). The idea that there might be a public health obligation to *protect* sex workers from infection *by men* continues to seem somehow incomprehensible: 'The implication, and indeed the practice, of public health is to disregard the safety of women sex workers because they are viewed only as sexual receptacles presumed to be already infected' (Patton, 1994: 109).

AIDS discourse generally constructs a familiar model of woman-as-risk-to-man, both sexually and maternally (through vertical transmission of HIV during pregnancy/birth). Prostitutes in particular, and women generally, are described as 'reservoirs of infection' or 'an index to the spread of heterosexual AIDS' (Panos Institute, 1990a; Treichler, 1988a), while the needs of women *as* women remain marginalized or completely invisible. As Cindy Patton puts it, with characteristic bluntness, 'When women are not vaginas waiting to infect men, they are uteruses, waiting to infect foetuses' (Patton, 1994: 109). Within this naive and offensive heteropolarity lesbians are erased from existence and non-lesbian women's sexual agency and subjectivity becomes inconceivable.

The possibility that a woman who is HIV positive may transmit HIV to her unborn child has given rise to another good woman/bad woman dichotomy. Throughout the world it remains the case that motherhood is a woman's central duty and responsibility, and sometimes her only route to adult status. 'Every society . . . accords status and respectability to women as childbearers. Childless women face stigma in many cultures; sometimes the penalty is desertion or divorce' (Panos Institute, 1990a: 25). It is also true that reproduction remains bound up with nationalism. Pregnancy and mothering are, then, profoundly burdened with signification on a social, psychological, cultural and political level.

Whether a mother is an innocent victim or guilty perpetrator in AIDS discourse usually depends on how she became infected. Receipt of contaminated blood products, either by the woman herself or by her lawfully married husband, marks her as innocent victim. Infection from an absent husband or partner whose own infection was due to drug use or bisexuality about which the woman remained ignorant also enables her to claim innocent victim status. Almost any other cause of her infection is suspect and likely to render her blameworthy. But concern for the baby *always* outweighs concern for the mother, and a mother who, along with giving life, gives her baby a fatal illness becomes the opposite of a mother:

> Sex partners of 'drug addicts', who, like transfusion cases, are often infected without their knowledge (even knowledge that their partner may be at risk for AIDS) are sympathetic 'victims' – up to the point when they become pregnant, when they become baby killers. (Treichler, 1988a: 210–11)

Once again we are confronted with the invidious interpenetrations of ideologies of femininity with national and familial ideologies. The role of the woman *is* to be a receptacle for sperm whether in the context of providing sexual services for men or children for the nation/race. As such, she may, by behaving in a *morally* 'unhealthy' way (that is, in a way which asserts her independence from male control), also become a receptacle for disease, which then threatens the health and safety of men and children. That gay men have, for a time, served as 'the women' in this epidemic has only delayed and finally reinforced the re/presentation of this heteropolar narrative. Writing at the time of the Gulf War, Cvetkovich and Gordon expose the precise connection between gender, AIDS and militarism:

> The masculinity that is consolidated, legitimated, and celebrated when a soldier dies with honour or when the United States engages in military combat – a masculinity marked by virility, strength, freedom and individualism – is precisely the definition of masculinity that a homophobic and sexist culture sees as threatened by homosexuality and AIDS. (Cvetkovich and Gordon, 1994: 42)

It will take more than a global pandemic to disturb the heteropolar narrative of gender which locates chaos, entropy, sex, disease and death in the female body and constructs a (somewhat disembodied) masculinity out of order, activity, health and life. It is unsurprising that malestream AIDS discourse has so obediently recycled what are, after all, the foundational gender narratives of Western culture.

A feminist oxymoron?

But what of the feminist challenge to hegemonic narratives of gender? This challenge is undoubtedly more powerful than at any previous time in the history of sexually transmitted diseases. Any such challenge which might have developed in the Middle Ages and Enlightenment is not on record, and the resistance of nineteenth-century women is currently being pieced together from the disregarded margins of malestream history. Feminists today, however – at least those not silenced on account of their class, 'race', sexuality and nationality – have access to a relatively privileged speaking position, and have made use of this to challenge the ways in which women have been represented in the context of AIDS and to resist the marginalization of women's needs for information, support and care. With a few exceptions, feminists have been slow to take on board the implications of gendered AIDS representational practices for women.

There is an additional problem, in that feminist interventions into the textual/representational construct of AIDS may, ironically, be counter-productive. Marge Berer argues, for example, that the feminist critique of safer sex promotional policies fails to engage adequately with the com-plexities of power:

> Many criticize the fact that women are being asked to take responsibility for safer sex with men, as with birth control. As if responsibility were not power. As if women could become empowered without taking responsibility. (Berer with Ray, 1993: 181)

Of course, responsibility is *not* the same as, nor even necessarily associated with, power. It is as likely if not more likely to be located with the powerless and to be assigned to them by the powerful. I remain convinced that the universal tendency to dump responsibility for sexual safety on women is both driven by and expressive of *men's* power, not women's (see Wilton and Aggleton, 1991; Wilton, 1992a). However, it is important to recognize that feminist interventions may tend to reify the interpenetrations of power and gender in what may ultimately prove an unhelpful way. As Berer again insists:

> While there are many cases of women who deny the risks they face and find it impossible to protect themselves from HIV, others are challenging gender and sexual roles. Concentrating only on cases of women who have not yet managed to overcome the obstacles can help to make the image of women as victims a self-perpetuating one. (Berer with Ray, 1993: 181)

Certainly the feminist discursive construct of woman as victim of male power can easily collude with and reinforce the heteropolar narratives of gender; narratives which, in their constitutive relation to subjectivity and the social, may be instrumental in impeding women's ability to protect themselves from HIV infection. It is also true that feminism too has its 'others', its outsiders. Women who inject street drugs, sex workers and destitute women tend to be constituted as the object rather than the subject of feminism. Minority women and lesbians continue to occupy an uncertain position on the borderline of feminist discourse, still obliged to resist their silencing and marginalization.

These are precisely the women positioned as outsiders, as sexually dangerous, as diseased and contaminating, in heteropolar discourse. If feminist interventions into HIV/AIDS representational practice are to avoid reproducing the traditional narratives of sex/gender, they must coalesce precisely around the ab/jected, dangerous 'other', must incorporate the 'woman' who *is* sex, disease, danger, chaos and death, and construct a disobedient reverse discourse. This is not confined to resistance in the context of AIDS, but is important to feminist politics more generally. A radical feminist rupture of hegemonic discourses and ideologies of heteropolarity has yet to be established.

Notes

1. This might, of course, mean that neither men nor women had access to sex for money. We can only guess at what would happen to the commercial sex market if gender were not a relation of power.

2. An alternative explanation is that the syphilis spirochete, long present in European populations, became suddenly and dramatically more virulent.

3. Brandt, Llewellyn-Jones and other commentators suggest that the 'feminization of the venereal diseases' begins at least as long ago as the Middle Ages. Gilman is unusual (and, I think, inaccurate) in pinpointing the Enlightenment as the origin of this construct, although there does appear to have been a looking away from men and an intensification of the male gaze at women at this time. This is an area which needs more research.

4. I hope it is unnecessary to comment that, if HIV was 'imported' into Western gay communities in this way, the epidemiology of the disease in the early stages of the epidemic would have been very different.

5. This is certainly the case for those sex workers who are organized, identify as sex workers and have access to peer networks. It is far more problematic for those women whose sex work is chaotic, desperate or associated with the need to fund addiction to street drugs. As Beban Kidron's film *Hookers, Hustlers, Pimps and their Johns* (1993) makes clear, there are enormous differences in status and power between, e.g. those women who work as escorts in nightclubs and homeless destitute women who walk the streets in an unending struggle to stay alive. HIV is a low priority in the lives of these women, and safer sex is often not an option open to them.

5

Whatever Turns You On – Safer Sex Promotion

We have seen that current hegemonic narratives of gender/sex are predicated upon and in their turn perpetuate the co-dependency of gender (being properly or adequately male or female) and of the erotic (demonstrating properly or adequately male or female desires and sexual behaviours). My use of the term 'heteropolarity' is intended to highlight the chronic inseparability of 'gender' from the erotic within this paradigm and to foreground the foundational assumption of the naturalness, properness and rightness of heterosexuality. It also signals a peculiar interplay of the biological, the moral, the ideological and the erotic which lies at the heart of humanity's failure to stop the spread of HIV infection around the globe.

The biological functionalism which underpins the complex institutional expression of 'gender' depends not merely upon heterosex, but upon heterosexual *penetration*, that is, the penetration of the vagina by the penis. Furthermore, it depends on *productive* heterosexual penetration, coition which results in pregnancy. Despite the theoretical lead taken by exponents of the new Queer Theory in deconstructing gender, the question of reproduction has largely been ignored. Partly, no doubt, this is due to the more distant relationship which the queer constituency – lesbians, gay men, bisexuals and transgenderals – have to pregnancy and childbirth. I suspect, however, that it is also due to the difficulty of fitting the business of reproduction into the performative model of gender. However sophisticated the surgical techniques of gender reassignment may be (and they are not very), however appealing the cinematic fantasy of a heavily pregnant Schwarzenegger (and it wasn't very), a genetic male cannot conceive, give birth or breastfeed a child. He can perform 'woman' until his prostheses burst but will remain barren. Similarly, a genetic woman may be as butch as a bull elephant seal but neither the hormones and scalpel of medical science nor the leather and strap-ons of bull-dyke scene cred will enable her to impregnate a woman. Had someone whispered into my ear while I was in the swearing stage of labour (the stage that lasts right the way through) that I was putting on a really convincing gender performance I think I'd have (queerly) bitten their head off.

Not amenable to incorporation within a gender-performativity paradigm and resistant to deconstruction, sexual reproduction remains the keystone of heteropolarity. It is not just the supposedly passive behaviour of the female body during heteropenetration which has provided the biological justification for the cultural construction of femininity *as* passivity, but the role women play in birthing and caring for children. The stereotypical qualities of nurturance, emotionality, intimacy and childishness which run so strongly through the dominant cultural construction of the gender 'female' in the industrialized West are not associated with being penetrated vaginally but with caring for vulnerable young. Proper female sexuality within heteropolar discourse is motivated not by erotic desire but by the desire for children, and womanliness is most convincingly achieved by motherhood. Similarly, the ultimate proof of masculinity is to father a child (Panos Institute, 1990a; Davidson, 1990), achieving vaginal penetration being a rite of passage towards this goal. In capitalist societies masculine status also traditionally inheres in the ability to support financially both wife and children (while women traditionally worked for 'pin money'), and the shame and stigma of gender failure attends male unemployment and the entry of women into well-paid 'men's jobs' (Giddens, 1992; Cockburn, 1991).

The heteropolarity which structures post-industrial Western societies is, then, specifically reproductive, and as such represents an almost insurmountable obstacle to the promotion of safe or safer sex. The only way of avoiding the sexual transmission of HIV altogether is to engage in sexual activities other than penile penetration (whether of anus or vagina), while the next-best option is to use condoms and lubricant for penile penetration. Clearly, neither non-penetrative activities nor the use of condoms makes pregnancy possible (this is, of course, the stated motivation for the Roman Catholic Church's continued hostility to condoms), so neither counts as 'real' sex. Significantly, both condom use and non-penetrative sexual activities constitute a tacit threat to heterosexual identity as 'real' man or woman. Any AIDS educational material which aims to promote the adoption of safer sex must engage with reproductive heteropolarity and must contribute to the process of challenging its status as naturalized and totemized norm. Material which unthinkingly reproduces or colludes with hegemonic constructs of gender and/or sexuality merely adds to the vociferous monovocal text of heteropolarity, and it is this text which has been the most potent social factor contributing to the rapid global spread of HIV. As Tessa Boffin argued in the phrase which I have taken as an epigraph for this book, 'The most important work for saving lives must take place in the minefield of representation' (cited in Cooper, 1994: 306).

Health education as discursive practice

As is the case for most health educational publications, safer sex educational materials are produced within the statutory sector (by national or local government departments, local health authorities, etc.), within the voluntary sector (by AIDS service organizations, prostitutes' collectives, gay community groups, etc.) and within the private sector (by condom manufacturers, gay commercial organizations, etc.). Often there are strategic and political alliances. For example, the statutory sector may fund the voluntary sector to produce materials which, because of their explicitness or openness about sexual practices or injecting street drug use, must not be associated too directly with government agencies in the mind of the electorate.

This in itself gives rise to the encoding within safer sex promotional materials of covert political narratives of gender and the erotic. The political Right has historically been closely associated with conservatism in matters of both gender and sexuality: Hitler wrote in *Mein Kampf* that the family was 'the final goal of genuinely organic and logical evolution . . . it is the smallest unity, but also the most important structure of the state', while Mussolini addressed Italian women as 'illustrious, prolific mothers' (cited in Cockburn, 1991: 220–1). The New Right of Thatcher's Britain and Reagan's United States was vigorous in its familialism and its promotion of a punitively restrictive sexuality (Weeks, 1991). The ideologies of heteropolarity and Fascism have much in common; 'Essentialism and the idea of complementarity find their fullest expression in Fascist thought' (Cockburn, 1991: 221). Indeed, Maria-Antonietta Macciocchi strongly suggests that Fascism is predicated upon patriarchal notions of sexual difference and the totemization of motherhood in particular, together with a model of gender as a property relation which purports to render anachronistic the notion of class inequality:

> . . . fascism takes as its point of departure the subordination of one sex to another, in so far as women voluntarily accept the 'royal attributes' of femininity and maternity . . . Ownership of women is the same for all men, who, precisely because they own this chattel, woman, which cannot be expropriated, are considered, from boss down to worker, equal to one another and with the same rights. (Macciocchi, 1979: 77)

A regime which locates the power-base of the nation state so overtly in the reproductive heteropolar family is deeply threatened by those who cannot or will not conform to its proscriptive norm. The impulse to control which marks the political Right inevitably mandates the eradication of that which is excessive, beyond control. Thus the discursive package which encompasses unruliness as woman, sex, disease and death and regards them as treacherous to the nation state is deployed with particular relentlessness under the aegis of right-wing political ideologues.

Right-wing governments are characterized by rigid moralism, often associated with religious fundamentalism, and by their anxious and punitive regulation of sexual behaviour. That the initial recognition of the AIDS epidemic came at a time when the political Right was in ascendancy in the United States, Britain and many other European countries was disastrous as far as the ready adoption of safer sex went. Among the stated objectives of New Right political ideology were the reinstatement of the 'traditional' nuclear family and the repression of homosexuality, extra-marital sex and street drug use, all identified as threats to that mythic family. In Britain legislative measures to prohibit the 'promotion' of homosexuality, to coerce young people into extended economic dependence on their families of origin, to restrict the provision of donor insemination to certain groups of women and to force biological fathers to take economic responsibility for their children (however tenuous or hostile relations between the biological parents), were accompanied by vigorous campaigns against street drug use. Similar measures were enacted in the United States. Against this political background, attempts to get AIDS education campaigns off the ground were rendered all but impotent by the politically motivated imperative to promote a specific *moral* message rather than to provide adequate and appropriate information:

> When Mrs Thatcher saw the draft of the first advertising campaign around AIDS she is reported to have vetoed them [*sic*] with the comment: 'It's like writings on a lavatory wall.' It apparently took the concerted efforts of the permanent head of the Department of Health and the Chief Medical Officer finally to persuade her to action. (Weeks, 1990: 245)

Early British safer sex educational materials produced by statutory bodies promote abstinence, monogamy, marriage and mutual fidelity as the principal means of preventing HIV transmission, resolutely constituting gay men as outwith 'the general public'. The body politic is unproblematically heterosexual. Within this framework, they recommend vaginal penetration with a condom, leading Bea Campbell (1987) to dismiss AIDS health education as 'penetration propaganda'. However, this monolithic moralism has shifted significantly in a relatively short period of time. The epidemic, and in particular the energetic activism of the gay community in Britain, has forced statutory bodies to recognize the existence of sexual behaviours and identities other than the reproductive heteropolar norm and to produce health educational materials which reflect that.

This new recognition has not implied a radically new establishment approach to the erotic. The language used by bodies like the Health Education Authority continues to represent sexual activity as suspect and distasteful, and to stress risk and danger over and above pleasure. Although there has been a growing tendency within such materials to make use (somewhat reluctantly and often inappropriately) of street terminology to describe sexual activities, there is no attempt to present safer sex as pleasurable or erotic. The notable exception to this is in the material which is specifically targeted at gay men on the scene (and very little is targeted at gay men *not* on the scene), which is often slick, sexually suggestive and expensively produced (see p. 82).

The urgent need to promote the most specific changes in intimate sexual behaviours across populations has required health educators to develop effective tools for informing, advising and supporting disparate groups with wide-ranging beliefs about sex. The textual/representational practices of health education are not, however, a 'special case' in terms of the discursive constitution of gender. Rather, they are an integral part of the polyvocal, protean conversation about masculinity and femininity ceaselessly engendered in the permeable interface between the subject and the social. Individual and social/cultural norms of gender – what real women and men are and do – are contingent upon and shaped by the cultural reservoir of meanings available at any particular time at any particular place. In Britain, for example, a real woman is no longer someone offended by the sight of an undraped piano leg, as some would have us believe was the case for the Victorians. Health education discourse embodies certain sets of meanings about gender and, as such, may not be thought of as operating outside or in detachment from the wider cultural reservoir of gendered meanings. It is crucial that we ask what meanings for gender and the erotic are being promoted in AIDS discourse generally (see previous chapter) and in the representational practices of AIDS health educational materials in particular.

Sexy genders, gendered safety

The first point about AIDS health education which concerns us here is that such materials, broadly located as they are within the commercial advertising paradigm and hence motivated by the assumptions of that profit-motivated paradigm, are generally targeted at very specific groups. This targeting is more coarsely or more finely tuned depending on the size of the anticipated audience and the potential for restricting access to the materials concerned. Thus a safer sex 'commercial' broadcast on network television will be aimed at a presumptive 'general public', whereas a similar commercial broadcast as part of a magazine programme for lesbians and gay men assumes and targets an audience of gay men.[1]

There is no space here to address the massive body of safer sex promotional initiatives which have been developed in the West since the start of the epidemic. This body of work includes television and radio broadcasts, art activism by groups such as AIDS Coalition To Unleash Power (ACTUP) and Gran Fury, theatre performances, zaps, demonstrations, specially designed condom packets, fashion statements, ephemera (such as match books, games, pick-up cards, badges, or puzzles),[2] designer accessories, books and videos as well as the more traditional posters, press ads and leaflets. I have chosen here to focus most directly on press ads, leaflets and posters. This is partly pragmatic – such materials are easy to collect and to send through the post and I have acquired a large collection of them – and partly because such materials have traditionally been the mainstay of health education in the industrialized West since the First World War (Naidoo and Wills, 1994).

Such small-scale materials as posters, press ads and leaflets are more amenable to targeting than are mass-media campaigns, and targeting is in itself significant in the discursive constitution of gender and the erotic by/ within AIDS health education. As I have written elsewhere (Wilton,

1994a), the act of targeting safer sex educational/promotional materials cannot be seen as a transparent practice simply reflecting a pre-existing set of organizational categories: 'gay men', 'heterosexual women', etc. Rather, the practice of targeting in and of itself *assigns* sexual/gender identities to specific groups, both constituting and deploying identities in a process which I have called identifaction/identificating. Moreover the taxonomic imperative which motivates and is expressed through targeting is predicated precisely upon specific sexual *acts* as both foundational to and marking specific sexual *identities*.

Targeting is enough by itself to discursively constitute the groups so addressed. The category 'men who have sex with men' (sometimes abbreviated to MSM) is arguably an entirely new sexual category, and one which illustrates admirably the notion of identifaction. Researchers such as those working for Project Sigma, a longitudinal study of the sexual behaviour of gay men in the context of AIDS, discovered that surprisingly large numbers of men who had sex with other men did not identify as gay. Indeed most of them maintained a heterosexual identity and many were married (Davies et al., 1990). This was not in itself new; Land Humphreys in the United States had recognized this phenomenon a decade before the start of the AIDS crisis (Humphreys, 1970); but it was not something which had needed to be addressed in policy before. In the context of AIDS this group represented a health educational problem, since although they were having sexual contact with other men they were unlikely to have access to gay community networks or to come into contact with safer sex information circulating within or addressed to that community. They were therefore labelled 'men who have sex with men'.[3] This label, useful though it was to health educators and researchers, was neither chosen by the men themselves nor adopted by them once coined. It was, in other words, an *entirely* assigned identity, not subject to the usual processes of resistance, incorporation, performance and negotiation which constitute sexual and gender identities.

Cindy Patton suggests that a similar process has taken place with regard to the term 'prostitute' which, she argues, encompasses such a diverse range of economic, social and cultural meanings as to be incoherent. In terms of the epidemic, where detailed knowledge of risk behaviours made the use of such a vague term inadequate, 'the Centers for Disease Control replaced the term "prostitute" with the phrase "people who trade sex for drugs or money"' (Patton, 1994: 56). Meanwhile, depending on social, geographical and cultural location, male and female 'prostitutes' may describe themselves as hustlers, hookers, call girls, working girls, sex workers, professional entertainers, second wives or escorts (the list is far from exhaustive). The cultural and economic conditions under which sex is exchanged for material reward vary enormously, and the resultant behaviours range from legally sanctioned marriage to the most alienated of brief encounters. The identity of a destitute woman exchanging sex for drugs on the streets and that of a well-off hustler offering a personal service to clients from his luxury apartment are likely to be shaped in incomparably diverse ways by the fact that both exchange sex as a commodity in a marketplace. As such, safer sex education unproblematically addressed to 'prostitutes' or 'sex workers' colludes with and reproduces the discursive constitution of an entirely imaginary group and, as such, is likely to be ineffectual.

Most AIDS health educational material may be categorized by target audience. Material is intended either for supposedly discrete groups such as haemophiliacs, gay men, women, young people, etc. or for wider constituencies such as 'the general public' or 'people travelling abroad'. For the purposes of this chapter I have divided the materials used for my research into seven categories: those aimed at gay men, at lesbians, at 'women', at 'men', at sex workers, at injecting street drug users and at 'young people'. There is a further category, materials which aim specifically to promote condom use, which comprises materials which do not *overtly* constitute their target audience as either gendered or of any particular sexual orientation.

The *amount* of material addressed to specific groups is also highly significant. The degree of attention accorded various sexual constituencies in the AIDS crisis demonstrates widely held assumptions about the degree and nature of risk which the sexual behaviours of those groups variously exposes them to. It also, arguably, indicates the wider social value accorded to sexual constituencies and the degree to which their existence as a group is recognized. There have been, for example, very few safer sex campaigns addressed to elders (of whatever sexual orientation), to disabled people, the homeless,[4] the 'mentally ill' or lesbians.

The vast majority of safer sex promotional leaflets and posters produced in the US, the UK, Australia and New Zealand (which make up the bulk of material I used to research this chapter) are targeted at an undifferentiated 'general population'. This changes dramatically, however, if press ads are included, since the gay press in all four countries carries such ads with much greater frequency than the 'straight' press. A random sample of back issues of six British lesbian and gay publications – *Gay Times, Square Peg, Rouge, Phase, The Pink Paper* and *Gay Scotland*[5] – produced a total of six ads promoting safer sex together with nine substantial articles on AIDS and eleven ads which directly relate to AIDS (ads for AIDS charities, helpline ads, etc). A similar sample of recent back issues of six 'straight' publications – *Ludus, Elle, New Woman, Bite, Cosmopolitan* and *GQ* – produced a total of precisely one ad promoting safer sex – a condom promo from the Terrence Higgins Trust on the back cover of *Ludus* – together with a commercial ad from condom manufacturers Durex promoting their brand 'Assure'. There were no articles about HIV/AIDS and no ads relating to AIDS, although there *was* a commercial advert for, of all things, a brand of vitamin pills, which used the caption 'Ten years ago, you might not have thought of using a condom either', suggesting that condom awareness is assumed to be generally high among the magazine's readership.

Perhaps more worrying is the clear trend among publications addressed to a specifically heterosexual readership to play down the threat of HIV or deny it altogether. Exemplary of this tendency is an article in British men's sex magazine *Knave* which sets out to reassure prospective heterosexual male sex-tourists to Thailand:

> Basically, if you're healthy enough and heterosexual enough to get to Patpong in the first place, all you need to worry about is food, drugs and booze – plenty of good food and moderation with the others. Then go . . . safely up market [for your prostitutes]. That way you are very unlikely to catch HIV and in good condition to tolerate it even if you do. (de Groot and Nicholls, 1992: 15)

Not only are heterosexual publications unlikely to carry safer sex ads or to inform their readers about HIV/AIDS, they are quite cavalier about promoting dangerously misleading information with a disregard for consequences which can only be described as reckless.

If press advertisements and informative articles are set aside and only leaflets and posters considered,[6] the following results emerge: the great majority of such materials are targeted at a supposedly undifferentiated 'general public', followed by those targeting young people. Then come (in order of decreasing numbers): gay men, 'women', parents and carers of children, lesbians, injecting street drug users, prostitutes and, with only three leaflets explicitly addressed to them, 'men'. A significant gap occurs between the top four categories – the general public, young people, women and gay men – and the categories below them, all of which added together account for only a handful of materials. Also significant, I suggest, is the lack of material explicitly addressed to self-identified *heterosexuals*. The only HIV/AIDS health education publication I have come across which addresses itself overtly to heterosexuals (as opposed to being permeated with heterosexist assumptions and illustrated with heterosexual iconography) is an anonymous booklet, dated 1988 and printed in Sussex but otherwise unattributable, which has on its front cover 'AIDS and MEN: What EVERY heterosexual man needs to know . . .'

The relative attention paid to different sexual constituencies by targeted HIV/AIDS health education publications is instrumental in the social construction of risk. Groups which are volubly addressed are thereby constituted as groups at great risk of infection. Since the association of sexual risk with specific groups carries with it the cultural package of sex-disease-chaos-death, together with more straightforward burdens of stigma, it is unsurprising that the groups at the top of the list are groups already constructed as partaking of that discursive complex: women, young people and gay men.

The social construction of 'youth' is predicated upon notions of excess, risk and rebellion. Adolescence is historically a very recent social phenomenon, having to do with shifts in employment practice, economic relations and educational policies rather than with extra-social biological processes. It is discursively constructed as a time of biological excess –

excessive hormones, secretions, sexuality and gland-driven emotionality – and of 'experimentation' with drink, drugs, sex, politics, music, fashion and (in the case of young men) reckless driving or other criminal behaviours. Adolescents are, perhaps above all, widely believed to *take risks*. Indeed, some commentators suggest that this risk-taking is an inevitable part of the process of growing up, as though risk were a biological rather than a social entity (Wilton with Aggleton, 1991).

In the context of a sexually transmitted disease, it becomes easy to see how 'young people' are positioned alongside women and gay men as excessive, uncontrollable and dangerous. This, I suggest, is what gives rise to the quite phenomenal amount of safer sex promotional material addressed to 'young people'. Nor should we fail to note that these materials by and large *assume heterosexuality* in their young readership. A few make token gestures in the direction of a possible gay male reader – typical of this approach is a comic-style publication *AIDS: Coming Soon* by Central Independent Television's Community Unity (n.d.) which refers to the lead taken by gay men in adopting safer sex and comments 'If you are gay, you probably know more about AIDS than most of us'[7] – but I have found none which include young lesbians in their addressed readership. A 1991 booklet *AIDS and HIV: Information for Students in Brighton* does mention dental dams, but simply notes that they 'can be used as a barrier during oral sex', without even specifying that cunnilingus/ anilingus, rather than fellatio, is meant. Most material addressed to 'young people' fails to provide a reading position for lesbian or gay young people, usually containing such gems as, 'Some young people think that AIDS is something that *other people* need to worry about – gays, drug users, people who sleep around' (Clift and Kanabus, 1993: 12, emphasis in original).[8]

Making up men and women: gender/sex in health education materials

HIV/AIDS health education is unique, in that it is a self-consciously ethical discourse which is, nevertheless, obliged to be fairly explicit about sexual activities. It is also, as we have seen, usually targeted at specific groups *categorized precisely by their sexual behaviour*. In this its only parallel is pornography, not generally thought of as an ethical discourse and not usually published or disseminated by statutory or voluntary agencies. There is a further, disquieting, parallel between 'pornography'[9] and HIV/AIDS health education, in that both sets of texts give voice to almost indistinguishable constructs of sex/gender identities. In this section I want briefly to examine the constitution of four sex/genders in HIV/AIDS health education and in 'pornography'. The four I have chosen are 'woman', 'gay man', 'lesbian' and 'non-gay man', and the 'porn' I have chosen to focus on is telephone sex line press adverts.

Gay man

Telephone sex line ads aimed at gay men are dominated by black and white line drawings of seductive hunks, with a scattering of black and white or meaty colour photos.[10] The artwork is explicit and teasing, and the sex lines themselves offer a varied and wide-ranging menu of erotic interests. This menu has clear and sacrosanct limits; there is no suggestion that men's desire might be anything other than gay, the erotic boundaries of the gay identity are impermeable within this discourse. Nor is there any space for effeminacy or for anything else which blurs the boundaries of gender. These men are hypermasculine; embodying, in their exaggerated musculature, their obsessive gorging on the phallus, their piercings, tattoos and leather, an almost parodic masculinity forever threatening to burst out of the containment of the mere body. In this 'gay man' both the 'gay' and the 'man' are (perhaps anxiously) belted out at full volume, monolithic and unmediated. This is not for vegetarians.

How does this discursive monovocality compare with health education? The 'gay man' constructed by HIV/AIDS health educational materials is almost exclusively a sexual creature. Despite the active role many gay men play in caring for PWAs, the fact that there are gay men who inject street drugs or who have sex with women (Davies et al., 1990), there is no mention in these materials of gay men as carers or drug users, and no advice on safer heterosex. HIV, in the context of this discourse, is precisely a (homo)sexually transmitted infection.

Not only is this 'gay man' highly sexualized, but he is assumed to be imaginative, knowledgeable and inventive when it comes to sexual activity, and to have a positive and accepting attitude to sexuality. Most safer sex material addressed to and constituting this erotic paragon is produced and distributed by voluntary groups, but this does not mean that its production values are either cheap or amateurish. Most leaflets and posters are lavishly illustrated (see Figure 5.1), often in full colour, with highly sexualized and sex-positive images (usually photographs of healthy, beautiful young men), and extremely explicit. Compare, for example, this extract from a 1992 THT leaflet *Hot Sex Now* with the advice given to women below (p. 92):

You can still do almost everything else that turns you on safely . . .

- You could suck, kiss, lick, fondle, bite, nibble and squeeze all over his body – his nipples, arse, calves, toes, neck, ears, thighs, nose, crotch, balls, armpits, fingers . . .
- You could give him a soft sensual massage or get together with wrestling, rough and tumble or spanking
- You could wank each other off – dry or using lots of lube – or press, rub and slap your dick against his dick, buns, face, chest, thighs . . .

Figure 5.1   *Terrence Higgins Trust, 'Hot Sex Now' leaflet illustrations (Terrence Higgins Trust, London, 1992, p. 6)*

HOT
SEX
NOW

- You could have sex in front of mirrors; take Polaroids and videos; or watch each other jerking off . . .
- You could dress up or strip down to sports gear, lycra, leather, rubber, jock straps, uniforms, work gear, torn jeans, boots, socks . . .
- You could use cock-rings, nipple clamps and other sex toys, or play with mud, piss, oil, or beer . . .
- You could play with his arse – finger him, put dildos or butt plugs up him . . .
- You could talk dirty, and tell him about your wildest fantasies . . .
- You could get into role play and domination fantasies; binding, roping and restraining; or cross dressing . . .

(Terrence Higgins Trust, 1991: 8)

The leaflet also includes explicit advice on fucking with a condom, rimming and sucking, while activities suggested in a similar New Zealand booklet (New Zealand AIDS Foundation, n.d.) include; wrapping each other in cling film, whipping/tickling each other with pampas grass feathers and spraying each other with whipped cream then licking it off. In London, SM Gays offer a 16-page booklet, *Rough Sex, Safer Sex*, containing clear and detailed advice on a range of minority sexual practices and illustrated with explicit photographs. Taking explicitness to new levels is one of a series of postcards promoting safer sex produced by Gay Men Fighting AIDS (GMFA) and intended for distribution through gay bars and clubs and at the annual Lesbian and Gay Pride march and party. This has a black and white close-up photograph of a hairy butt descending onto a condom-clad erect penis, across which are the large white letters 'FUCKING SAFE'.

There are problems with such materials. They tend to rely overwhelmingly on photographs of young, able-bodied, white men, and men who can afford expensive clothes and lots of time at the gym, to boot. The explicitness and intense focus on raunchy sexuality also speaks to certain gay men and excludes others, who may ironically have invested much energy in challenging the heterosexist view that being gay is all about what you do in bed. But the queer communities who consume these materials are nothing if not critical, and some recent materials from the THT and GMFA reflect a new concern to be more inclusive. The THT *Hot Sex Now* campaign includes *Tales of Gay Sex*, a collectable set of fold-out photostory booklets (about the size of a pack of condoms) which deal with some important problems which gay men might experience in practising safer sex. These include: young gay men believing that AIDS is only a problem for the older generation, negotiating safer sex during an SM/bondage encounter, moving to the sexual delights of the big city, proposing non-penetrative activities to a new partner, introducing and maintaining safer sex in long-term relationships, heavy drinking and condom use, getting used to condoms, having sex with an HIV positive partner and maintaining safer sex with many partners. Several of the models are from a range of minority ethnic groups, and some are older men. Meanwhile, on the opposite end of the pervy continuum from their butt-fucking card, GMFA have produced a set of playful pick-up cards, full of light innuendo, which have space for the cruiser to insert his name and phone number in the context of a message inviting a cruisee to partake of safe sex.

Whatever criticisms may be made of HIV/AIDS health educational material addressed to gay men (and there are important ones, see pp. 106–10), they are far more imaginative, engaging, erotic and simply informative than those addressed to any other group. Those produced by statutory bodies certainly use more circumspect language when describing sexual activities, and tend to emphasize risk rather than pleasure,[11] but they are generally slick, high quality and explicit, and make a real effort to be both (mildly) erotic and sex positive. This cannot be said for *any* HIV/AIDS educational material addressed to women.

'Woman'

Pornography for women is something of an ideological oxymoron. Heteropolarity constructs *men* as the consumers in the sexual marketplace and women as the goods and services on offer. Moreover, sexual desire and agency are discursively allocated to men and almost universally written as *intrinsically masculine*. Not only is there, as many feminists have commented, no word for sexual power in women equivalent to 'virility' or 'potency', the English language lacks even a word for women's sexual fluids. AIDS has accustomed us to reading of what is variously described as 'cervical and vaginal secretions', 'vaginal juices', 'female bodily fluids' and other such clumsy phrases alongside the straightforward and universally understood 'semen'. Within the reproductive heteropolar paradigm women's sexuality resides in and is limited to their performance *as sex objects for men*. The iconographic expression of 'female sexuality' consists in signifiers of sexual *availability* and sexual *attractiveness*. The black lace, suspenders, garters, stockings, basques, G-strings, crotchless panties, peep-hole bras and so forth signify not female lust but stimulation and ready access for the lustful male. Outwith a queer milieu there is no vestimentary paraphernalia with which a man may eroticize his body for female consumption. There are no black lacy crotchless Y fronts,[12] no peep-hole T-shirts, no tottery nine-inch stilettos for straight men within the traditional heteropolar sartorial repertoire.[13]

Since 'sex' has been so vociferously located in the bodies of women, and since women's sexual desire has been so inextricably elided with sexual danger for men, dominant heteropolar discourse constitutes what I can only call 'womansex', a construction, 'woman', which embodies, performs and exists for the stimulation and gratification of male sexual appetite. Please note, I am not here suggesting that all women are trapped in the position of victim in relation to heterosex or, indeed, to men. I am commenting on the dominant meanings for 'woman' produced in sexualized representational practices. Such meanings exert a powerful influence on the subjectivity and world view of individual women and men, but they are challenged, resisted, disrupted and opposed almost as widely as they are accepted or taken for granted.

Nevertheless there has been, in recent years, some attempt to produce commercial pornography for consumption by women. To find telephone sex line ads addressed to women it is only necessary to look in women's sex magazines, such as *Ludus* or *Women Only*.[14] It takes only a quick glance at these ads to see a dramatic difference between them and those addressed to gay men. Firstly, the erotic boundaries of the 'woman' addressed and constituted by them are permeable and liable to leakage. Paradigmatic of the genre are three pages from *Women Only* which advertise, in full colour, the services of the same sex line company, Mainline (see Figure 5.2). Each page is divided into four boxes. The first page, headlined 'Erotica to arouse every woman's desires', features *Order an Orgy*, *Raw Men*, *Gay Guys* and *Lesbian Lust Box*. The second offers *Female Fantasies*, *Passion Rampage*, *Gay Fantasies* and *Lesbian Lines*, while the third , headlined 'Just Juice', has *For Women Only*, *Wild Sex*, *Butch Boy* (gay-themed) and *Listen in on Lusty Lesbos* (that's lesbos as in plural of 'lesbo', not the island).

These pages construct a female sexuality entirely unattached to a *sexual* identity. Woman's desire is so unfamiliar that the textual targeting conventions have no information to go on and the result is a frantic firing of messages at all known sexual constituencies thought to experience feminine desire – straight women, lesbians and gay men. Heterosexual women's desire is so complete an oxymoron in terms of the reproductive heteropolar paradigm that even so direct a discourse as this constructs it as always already fractured, as shot through with lesbian and gay male desires, as omnivorous (and hence not heterosexual). How does this compare with the 'woman' constructed in AIDS health education?

Gay men, as addressed/identificated by AIDS educators, are resolutely gay and highly sexual. Their gender identity is excessively masculine, their sexual identity excessively homo/*sexual*. In complete contrast, the 'woman' constituted in the representational practices of AIDS health education is minimally sexual, firmly located in relations of caring where she cares for vulnerable others (PWAs and children), and equally firmly located in a system of hetero-relations represented, when the address is to women, as relations of *responsibility* rather than of power.

Very interesting . . . but boring

The copious body of leaflets and posters addressed to women are stubbornly non-erotic. The Terrence Higgins Trust, which produces some of the most explicit, erotic and beautifully illustrated materials for gay men, addresses 'women' by means of plain covers decorated with an abundance, not of delicious flesh but of typographical variation, originally in funereal tones of grey and purple (see Figure 5.3), later updated to incorporate faintly jolly-looking childish graphics. As with telephone sex line ads, the

Figure 5.2   *Telephone sex line advertisements from soft porn magazine for women (Mainstream, London, 1994)*

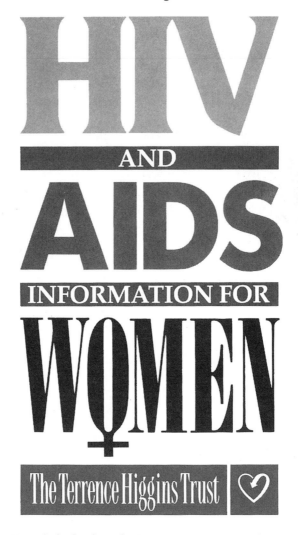

Figure 5.3   *Women's leaflet from the Terrence Higgins Trust (Terrence Higgins Trust, London, 1993)*

direction of the address to women in AIDS educational materials is highly significant. With the exception of a tiny proportion of leaflets specifically targeted at lesbians (see p. 93), these materials assume and constitute an undifferentiated 'woman' whose desires may be heterosexual or lesbian. Although most carry a subtext privileging heterosex, the majority carry some reference to sex between women. This is in clear contrast to gay men's materials, which do not admit of the possibility of sex between a man and a woman. In this discursive constitution of femaleness *gender* is overtly privileged over the erotic as the source and marker of female identifaction.

While the erotic circumscribes a relatively restricted set of activities and behaviours, gender is a much wider semiotic field, encompassing a broad range of expected social roles. Within reproductive heteropolarity women's gender role is primarily familial/functional. Thus, whilst gay men's materials focus on sex, this is true of only a tiny fraction of those addressed to women. The vast majority contain information about pregnancy, children with HIV/AIDS, caring for PWAs or, in several instances, getting involved in voluntary AIDS work. In other words, their traditional *caring* function, the unpaid labour on which the heteropatriarchal state depends, is deeply implicated in the address to and representation of 'women'. One booklet, published late in 1987 by Manchester AIDSLINE, contains this advice to women:

> *The most important thing women can do is help prevent AIDS by spreading the word.* Get the issue discussed at work, with family and friends, in local women's groups and associations . . . *For the sake of ourselves, our partners, our families, our unborn children, women have to take control of our sexual lives and insist on safer sexual practice.* (Manchester AIDSLINE, 1987: 15–16; emphasis in original)

Sex is here seen, not as a source of pleasure but rather as a matter of *responsibility*. This, of course, has been an important theme of some gay men's safer sex materials too. Gay men have been urged to adopt safer sex in order to protect other gay men and, at a wider level, the gay community itself (Patton, 1994; Kayal, 1993). But take a look at the groups for whose safety women are held responsible: themselves, their partners, families and unborn children. Just about everybody in their intimate circle!

Although advice about safer sex is presented in this booklet, it is set in the context of a wider gendered position. To the anxious query, contained in a speech bubble 'What basic precautions do I need to take?' the booklet instantly gets right down to basics:

> *Common sense hygiene in the home*
> Normal standards of hygiene will be enough to protect you from any germs that share your house. For example, it makes sense for **EVERYONE** to follow the following common sense tips: –
>
> ● Cover up cuts or sores.
> ● Wash hands after using the lavatory, handling pets or cleaning litter trays.
> ● Use different cloths for cleaning kitchen and bathroom. (ibid.: 17; emphasis in original)

With the exception of specialist publications for those buddying or caring for people living with HIV or AIDS, I have not found advice on housework or pet hygiene in similar material addressed to any other group.

Since it is the functionalist aspect of their gender responsibilities which primarily constitute the female gender role, there are very few leaflets addressed to women which consist solely of advice about safer sex. The majority follow the model exemplified by a leaflet published by the San Francisco AIDS Foundation entitled, seductively, *AIDS KILLS WOMEN*

AND BABIES. This leaflet, intended for use in women's prisons, has line drawings on the front cover of a young woman in head and shoulders profile and another young woman holding a baby girl who might be asleep or might be dead. The total sum of advice given is:

> You can get AIDS from sex or sharing needles.
> You can stop AIDS:
> Never share needles or works.
> Always use a rubber (condom) when you have sex.
> You can't tell who has AIDS by how they look. Someone can feel and look OK and still give AIDS to you if you have sex with them or share needles with them.
> You can give AIDS to your unborn baby without knowing it. Get medical help right away if you are pregnant.
> You can't get AIDS from touching, food, sneezes, toilet seats, clothes or sheets.
> Signs of AIDS: swollen glands, diarrhea, night sweats, dry cough, tired each day, fever, unexplained weight loss.
> If you are worried about AIDS or feel sick, you can get help. (San Francisco AIDS Foundation, n.d.)

This leaflet, produced relatively early on in the epidemic, has the difficult task of presenting basic information about HIV/AIDS to a group of incarcerated women, many of whom have low levels of literacy. However, that it has chosen so powerfully to stress the lethal nature of the disease and, along with this, to elide women so firmly with motherhood (AIDS KILLS WOMEN AND BABIES), says much for hegemonic heteropolar constructs of femaleness.

One brave exception to the unwritten (and undoubtedly unconscious) 'no safer sex leaflets for women' rule was Frenchay Health Authority in Bristol, England. They published a leaflet, *Safer Sex for Women* (n.d.: see Figure 5.4) which was subsequently updated. This self-consciously avoids addressing women through sexual identity, referring rather to 'safer sex for women having relationships with men or women at risk' – it does not make clear what 'at risk' means in this context, nor does it distinguish between the level of risk inherent in women's having sex with men or with other women. The initial bravery of this initiative is, however, fairly thoroughly undercut by its presentation and content. Conspicuous on the front cover in red, upper-case type are the words 'THE ADVICE IN THIS LEAFLET IS EXPLICIT PLEASE DO NOT READ IT IF YOU ARE EASILY OFFENDED'. There is no suggestion as to what alternative sources of information are available to an easily offended woman. The 'explicit advice' contained in the leaflet, far from listing a tempting menu of safe and safer sexual activities, presents lists of 'high-risk sexual practices', 'medium-risk sexual practices' and something simply headed 'no risk'. In other words, risk rather than pleasure is once again being prioritized. The list of supposedly high-risk activities is as long as the other two combined – clearly most sex is very dangerous – and, rather strangely, includes 'oral sex if the active partner [*sic*] "comes" in the mouth of a passive partner [*sic*]

Figure 5.4 *Frenchay Health Authority safer sex advice for women*
(Frenchay Health Authority, Bristol, n.d.)

who has bleeding gums or mouth ulcers'.[15] Is female orgasm risky in this context, or does oral sex only refer to fellatio? Even more strangely the first edition of this leaflet distinguishes between cunnilingus as performed by a man and as performed by a woman. When a woman goes down on another woman the (medium) risk lies in the 'active partner' having 'bleeding gums, mouth ulcers etc.'. If a man goes down on a woman, there is a (medium) risk 'if he has broken skin in or around mouth'. The association of 'bleeding gums, mouth ulcers' with lesbian sex and the much more neutrally loaded 'broken skin' with heterosex is telling.

If a woman looked to this leaflet to support her in adopting low-risk activities, she would be obliged to restrict herself to:

Kissing – providing there are no bleeding gums or mouth ulcers.[16].
Solo masturbation.[17]
Stimulation using hands, stroking, body kissing.
Sex toys – provided they are not shared.[18]

Wow! Don't get too excited now, girls! It is instructive to compare this list with the one addressed to gay men (see p. 84), a comparison which causes the nervous erotophobia of this women's leaflet to become sharply visible. The advice to *men* intending to have sex with a man could usefully and appropriately be shared by *women* intending to have sex with a man, with the simple alteration of suggested actions involving 'your dick'.

Safer sex promotional materials, then, address and identificate 'women' as prudish, sexually uninterested, unimaginative and unsophisticated and as more appropriately addressed in terms of *danger* than of pleasure.

This is entirely coherent with generally hegemonic notions of femininity. The Panos Institute (1990a: 86) cites anthropologist Vincent Gil: 'In many cultures women "grow up being protected from sexual knowledge in the traditional sense . . . sexuality is often viewed as polluting".' AIDS educational materials might risk incoherence if they attempt to challenge dominant discursive conventions. Sex is something women should be frightened of/off, and women's *responsibility* – for families, children, unborn babies, the sexual safety of themselves *and* their partners – is more intrinsically foundational to their gender identity than sexual pleasure or desire. In fact, I suggest, 'women' *do not have* sexual identity, unless they call themselves lesbians; they only have gender identity. They are discursively constituted within/by reproductive heteropolarity as *functional in the context of masculine sexuality/reproductivity*, not as sexual agents/actors.

Lesbians

There is a handful of AIDS educational materials addressed to lesbians. It might be thought that this scarcity is innocent, due merely to the assumption that lesbian sex is the least efficient transmission route for HIV (as is indeed true). However, such is not the case for heterosexual men, and health educators pay even less overt attention to them than to lesbians.

This suggests to me – especially since lesbians have been demanding safer sex information since the very beginning of the epidemic – that there is something other than a straightforwardly realistic risk assessment going on here.

The same scarcity operates in the field of 'pornography'. There exists very little sexually arousing material for consumption by lesbians, although this has been a burgeoning area of lesbian cultural activity in recent years. Interventions such as *Drawing the Line*, the photographic exhibition and subsequent postcard book by Canadian lesbian group Kiss and Tell (Kiss and Tell, 1991; 1994), and the publication of lesbian sex magazines – such as *Quim*[19] in Britain, *On Our Backs* and *Lezzie Smut* in the US or *Wicked Women* in Australia – have been imaginative and of high quality, but there has been precious little increase in material addressed to lesbians in the 'mainstream' gay press. The few telephone sex line ads which target lesbians use strangely non-sexual, romantic images of couples rather than the overtly sexualized *fleisch*-fest offered to the gay male gaze, and there is not the same emphasis on instrumentality – the 'menu' presentation of sexual acts, fantasies and fetishes is a resolutely gay male prerogative (Wilton, 1996a).

If scarcity characterizes the body of material for lesbians in both these sets of texts, the same consistency can be identified with regard to content. I have yet to come across erotic HIV/AIDS educational materials for lesbians (see Figure 5.5). True, the THT booklet *HIV and AIDS: Information for Lesbians* (1990, updated version, 1993) includes a faintly erotic image of two young, attractive, white women embracing in a shower/bathroom. But, in contrast to its steady stream of newly produced erotic images of gay men, this is the *only* erotic photograph of lesbians THT has yet produced. It is part of a series of six posters, *Get Set for Safer Sex*, produced by the Trust in 1990 'promoting safer sex to young people. Advocating non-penetrative sex as an option'.[20] The six posters all depict couples in sexual encounters; four are heterosexual, one gay and one lesbian. Of the six, the lesbian image is the one which remains most obedient to the traditional semiotic codes of soft porn and which segues most easily into an erotic commodity for straight men (Wilton, 1992a). In the context of the current productivity of lesbian erotic photographers it is depressingly significant that THT, which serves up such luscious fare for its gay male audience, is content to recycle tired and dubious images for lesbians.

Other safer sex materials for lesbians have been produced by queer/lesbian and gay community organizations. Gay Men's Health Crisis in the US has published a safer sex handbook for lesbians, in Australia the AIDS Council of New South Wales (ACON) Women's Team has produced a 52 page booklet, *Lesbian Sex*, which includes advice on HIV and safer sex, and in Britain Leicester's Lesbian, Gay and Bisexual Communities Resource Centre commissioned photographer Laura McGregor to produce a set of eight fairly explicit safer sex postcards. In comparison to the enormous range of material available for gay men, however, such initiatives

LESBIANS
HIV &
SAFER SEX
- LOW RISK
ISN'T NO RISK
LESBIAN AND GAY
Switchboard
071·837·7324
24 HOURS A DAY
SWITCHBOARD

remain few and far between. It is certainly not easy for women to get hold of the information they need about safe lesbian sex.

In uneasy collusion with material addressed to 'women', *all* the leaflets or booklets for lesbians which I looked at contained advice on sex with men and on pregnancy (particularly through donor insemination). Whilst not denying that the information is valuable, this does reintroduce reproductive heteropolar gender identity into a lesbian context, thereby reasserting the primacy of gender identity over and above sexual identity even for lesbians. Sex between gay men and women is now recognized to be an occasional (if uncommon) occurrence, and there are certainly numbers of gay men involved either in co-parenting of their biological children or in donating semen to lesbians who wish to become pregnant. The presence of such information in lesbian material combined with its absence in gay men's material constructs gender identities for both lesbians and gay men in somewhat pathetically docile obedience to dominant heteropolar doctrine. Moreover, the ACON booklet contains advice for post-operative male to female transsexuals who identify as lesbian. Is it perhaps over-cynical of me to suggest that they had to get queer men in there *somehow*?

The only lesbian leaflet which restricts itself to information about sexual practices is one addressed to S/M dykes and produced in 1990 (3rd edn) by the Safer S/M Education Project of the AIDS Committee of Toronto. This contains direct, explicit and thorough information about safer sadomasochistic practices (including with men), but is (significantly) *not* illustrated (apart from two sparse line drawings of a dildo and a pair of handcuffs) and *not* intended to be erotic. Despite the assumption that safer sex materials *must* be erotic if they are to work (Watney, 1987; 1990) which informs and directs most materials addressed to gay men, I suspect that this leaflet is among the most effective and useful ever produced. The advice given is clear and exhaustive, the intended audience clearly indicated, and the text is both sex positive and community affirmative.

'Nowhere Man'

If there is a scarcity of lesbian HIV/AIDS educational material there is a veritable textual black hole where leaflets addressed to heterosexual men should be. The scarcity of material is not simply to be deduced from the small number of leaflets in my sample; after all, it is perhaps to be expected that, as a lesbian, I would have less access to material addressed to heterosexual men than those addressed to my three sets of peers: women, lesbians and (*qua* 'feminine' and *qua* 'queer') gay men. Many commentators have, however, also noted this scarcity.

The Panos Institute (1990a: 89) cites Professor Constance Wofsy, co-director of San Francisco General Hospital's AIDS team, who complains, 'heterosexual men by and large are not being targeted – they may be targeted coincidentally as part of a couple, the partners of sex workers say – but there's little attempt to reach men more generally'. The over-whelming tendency has been to address men *only* as 'at risk' in the context of prostitution, in other words to replay the tired and offensive construct of the contaminated and deadly prostitute. Cindy Patton comments that 'advice to men about using condoms centers almost exclusively on the risk to them of sex for payment' (1994: 109). Even when overt concern is expressed to allocate men their rightful share of sexual responsibility, it seems impossible for educators to imagine what such an initiative might look like. Thus, an editorial in the Royal Tropical Institute/SAfAIDS newsletter *AIDS Health Promotion Exchange* (1991, no. 4) which was optimistically entitled 'Men's responsibility and partnership in the preven-tion of AIDS', concentrated *exclusively* on outreach work to the clients of sex workers and on 'sex tourists'. Matshidiso Moeti, writing in the same newsletter – which had by now been retitled *AIDS/STD Health Promotion Exchange* – (1995, no. 3), comments that 'The increasing awareness of the importance of gender in HIV/STD risk and transmission has, as yet, resulted in little focus on men.'

There is no scarcity of material in the realm of 'pornography', and telephone sex line ads targeting straight men are many and colourful. A flick through just one magazine, *Knave* (1992, 24(9)), revealed twelve and a half full-colour pages of such ads, liberally scattered with colour photographs of naked or fetish-clad women in a farcical series of 'fuck-me' poses, often directing their genitals at the camera/punter.

Significantly, these ads construct 'heterosexual man' as sexual agent precisely by allowing him to occupy the invisible and privileged viewing position *behind* the camera. His masculinity inheres in his status as consumer in this sexual marketplace, and his positioning as consumer is constantly and anxiously reinforced in relation to its negative referent, the blatantly displayed goods on offer to him. There is no construct of 'heterosexual woman' in this discourse, for women are not defined by their desires. Indeed, their desires are redundant, for many sex lines offer 'lesbian' commodities for straight men's consumption. There is only 'woman' – or rather, 'birds', 'girls' – and it is a 'woman' constructed entirely of sexualized body parts and processes. An accretion of 'shaven haven', 'dripping pussy', 'large jugs', 'sex scream', 'titties', 'boobs', 'hard cherries' and 'ripped panties' chaotically re/presents this 'woman'. There is also an anxious insistence on authenticity: 'girls do it for pleasure', 'we didn't know they were doing it, and we don't care', 'we got them to do the business and we held the microphones really close'; perhaps to protect the 'real' masculinity of the punter who is, after all, supposed to get 'really' aroused.

Masculinity within this specifically sexualized discourse inheres in and is expressed precisely by invisibility. It is the prerogative and property of masculinity to look, to label, to listen, to choose, to consume. It is the property of femininity to be looked at, labelled, heard, chosen or rejected and consumed. And this is as true for scientific or health education discourse as for commercial porn.

It is this imperative to keep masculine sexuality hidden, rather than any rational assessment of risk, which I suggest dictates the overwhelming absence of non-gay men from HIV/AIDS educational materials. Of the three leaflets in my sample which are specifically addressed to men one (from the Aled Richards Trust, a Bristol-based voluntary AIDS service organization) includes both gay and non-gay men in its target audience. This leaflet gives advice such as 'If you want to be extra careful use a FLAVOURED CONDOM for sucking/licking the Penis, or use a DENTAL DAM – a LATEX SQUARE – when licking the Vagina/Anus.' Such advice, while it suggests care has been taken to make no restrictive assumptions in addressing the generic 'men', constitutes 'men' as wildly polymorphously perverse, making little or no distinction between the penis, vagina or anus just as long as they can suck/lick *something*. In the context of gendered relations of power (and no such text may be read outside that context), to constitute masculine desire in this way simply makes no sense.

The second leaflet, published by the Gamma Project in Australia, is addressed to *bisexual* men, although this information is offered in *very* small type on a front cover promising 'information for sexually active men'. This A4 gatefold leaflet restricts itself to fairly dense type, with no images at all, erotic or otherwise. The third, which is the only one I have yet come across that proclaims its targeted readership to be 'heterosexual men', is strangely unattractive (see Figure 5.6). The cover, in a peculiarly distasteful rust brown, features three head-and-shoulders portraits of fully dressed men, stereotypes of the hooray Henry[21] in cravat, the wimpy New Man in donkey-jacket and fluffy hair and the working class oik in leather/plastic jacket with shapeless beard and smug grin. The contrast between these three and the men pictured in gay men's leaflets could not be greater. The relationship between the three men and the epidemic is *negatively* presented. Thinks bubbles above their heads declare 'It doesn't affect me', 'I don't have sex with other men' and 'I don't sleep around much'. The intention is clearly to encourage the reader to interpret this as a set-up; these may be the excuses *he* is making, but he is about to be proved wrong. However, the statements also reinforce the construction of heterosexual man as unconcerned about the risk of HIV, a construction which is reinforced by the booklet's text. The imagined straight male reader is given a voice in the form of talk bubbles scattered throughout the text. Thoughts given voice to in these bubbles include:

Oh no, not AIDS again!
I can see lots of problems in encouraging men to start using condoms though.
But condoms cost too much and are embarrassing to buy.
But I don't like using condoms.
What if I'm not going to use condoms?

Figure 5.6   *A rare leaflet targeting heterosexual men (n.p., 1988)*

It would probably be argued by the authors of the booklet (and there is no indication of when, where or by whom it was produced) that the intention is to reflect the attitude of straight men to condom use in order to challenge it. Unfortunately, this naive approach – common to much AIDS health education – makes no allowance for the *constitutive* effects of representational practices. By presenting 'heterosexual man' as childishly irresponsible, resistant to using condoms and, in the end, as *threatening not to*, this text powerfully reinforces the construct of straight men as irresponsible and uncaring. This in itself gives men who read this text 'permission' to behave in this way, however hard the 'voice' of authority insists that they are mistaken. Indeed, masculinity is so strongly elided with sexual irresponsibility in mainstream popular culture generally that this text colludes with the *cultural sanctioning* of that elision.

Incredible how you can see right through me[22]

It is not only the rare material addressed to heterosexual men which is instrumental in reinforcing/reproducing the hegemonic construct of masculinity as sexual irresponsibility. Material addressed to 'women' does too. By assuming that women will have problems in persuading their male lovers to behave responsibly, by suggesting assertiveness training *for women* (never for men) in order to give them the skills to insist on safer sex, this textual address sets up uncaring masculine sexuality *as the norm*. Phrases used in material addressed to women include:

Most people will have to change their sexual practice and a lot of men are reluctant to do this. Hopefully the DHSS campaign, local health education programmes, booklets like this one and women themselves will help to change this. (Manchester AIDSLINE booklet)

Women are . . . very often left with the responsibility [for safer sex] because, in the same way that they haven't had to worry about contraception over the years, men often don't want to see it as an issue for them . . . Some women are afraid of physical violence or abuse from their partners, if they try to make changes in their relationship . . . Assertiveness training may help, but . . . cannot change the problem. (THT booklet)

'Boys won't want to sleep with me if I insist they use condoms' . . . 'If you try to explain that it is to protect both of you and keep a healthy sexual relationship going he might change his mind. If he doesn't then it would be far better to find someone who is more considerate.' (Health Education Authority leaflet)

'What if he won't use one [condom]?' . . . 'There's no doubt that asking a man to wear a condom can be daunting, but when you know it's your health at risk, it is sensible to forget your embarrassment and stand your ground.' (Durex Contraception Information Service leaflet)

The assumption that it is the woman who takes responsibility for sexual safety and the man who resists is centuries old and deeply embedded in most Western cultures. The theme of male sexual irresponsibility with its dire consequences for hapless females runs through folk tradition, as the British ballad 'Long Pegging Awl' demonstrates:

> Then home to her parents she went straight away
> And unto her mother these words she did say:
> 'I'll follow my true love whate'er may befall.
> I'll follow my love with his long peggin' awl.'

> 'Oh daughter, oh daughter, how can you say so?
> For young men are false, you very well know;
> They'll tell you fine things and the devil and all,
> And leave you big-bellied with the long peggin' awl.' (in McCarthy, 1972: 67)

So deeply ingrained in the traditional construction of gender is this set of assumptions, that it is extremely difficult to step out of the paradigm and problematize it. Additionally, the construct of gender whereby men's sexual irresponsibility endangers and victimizes women has been ironically reinforced by feminist discourses of sexual violence and male power. It is only by artificially disrupting the semiotic conventions – for example by reversing the direction which gender takes in particular texts – that we may make explicit the power relations that inhere in them:

> Most people will have to change their sexual practice and a lot of women are reluctant to do this. Hopefully the DHSS campaign, local health education programmes, booklets like this one and men themselves will help to change this.

> Men are . . . very often left with the responsibility [for safer sex] because, in the same way that they haven't had to worry about contraception over the years, women often don't want to see it as an issue for them . . . Some men are afraid of physical violence or abuse from their partners, if they try to make changes in their relationship . . . Assertiveness training may help men, but cannot change the problem.

> 'Girls won't want to sleep with me if I insist they use condoms' . . . 'If you try to explain that it is to protect both of you and keep a healthy sexual relationship going she might change her mind. If she doesn't then it would be far better to find someone who is more considerate.'

> 'What if she won't use one?' . . . 'There's no doubt that asking a woman to use a condom can be daunting, but when you know it's your health at risk, it is sensible to forget your embarrassment and stand your ground.'

This gender reversal exposes in a very direct way the complex and many-layered discursive *habits* which construct the sex/genders 'male' and 'female' in the reproductive heteropolar paradigm.

OK, so what?

Clearly AIDS education not only fails to challenge reproductive hetero-polar constructs of gender and sexual identity, it actively colludes with and reinforces them. But why should this matter? My answer is that it matters on two related levels.

Firstly, there is the specific context of safer sex promotion. Do the materials we have seen fulfil the health promotion mandate to make the healthy choice the easy choice? Do they make it easy for people, whatever their sexual and gender identities, to practise safer sex?

In the case of gay men, the answer is undoubtedly 'yes'. But there is a unique and, I suspect, inimitable relationship between gay identity, community and safer sex and this is reflected in, capitalized upon and reinforced by the representational practice of much AIDS educational material addressed to gay men. In the context of homophobia, when the heterosexual media have overtly expressed the view that AIDS is the inevitable consequence of perverted sexual practices and have *celebrated* the death toll among gay men (Wilton, 1992a; Baaden, 1991; Armitage et al., 1987), the practice of safer sex could not but be defiant, radical, a survival strategy that was truly subversive. The fact that safer sex material produced by and for gay men (and lesbians) was so often censored, impounded or labelled obscene only added to the intrinsic deviance and disobedience, the *queerness* of such materials.

Against this background the act of two men having safer sex with each other becomes in and of itself a snook cocked at a hostile society out to eradicate homosexuality. The more distant gay sex can be from the reproductive heteropolar norm, the more revolutionary it seems. The proliferation of high-quality representations of gay male sex and of luscious objects of gay male desire which AIDS health educators have produced would be by themselves a triumphant assertion of specifically *sexual* pride and determination to survive. The fact that such materials contain information that celebrates gay sex *and* makes continued health and long life more likely makes them potent indeed. Gay men have been able to construct safe sex as pleasurable and transgressive, and the close research attention paid to gay men's sexual behaviours has enabled health educators to respond swiftly and accurately to subtle shifts in attitudes and behaviours. The eroticism of gay men's AIDS health educational materials is an important and effective tool in the community strategy to survive the epidemic, but it cannot be seen in isolation.

For lesbians, there has been a very high level of community awareness of and involvement in AIDS. Lesbians have been producing safer sex information since the early years of the epidemic (Patton and Kelly, 1987) and have been active in criticizing health educational material and in demanding research into woman-to-woman transmission and appropriate and accurate safer sex advice for dykes (Califia, 1995). This has not, however, been reflected in the amount or the quality of the materials available. Most of these are cheaply produced, unimaginative, uninformative, highly tentative about sexual activities and utterly unerotic. Given the celebratory proliferation of sexualized lesbian imagery in the last ten years or so, this indicates the social marginalization of lesbians (who lack access to the machinery of representation which gay men enjoy) and the low priority accorded lesbians in the reproductive heteropolar regime. I know from many conversations with lesbian AIDS health educators that an additional problem is the perceived hostility of a certain lesbian-feminist critique of pornography. It seems that some lesbians would rather produce ineffectual safer sex information than risk the wrath of the anti-porn lobby (see p. 106).

The result is that there is almost no support within lesbian communities for the practice of safer sex, and the leaflets and posters addressed to them reflect and reproduce, rather than challenging, the invisibility and marginalization which makes lesbian safer sex so problematic.

For non-lesbian women, the bulk of HIV/AIDS educational materials make the adoption of safe or safer sex more rather than less difficult. This is in part because it is made out to be so difficult and also because little effort is made to encourage men to adopt safer sexual practices. Women's desire for men remains invisible in health educational materials, female sexuality is constructed as responsible, reproductive and innocent of desire. Catharine Stimpson (1988) has suggested that the cultural construction of women as innocent of sexual desire makes logically necessary the image of women as *victims* in pornography. If women have no desire of their own and experience sex as something repugnant and offensive (remember that the assumption in even the most faintly explicit safer sex materials is that women will find them offensive), then the *proper* way for a man to get sexual pleasure is by ignoring the wishes of his female partner, not bothering to be concerned with the (non-existent) likelihood of her pleasure and concentrating on his own desires.[23] Given that he is encouraged by health educators to regard himself as an irresponsible non-condom-user, the implications of this discursive structure for HIV transmission are profound! Gill Gordon sums up:

> Unless men are treated as responsible, caring human beings, rather than irresponsible children who have to be seduced or cajoled into good behaviour, the promotion of safer sex is unlikely to make much impact. (cited in Panos Institute, 1990a: 80)

AIDS health educators have singularly failed to treat (and hence, constitute) men as responsible adults, whether in material addressed to women or 'the general public' or in the handful of materials addressed overtly to men.

The final important point about the discursive construction of masculinity in/by AIDS health education is that the risk of heterosexual transmission is positioned overwhelmingly as unidirectional, *from* women (particularly prostitutes) *to* men. This despite research findings which strongly suggest that women are at greater risk from heterosexual transmission than are men (Bury, 1994). Thus a Department of Health and Social Security (as it then was) booklet *Before You Go: The Traveller's Guide to Health* (1988) warns:

> Do not have sex with anyone other than your usual partner. If you do have sex
> with someone else always use a condom (sheath, rubber). Remember, in some
> countries many prostitutes are infected. (DHSS, 1988: 8)

This last hint not only identifies foreign prostitutes as a risk to British men
(imagine this passage reading 'if you intend to have sex with local prostitutes, remember to use a condom to protect them from possible infection'),
and British men as concerned with their own sexual safety rather than that
of their partners, it also lets slip the gender of the *assumed* audience.
'Traveller' may be gender neutral, but in this text it is presumptively male.

Health educational materials, then, make it more rather than less difficult
for women (whether lesbian or not) and for heterosexual men to adopt
safer sexual practices. They also, by their obedience to hegemonic conventions of gender representation, reinforce a wider discursive construction of
gender and the erotic which impedes the widespread adoption of safer sex.
In the next chapter I want to interrogate the assumption that gay men's
AIDS education is successful *because* it is erotic, and that what Simon
Watney calls 'a pornographic healing' is necessary to the development of
truly effective HIV prevention initiatives.

Notes

1. The commercials referred to here, a short series of video narratives made by Gay Men
Fighting AIDS and broadcast nationally in Britain as part of Channel 4's 1994 series of *Out*,
made no attempt to address the needs of lesbians for information about or support in
practising safer sex.

2. In the case of the Swedish lesbian and gay rights organization RFSL an imaginative
campaign in the early 1990s included the production and distribution of small perspex cube
puzzles, neat packets of mint breath fresheners, chewing gum and pens all emblazoned with
sex-positive safer sex messages.

3. There was a phase of using MSM to encompass *all* men who have sex with men, whether
self-identified as gay or not, but this was, quite rightly, effectively challenged by researchers
and gay commentators.

4. The homeless have been invisible in statutory AIDS health education until recently. In
1994 the Health Education Authority published a handbook on HIV/AIDS education with
homeless young people, the first of its kind since the start of the epidemic in Britain. This is in
contrast to policies in many poorer countries, where relatively larger numbers of destitute
people have obliged statutory and voluntary agencies to devise means of educating them. In
the Americas 'socially apart' youth are recognized as a priority group for AIDS education.

5. Gay magazines researched were: *Square Peg*, 27 (n.d.), *Phase*, 2 (April 1994), *Gay Times*,
189 (June 1994), *Rouge*, 2 (Spring 1990), *Gay Scotland*, 37 (Jan./Feb. 1988) and *The Pink
Paper*, 110, (week ending 17 Feb. 1990). 'Straight' magazines were: *Bite* (Dec. 1993), *Ludus*
(June/July 1992), *Cosmopolitan* (Oct. 1992), *Elle* (Nov. 1994), *New Woman* (Jan. 1993) and *GQ*
(Oct. 1991). All were published in the late 1980s or early 1990s, by which time the HIV/AIDS
epidemic was well established in Britain.

Both *Phase* and *Square Peg* are, at the time of writing, sadly defunct.

6. By 'posters' here I mean small-sized posters (A2 or smaller) intended for display in clubs,
schools and other public buildings, *not* the vast hoarding-sized ads used in mass publicity
campaigns.

7. So, luckily for us, we don't need to take the trouble to address your needs here in this
straight folks' publication . . .

8. This particular publication continues by denying, not that some young people *are* gay, but that 'All young people, whoever they are . . . need to take the threat of HIV seriously.'

9. I am using 'pornography' here very loosely, in its generally accepted sense of materials intended to arouse. I would stress that my own definition of what constitutes pornography is far more specific than this, and I refer the reader to the last part of chapter 6, where this will be clarified.

10. I looked at such ads in four publications, *Gay Times* and *The Pink Paper* from Britain and the *Advocate* and *New York Native* from the US.

11. Compare, for example, the description of the risks involved in rimming as outlined in the Health Education Authority's leaflet *Safer Sex for Gay Men* with that in the THT's booklet *Hot Sex Now*. The HEA warns: 'Although there is no evidence that you can contract HIV by rimming (licking his anus) both partners are at particularly high risk from other infections including hepatitis. This in turn *may* increase the risk of developing AIDS if you are already infected by [sic] HIV'. The same information, with important additional details, is presented in a subtly more positive way by THT: 'Licking arse is safe *unless* there's any blood in or around the arse. However there are some risks to your health from rimming from other types of infection e.g. hepatitis, salmonella and some parasites. If you have HIV, these can be very serious. Remember that you can get vaccinated against hepatitis B.'

12. Indeed, one episode of the BBC television comedy series *Bottom* relied on the lack of crotchless panties for men for one of its jokes. Rick Mayall, packing for a wild holiday, takes his 'crotchless Y-fronts', and holds the absurd garment up for the camera.

13. This has not always been the case, of course. At various times in European history men have worn high heels, exaggeratedly elongated toes on their shoes (thought at the time so overt a reference to the penis that they were banned as obscene), short breeches and hose, codpieces, kilts, sporrans, etc. All this display was with the avowed intention of arousing female lust. The episode in *Twelfth Night,* where Malvolio is duped into wearing yellow stockings with cross garters supposedly at the lascivious request of Viola, makes no sense outwith the Elizabethan model of heterosexuality, which allocated women a much fairer share of carnal lust than our own.

14. These magazines are British. I suspect that this commercial venture is more advanced in the US, but I have been unable to obtain any examples. The humble British product will have to suffice!

15. Something about this particular active/passive divide makes me wonder if I've been doing it wrong all these years . . .

16. Better stick to kissing men, then!

17. What exactly the risks of mutual masturbation might be (it is included as 'medium risk'), I have not been able to discover.

18. There is no advice here on the safe sharing of sex toys, by washing them between partners or, where appropriate, using condoms. The object, we might suspect, is to prevent people sharing their sex toys rather than to prevent infection being transmitted in this way.

19. 'Quim' is now sadly defunct, although the others mentioned are still, as far as I know, going strong.

20. Wording from THT promotional leaflet for the series (n.d.).

21. British slang term for the huntin' shootin' fishin' male who gets drunk on champagne in marquees and has recreational sex with young wealthy women – whom he probably refers to as 'fillies' – in ballgowns.

22. Apologies to the much-missed Freddie Mercury and to Queen for nicking this snippet from 'The Invisible Man'.

23. I hope it is not necessary for me to say that this is *not* my description of heterosexual relations. I am describing the logic of a very limited set of discursive practices which however have, I believe, a significant impact on the socio-cultural matrix in which hetero-relations are embedded.

6
Representation, Resistance and Community: Difficult Questions

We have seen that health educational materials which aim to prevent the sexual transmission of HIV differentially assign gender and sexual identities to (supposedly) discrete target audiences. They do this by addressing specific sex/gender constituencies with differing quantities of material, differently presented and encoding dramatically disparate meanings for sexual desire, pleasure, behaviour and identity. In particular, the textual address of these sets of materials identificates gay men as hypersexualized in an exclusively recreational-erotic paradigm, lesbians as barely present within the discursive field, 'women' as erotophobic bearers both of sexual responsibility and of the active male erotic gaze and straight men as invisible and proper originators/owners of erotic desire/pleasure/agency.

The discursive constitution of gender and sexual 'identities' within and by health education texts is, of course, an *unintended* outcome. Nevertheless, it is instrumental in facilitating rather than impeding the sexual transmission of HIV, and hence counterproductive in terms of the intended outcome of HIV/AIDS health education. It is in the nature of hegemonic constructs that they remain unproblematized and unrecognized as artefacts of relations of power. It is important to identify the constitutive function of HIV/AIDS health educational discourse in the social fields of gender and the erotic, both in order to interrogate (and hence problematize) its deployment/reproduction of hegemonic constructs and in order to develop effective educational instruments in the struggle against the pandemic.

Health education on its own is unlikely to be of much use in preventing the sexual transmission of HIV. The global community urgently needs to implement health *promotional* strategies across communities, and this is indeed the approach of many local AIDS prevention programmes around the world. From projects in many African countries which offer training in other marketable skills to women seeking alternatives to sex work, to jack-off parties in urban gay male communities in the US, to automatic syringe exchange machines on the streets of French towns (WHO, 1994), interventions which *make the healthy choice the easy choice* are many and ingenious.

How do the safer sex promotional materials discussed in the last chapter fit into this broader, urgent project of HIV/AIDS health *promotion*? In particular, what lessons may be learnt from the rich and erotic abundance of gay men's safer sex materials that might enhance the effectiveness of safer sex promotion across other population groups?

A pornographic healing?

There has been very little sustained critique of safer sex materials as discursive practice. Despite the oft-repeated allegation in Queer or AIDS-activist literature that the feminist critique of pornography is an impediment to effective safer sex promotion (e.g. Manchester City Council, 1990; Watney, 1987; Gorna, 1992), feminist critics have remained largely silent on the subject, and there have been no feminist interventions that I am aware of to prevent the production or distribution of AIDS educational materials. Clearly, however, some AIDS activists and (particularly) activist gay men initially felt obliged to dismiss the radical feminist critique of pornography in what seems to have been a (decidedly hostile) pre-emptive strategy designed to deflect potential criticism of gay men's safer sex campaigns anticipated from this source. From the beginning then – and not solely due to hostility to feminism, as I hope to demonstrate – what discussion of safer sex discursive practices as there was tended to be couched in defensive-aggressive terms.

The best-known exemplar of this genre is Simon Watney's *Policing Desire: Pornography, AIDS and the Media* (1987), which set the agenda for a particular cultural-political discourse around AIDS and sexual libertarianism, and remains an accessible and important study of early mainstream media accounts of the epidemic. Of interest to us here is Watney's impassioned assertion that the pornographic vernacular is the exemplary discursive matrix for effective safer sex promotion:

> Changes in sexual behaviour cannot be forced, they can only be achieved through consent, consent which incorporates change into the very structure of sexual fantasy. Hence the urgent, the desperate need to eroticise information about safe sex, if tens of thousands of more lives [sic] are not to be cruelly sacrificed on the twin altars of prudery and homophobia. (Watney, 1987: 129)

Watney's argument is that the erotophobia, prudery and homophobia of the (primarily) British and American establishments[1] have compounded the health crisis of the epidemic and have led directly to many preventable deaths. The principal instrument of this statutory genocide is, he argues, the legislative regulation and commercial manipulation of representational practices by governments and the media respectively. It is hard to disagree with this position,[2] and it is certainly the case that most individuals in Britain and the United States have been denied access to the kinds of explicit information about safer sexual practices which the gay community has fought so hard to provide for gay men. But is the solution as simple as Watney suggests? Should we fight for the eroticization of information about safe/safer sex? And what, given the immense and often catastrophic co-dependency of gender and the erotic, are the wider implications, both

politically and for HIV prevention, of so doing? In a self-conscious perversion of the apparently oxymoronic, Watney calls for a 'pornographic
healing' (ibid.).[3] Is this more than an attempt at semantic transgressivity?
Can pornography function as healing discourse in the context of this
epidemic?

In order to explore the full implications of this notion of pornographic
healing it is important to understand how pornography might be understood by a white, middle-class, urban gay man in the industrialized West as
performing a more general healing function. The answer to this is firmly
rooted in the recent social history of gay men, in particular the part played
in that history by gay activism and by the commercialization of the gay
'scene'.

The assertive, sexually confident, self-identified gay man is a very recent
phenomenon. The Wolfenden report in Britain (1957, leading to the 1967
Sexual Offences Act) and the Stonewall riots (1969) in the United States
both catalysed the growth of a newly non-apologetic lesbian and gay
community, in marked contrast to what had been possible before. Prior to
the 1970s there were certainly activist groups – lesbian, gay and mixed –
such as the Mattachine Society and the Daughters of Bilitis in the States or
the Order of Chaeronea (possibly dating from as early as the 1890s, see
Weeks, 1990) and the Homosexual Law Reform Society in Britain. Most
historians identify the change which took place in the 1970s as involving a
rejection of assimilationism, traditionally characterized by a somewhat
apologetic position on homosexuality (be nice to us, we can't help it), in
favour of a newly radical demand for rights. In Britain this is generally
presented as a conflict between the Campaign for Homosexual Equality
(CHE), representing the sober mainstream of the movement for gay rights,
and the Gay Liberation Front (GLF), representing the more intransigent
and less conciliatory new mood (Shiers, 1988; Weeks, 1990; Edwards,
1994). In Britain this dynamic continues in current clashes between the
lobbying group Stonewall, which has had much success in recruiting high-
status public figures to the cause, and the more unruly direct action group
OUTrage.

The new radicalism, with its in-your-face assertiveness and unapologetic
political stance, took gay *sex* as its foundational *raison d'être* and meta-
phor. More particularly, it took the homophobic construct of gay sex as
hedonistic, perverse, destabilizing of the family unit, subversive of proper
sexual morality and generally the enemy of social order and *celebrated it as
such*. As a response to homophobia, this represented a complete reversal
of familiar strategies. Rather than attempting to *disprove* homophobic
assertions about the perversity of lesbian and gay sex – by performing
homosexuality as decent, familial, responsible and 'straight' – the new
radicals constructed a reverse discourse of queer perversity, *claiming as
their own* the despised status of outsider and using that reclaimed outsider
position as a place from which to critique the heterosexual mainstream.
This, of course, locates the 'problem' of homosexuality firmly with

heterosexuals, where it originates/belongs, rather than with queers. The chant 'We're here, we're queer, get used to it!' potently epitomizes this reversal of responsibility.

Because the stigma and opprobrium attached to homosexuality coheres around homo*sex*, in particular around the symbolically overloaded and presumptively homodefinitional act of anal penetration, the discursive resistance inevitably did the same. The new gay male identity was powered by a proud and self-consciously transgressive reversal of discourses of sex. Features of gay men's lives which were consequential on surviving in a dangerously homophobic world – such as meeting in clubs, cottaging, cruising and having casual sex in public spaces such as parks or back streets – became celebrated as the quintessence of political radicalism, embodying a direct challenge to the punitively restrictive familial moralism which it was supposed structured the lives of straights. Tim Edwards (1994: 108) refers to this as 'the eroticisation of an oppressed position' and suggests that it operates as both social and psychic liberation:

> This liberation works on several levels: first, individually, as the idea is that public sex liberates personal hang-ups and inhibitions about sexuality; and second, collectively as 'every fuck is a fuck for freedom', a sign of community, and an opposition to the heterosexual monogamous and familial sexual ideology motivating state surveillance. (Edwards, 1994: 94)

Participation in and celebration of precisely those aspects of sex between men which were most stigmatized became the hallmark of the new gay identity. The gay political movement, which had for so long insisted that to be gay was far more than simply a matter of who you had sex with, became structured around the assertion that two men having sex together was the most politically radical action conceivable. In resisting a homophobia which was all too frequently lethal – gay men still comprise the largest number of hate crime murder victims in the States (Comstock, 1991) – sex was set against denial, erasure and death in a classic Eros/Thanatos polarity. For the new generation of gay men sex *was* life. Some gay men insisted that homosex was incomparably superior to anything possible within heterosex, declaring indeed that gay men had escaped the universal regime of repression, leaving the hetties behind them:

> the exuberant confidence of lesbian and gay male sexuality will inevitably seem at odds with the familial moralism of the mass media. Our frankness and articulacy and sheer gaiety disturbs the poky, repressive little world-of-the-family, and threatens to expose the brutal forces which hold it together across the entire field of 'public' representations. (Watney, 1987: 125)

The smugness and oversimplification of such anti-familial vitriol must be seen in context. Within the terms of the reproductive heteropolar paradigm homosex is positioned as sterile and hence purely lascivious and without justification. Lesbian and gay people, in some historical periods and in some cultures, have demonstrably internalized the notions of unnaturalness, barrenness, waste and (ultimately) death which coalesce around the queer rupture of the reproductive heteropolar imperative to breed. Along with this internalization of the hegemonic ideologies of gendered somatic functionalism came, for some, a despairing willingness to renounce sexual intimacy altogether:

> There is surely a place in the great scheme of things, even for the abnormal man and the abnormal woman, but it is not an easy place. Possibly it is a very high place: the place of clean living and renunciation. (Edith Lees Ellis, cited in Weeks, 1990: 103)

Developing as a reaction to the erotophobia and self-loathing engendered by such attitudes, it is hardly surprising that gay radicalism of the 1970s and 1980s (following on, let us not forget, from the sexual revolution which was such an integral part of the social upheavals of the 1960s) proposed sex itself as liberatory, health-giving, life-giving. The sterility which had seemed to a previous generation to be a mark of shame now became, in the discursive and ideological legerdemain so characteristic of all the important resistance movements of the time,[4] a sign signifying all that was most liberating and radical about homosex:

> Homosexuality is considered to represent a pure, unencumbered form of sexuality. Not engendering new life, divorced from the social and economic structures of heterosexual marriage, and apparently employing sexuality as the primary form of self-definition, homosexuality represents sex incarnate . . . This obsession [with sex], along with the impulse to personal freedom that makes sexual activity possible, is at the centre of the gay sensibility. (Bronski, 1984: 191)

Not only was homosex – and in particular casual, public, instrumental or anonymous homosex – allocated the burden of signifying resistance to hegemonic heterosexual norms and the homoerotophobia associated with those norms, it also took on additional significance in gay men's reassertion of their *masculinity*. Since gay men are anathematized by association with femininity, and since homosexuality is generally elided with failing to be one's proper gender (Butler, 1993), a resistant reverse discourse of homosex inevitably included a triumphal reclamation of the privileges, signs and performance acts of masculinity. From the early 1970s, urban gay culture in the industrialized West became resoundingly macho (Weeks, 1990; Edwards, 1994). The ritualization of gay sex – cottaging, cruising – which had been the consequence of criminalization and stigma, was co-opted as the performance of paradigmatic masculinity, unmediated by contact with women. 'Cruising sexuality, as instrumental, unemotional and orgasm-oriented is indeed male sexuality *par excellence*' (Edwards, 1994: 95).

This masculinization of the subculture gave rise to the 'clone' and to a new iconography of excessive machismo, typified in the drawings of Tom of Finland and performatively encoded in the denim, Wild West or lumberjack gear, blue-collar drag, military/police uniforms and – perhaps above all – leather, of the urban gay scene. This was not, however, in any sense a 'straight' celebration of machismo. Gay machismo, produced as it is from a position eccentric to the gender norms of the mainstream, is self-consciously performative. It also embodies a mocking critique of the unselfconsciously masculine which is expressed in parody and caricature. In other words, it is camp.

Understanding this unique aspect of gay machismo is important for an appropriate and sensitive deconstruction of the sexualized representational practices rooted in the urban gay context.[5] Tom of Finland's drawings, for example, have been cited as an important element in the defiant remasculinization of the gay subculture, and the artist stated that this was an integral part of his liberatory agenda: 'I work very hard to make sure that the men I draw having sex are proud men having happy sex' (Hooven, 1992: 8). Yet this exuberant body of work is characterized by a playful *parodic* construct of masculinity; indeed, the signifiers of masculinity employed in many of the drawings are so excessive as to spill over into their opposite, femininity. In particular the exaggerated pecs, currently so totemized in certain gay cultural milieux, are often drawn so spherical, the nipples so pronounced, as to 'read' as women's breasts. Many drawings depict men with these masculine breasts suckling one or more hypermasculine adult males, often resulting in a startling gender-fuck reinscription of the traditional high-art iconography of the Virgin Mary. This suggests, not a docile obedience to heteropolar ideologies of masculinity, but an astute recognition of the terror which underpins such ideologies – terror that the abject feminine will break through the rigidly policed bounds of the masculine – and the startling, *queer*, possibility of *celebrating* that rupture. Tom of Finland's drawings seem to me to embody the Queer Nation demand that queers 'PENETRATE the Rambo Bimbo DIVIDE' (Jarman, 1991). There is, I suggest, a strong argument for locating gay machismo in opposition to, rather than in collusion with, its straight counterpart.

Too sexy for your party – no way I'm disco dancing

But perhaps more significant than either the defiant celebration of homosex in the face of homophobia or the reinvention of a (potentially androgynous) masculinity has been the rapid commercialization of gay urban culture:

> Meanwhile, in the realm of consumption, the ongoing expansion of male homosexual, and increasingly lesbian, culture around the exchange of goods and services has led to the consolidation of entrepreneurial networks dedicated to the reproduction of 'homosexual lifestyle'. Via holidays and restaurants, shops and cafe-bars, insurance and legal services, it has now become possible to live a homosexual life in the large urban centres of Europe and North America. (Mort, 1994: 208)

The aspect of commercialization which most gay male commentators identify as especially significant is the proliferation of gay clubs, pubs and, most important of all, disco. It was disco culture which catalysed the dramatic sexualization of the most visible strand of gay male culture (and, more recently, lesbian culture), and which synchronized the celebration of sex and of masculinity within a safe space devoted to such celebration. In Britain, where disco culture was imported from the US, the transformation was startling:

> The most dramatic change came with the increasingly overt sexualization of the gay male subculture. Sex, and sexual need, had always been the glue that held the subculture together. But in the British moral climate it had been accompanied by a pervasive air of furtiveness, which the emergence of gay liberation in the early 1970s, with its bracing moralism, tended to underline rather than dispel. A change was signalled in the mid-1970s with the arrival in Britain of the mega-discos. (Weeks, 1990: 232)

Opinions differ among gay writers concerning the aspect of gay politics which was swept aside by the disco invasion. While Weeks refers to it as the 'bracing moralism' of gay liberation, others are more tentative in their account of the complexities of this shift. The aspect of gay male culture and politics which has been most thoroughly erased in the ascendancy of the commercial scene is its engagement with feminism, and in particular with the feminist critique of male power. In the 1970s many gay men were strongly influenced by this critique, and involved in a struggle against the rules of heterogender, a struggle which was at the same time deeply queer and deeply informed by feminism. At the time of writing, when queer has so publicly cast feminism as the reactionary disciplinarian mother and when many feminists represent queer as apolitical, reactionary and anti-feminist, this alliance seems unlikely, however devoutly to be wished. Gay men writing of this period today generally refer to their own feminist-influenced younger selves with mockery and embarrassment:

> The first time I went into the Union pub in Manchester, the doorman asked me jokingly if I 'give it or take it'! He was immediately subjected to a ten minute lecture from me about the oppressive and male-defined nature of penetrative sex and how he needed to escape from restrictive role-playing! (Shiers, 1988: 238)

This embarrassment is easy to understand, given the aggressive public hostility towards feminism, and *especially* towards those gay men brave enough or foolish enough to appear sympathetic to feminism, which is a staple of even the most 'intellectual' gay discourse today. Thus a gay man who dared to write to the *New York Native* asking for 'a creative pornography along lines other than power and the exchange of body fluids' was treated to the withering scorn of one gay writer on AIDS: 'This is the authentic voice of the feminist-identified gay man, spouting forth "on behalf" of other people perceived to be at risk' (Watney, 1987: 75).[6] In other words, gay men who have a public critique of gender relations as power relations risk being labelled by other gay men as the 'mummy's boys' of feminism, much as gay men have always been labelled mummy's boys in homophobic discourse.

Not all gay men are so naive in their dismissal of feminism. Shiers describes the events of the 1970s as leaving an unfinished question for gay politics:

> What in essence began to happen was the appropriation of heterosexual male symbolism and imagery, and its sexualization into gay male style. This process led to frequent clashes with many lesbian feminists over whether this amounted to the reinforcement of an oppressive form of masculinity, with overtones of Fascism. This is an issue which is still far from being resolved politically. (Shiers, 1988: 239)

Unresolved though it may be, it is important to recognize that the legacy of this commercialization and sexualization of masculinity, so apposite in the logic of resistance to homophobia, has been to align gay men *in opposition* to feminism. This is because the feminist critique of the relations of power which inhere in and are expressed by the reproductive heteropolar paradigm (a critique which, ironically, gives rise to a political position from which the most powerful challenge to heterosexism may be developed) is read by most gay men[7] as antagonistic to the fantasy of masculinity which lies at the heart of the 'scene'. And the scene is both most excellent sanctuary for, and potent catalyst in, the development of a confident gay identity.

Porn free

Implicit in the commercial sexualization of gay male culture was the boom in gay pornography. A somewhat simplistic reading of lesbian and gay autobiographical accounts suggests that porn performed for young, isolated gay men a similar function to that which lesbian pulp novels performed for young, isolated lesbians. In a society where the mirror of cultural production stubbornly presents an unvarying reflection of heterosexuality, *any* image of queer existence is a lifeline for confused and guilty lesbian and gay adolescents:

> I remember the very exciting feeling I got when I first saw one of those [porn] magazines before I came out. There I saw men kissing and holding and loving each other . . . It was proof of a homosexual community and it was through porn that I learned of its existence. (Gregg Blachford, cited in Richardson, 1991: 241)

And since homophobia, predicated precisely on execrated *sexual* behaviours, is the cultural oxygen of patriarchal social organization, the reassurances offered by porn are not something which lesbian and gay people can simply grow out of as we reach maturity. Some lesbians (e.g. Califia, 1995; Allison, 1995) and many gay men recognize the key role taken by porn in catalysing a confident gay identity:

> It's a curious thing that our 'subculture' is positively defined in terms of its porn production, because it is to do with self-image. News magazines carry sexual imagery, not because we're all sex obsessed, but because we define ourselves positively by it. We're almost obliged to find our positive definitions *there*, as a

resistance and response to the dominant's reduction of us to a sexual preference. (Mick Wallis in Dyer, 1989: 210)

Culturally marginalized, with our access to the machinery of representation compromised by our sexuality (and, for lesbians, by our gender – a much more significant factor in this context), queer people have a unique relationship to sexualized imagery. Images of heterosex predominate in the profligate outpourings of 'eye candy' which characterize postmodern culture. It is hard to find any commercial product, from toothpaste to life insurance, from knitting wools to health foods, which is *not* iconographically associated with familial or recreational heterosex. For us, 'Pornography is the only place where we can create our own images of lesbian and gay sex which celebrate its joy and beauty' (Richardson, 1991: 240).

Moreover, the sexualized representational practices of the queer community are subject to remorseless policing and constantly under attack. Gay bookshops are raided, gay publications taken to court, gay porn videos and magazines impounded (often illegally) by customs officers, individuals may have their homes raided and their private collections seized (Shiers, 1988; Dyer, 1989; Watney, 1987; Richardson, 1991). In the face of such overt abuses it is inevitable that the defence of lesbian and gay human and civil rights should encompass a defence of the right to produce, distribute and consume 'porn', *and* it explains why a continuing reflexive critique of the part played by porn in lesbian and gay communities is so necessary to the development of a radical queer politics.

> attacks on pornography quickly become attacks on the whole of lesbian and gay culture because the two are seen as one and the same. That is why we must oppose anti-porn forces in whatever guise they appear: which means being prepared to face up to pornography, to understand why we like it and why we find that so shameful. (Richardson, 1991: 233)

Gay men's cultural production/reproduction is located at the nexus of a unique set of social, cultural and political transformations in the field of gender and the erotic. These transformations are, in their turn, mapped onto a broader socio-cultural context where 'pornography takes most of the burden of talking about sex and . . . talking about sex is considered pornographic' (ibid.: 247). Sexualized representational and performative practices were the privileged markers and bearers of gay identity at the precise historical moment when AIDS began to be constructed as a coherent social/medical/moral entity.

Porn = sex = life: strategic fictions

When AIDS came,[8] it slotted neatly into the pre-existing struggle over sexualized representation. Although this struggle has never been restricted to lesbian and gay imagery, it was at the socio-political interface between queer and straight that most hostility, most legislative intervention, most police activity and most political energy focused on the question of porn.

The dramatic and ongoing transformations outlined above were precisely what enabled gay communities in the West to mobilize with such speed and effectiveness in response to the new health emergency. As large numbers of gay men began to die, gay men *as a subculture* moved through the inevitable reactions of shock, denial, anger and grief in an extraordinarily short space of time (although, for individuals, the rhythms of loss are more various and tend to follow closely the pattern of personal bereavement). As Jeffrey Weeks points out, the very subcultural norms which enabled the virus to take such a firm hold among gay men were what enabled the fight for survival to begin:

> Here we can see an important paradox in the history of the epidemic. The spread of the HIV virus in the gay male community was obviously due in large part to the growth during the 1970s and early 1980s of the highly sexualized subcultures, where sexual contact was easy, and internationalized. But what on one level increased the risks of coming into contact with the virus, also provided the social infrastructure for coping with the epidemic. (Weeks, 1990: 246)

The development of this infrastructure, which was soon to form the foundation of *all* HIV/AIDS work in the industrialized West, remains an extraordinary achievement unparalleled in social history. This marginalized and despised minority, coalescing around a sexual preference and in response to external hostility, had developed a coherent enough sense of community to be able to construct a complex network of services. Fundraising and organizing in the gay community gave rise to an imaginative, responsible, deeply compassionate and above all *effective* AIDS strategy which puts the response of *all* governments to shame. Intrinsic to this strategy from the earliest days has been the imaginative and sex-positive promotion of safer sex (Shiers, 1988).

Gay men in the US were advocating safer sex before the medical establishment had identified that a sexually transmissible virus was the cause of AIDS (Patton, 1994). The first detailed safe sex advice, *How To Have Sex in an Epidemic*, was published in 1983 by a group of gay men, including some with AIDS. Those people wringing their hands at the difficulties of promoting condom use to straight men would do well to pause and remember how much *more* problematic it should have been to get gay men to use condoms. This group (unsupported by professional health educators) was able to take an entirely alien and unfamiliar object and one closely associated, moreover, with the enemy territory of heterosex, and to interweave it with the strands of gay identity. What is more, having been startlingly effective in promoting condom use, gay men have also been able to promote the safest sex of all, non-penetrative sex. Such extraordinary large-scale transformations in sexual behaviour could only happen in a context of sexual articulacy:

> We were able to invent safe sex because we have always known that sex is not, in an epidemic or not, limited to penetrative sex. Our promiscuity taught us many things, not only about the pleasures of sex, but about the great multiplicity of those pleasures. It is that psychic preparation, that experimentation, that

conscious work on our own sexualities that has allowed many of us to change our sexual behaviours . . . very quickly and very dramatically. (Crimp, 1988: 253)

Of course the British and US governments, when they finally and reluctantly accepted that they had a responsibility to take action against AIDS, found the notion that gay promiscuity and sexual articulacy was advantageous ideologically intolerable – probably, one suspects, incomprehensible. Not only were gay men's safer sex promotional materials declared obscene and their distribution obstructed, but homosex *itself* was widely declared to be the cause of AIDS. A virulently homophobic discourse of diseased sexuality, focusing obsessively on homosexual buggery as the paradigmatic 'unnatural act', reinstated/restated the construct of gay identity *as* monolithically sexual and that monolithic sexuality as the originary source of disease, death and a corruption at once bodily, moral and social. In the US Peter Duesberg, the biochemist who continues to maintain that HIV is not the cause of AIDS, suggested that it was the decriminalization of homosexuality which was responsible for the epidemic:

We don't have a new disease. It's a collection of [old] diseases caused by a lifestyle that was criminal 20 years ago. Combined with bathhouses, all these infections go with lifestyles which enhance them. (cited in Crimp, 1988: 238)

Dennis Altman has pointed out that, since 'both homosexuality and America itself can stand as convenient symbols . . . of modern decadence', the association of AIDS with America was as significant, in terms of a moralistic agenda, as its association with homosexuality. 'The perception of AIDS as a gay American disease easily feeds into a particular moralistic view that depicts AIDS as a disease of modern decadence' (Altman, 1986: 175). In Britain, the moralism of the New Right seized control of the AIDS agenda and public discourse became saturated with homophobic rhetoric:

The reasons for the spread of AIDS were transparent to the former Tory Solicitor-General, Sir Ian Percival: because 'so many have strayed so far and so often from what we are taught as normal moral behaviour'. The virulently evangelical Chief Constable of Manchester, James Anderton, had no doubts about it either. He saw the spread of AIDS as a result of 'degenerate conduct', and he went on, 'People at risk are swirling round in a human cesspit of their own making.' (Weeks, 1990: 245)

At the very moment when they were mourning losses of unimaginable proportions; losses of opportunities, pleasures and safety as well as of friends, lovers, partners and community figures; gay men were subjected to vicious scapegoating from a self-righteous heterosexual establishment still entrenched in denying that AIDS had anything to do with themselves. As Douglas Crimp (1988: 171) succinctly puts it, 'Seldom has a society so savaged people in the hour of their loss.' It was a savagery whose consequence was uncountable numbers of preventable deaths, among heterosexuals as well as among gay men. The UK government banned the import of safer sex educational materials from gay groups in the US and HM Customs impounded AIDS educational materials during a raid on Gay's

The Word bookshop in London (Wilton, 1992a). Meanwhile advice to heterosexuals was to find, and stick to, a safe *partner* and the responsibility for condom use was dumped firmly onto straight women (Crimp, 1988). The political imperative to foreground a moral agenda deprived everyone, whatever their sexual orientation, of the information they needed.[9]

A dis/ease of homophobia

As Roberta McGrath has pointed out, the clinical characteristics of AIDS lend themselves to fearful fantasies of bodily and personal disintegration:

> [HIV infection] creates a body which turns upon itself, killing not through a single disease, but through a cumulation of our most feared diseases . . . diseases that attack skin, tissue and bone, our bowels and brains. These diseases not only mark the body on the outside, but dissolve it from within. This is total war waged on the body . . . and consequent breakdown, disintegration and disappearance . . . Furthermore, although various modes of transmission are recognised, HIV has been represented as fundamentally sexually transmitted. Thus HIV is the link between sex and death. (McGrath, 1990: 144–5)

It is hardly surprising that some gay men, beleaguered on one side by the ravages of an epidemic which gained access to the (but newly celebrated, recently confident) gay male body through sex and on the other by a vociferous resurgence in discourses of diseased homosex, should construct a reverse discourse predicated on the link between sex and death. Within the terms of this reverse discourse the historically recent structure of sex/porn/gay identity was co-opted as a discursive/representational package which carried meanings to do with life, health, survival, resistance. Aligned on the obverse of this queer pornutopian package were the presumed antagonists or opposites of the sex/porn/gay identity: erotophobia, any attempt to problematize pornography, heterosex, the establishment and a homogeneous feminism. Within this discursive matrix, porn signified not only resistance to homophobic erasure and the defiant affirmation of execrated sexuality but survival in the teeth of death itself.

The most assertive vocalizing of this queer pornutopian package has come from the US, where the virus made its earliest and most overwhelming inroads into gay men's lives. Here, the queer pornutopian gaze is directed towards the gay male body which, constructed within/by such discourse as the embodiment of celebratory lust, disintegrates under the touch of AIDS:

> Men who were once 200 pounds lie in bed reduced to 110-pound skeletons. Faces once brimming with life and lust are reduced to courageous death masks animated only with the desire to live. (Bronski, 1989: 226)

Within this discourse, AIDS is the thief which *takes away desire*, leaving the gay male body meaningless. A gay identity predicated so directly on specific rituals of sexual activity and located so relentlessly on the (shaved, perfumed, pumped-up, *controlled*) gay body is devastatingly vulnerable to biological hazard. Getting older, getting fatter or thinner, losing muscle tone, all take on the power to compromise sexual identity as, ironically, has long been the case for straight women. By stealing both erotic agency (desire and activity) and the body's erotic exchange value on the commodity market (good looks, fitness), AIDS erases the 'gay' from the gay body, leaving it just a body.

Towards a general theory of pornography

Those gay men who continued to problematize the values of the commercial scene, instrumental sexual encounters and particularly pornography were cast as the enemy within, traitors to the cause. Not only were they seen as on the side of the homophobic mainstream, they were now on the side of death and disintegration:

> To hate porn is to hate sex. To hate sex is to hate being human. Porn tells us that sexuality is great, and, in the age of AIDS, that's a particularly important message to hear. (Witomski, cited in Watney, 1987: 76)

This elision of porn, sex and 'being human' is profoundly problematic since it both depends upon and reifies a troubling biological essentialism while at the same time pretending ignorance of the *structural* matrices of sexuality: gender, racism, material inequality, geographical and cultural location. Is sex in some way *the same* as being human? Does this hold for women as well as men, for straight as well as queer, for Muslim, Christian, Jew, atheist, Hindu, Buddhist? In what perversely liberal paradigm can the statement 'sexuality is great' be made meaningful? What *is* this thing, 'sexuality', which remains 'great' even if you have been sexually abused, raped, institutionalized for your sexual behaviours or tortured? While the naivety of this position clearly makes sense as 'the eroticization of an oppressed position' (Edwards, 1994: 108), it is both arrogant and foolish to propose that Witomski's statement can usefully be read out of its (very specific) context.

This aggressive commandeering of the gay political agenda ironically parallels the way in which certain lesbians – those who had sex with men, were into S/M, played with dildos, etc. – were symbolically excommunicated from the church of lesbian feminism by self-appointed guardians of authentic lesbian identity. In the wider context of gendered relations of power and their inscription in the field of the erotic, it is perhaps unsurprising that attempts to produce politically pure sexual practice should diverge diametrically between lesbians and gay men. Thus, while lesbian 'fundamentalism' mandates notions of sexual restraint, gay men's 'fundamentalism' mandates the opposite; pornography signifies celebration of sexual energy within the queer pornutopian paradigm while continuing (rightly) to signify degradation within the radical feminist paradigm. While both positions offer an accurate, coherent and cogent critique of the status of sexualized representation within their respective political constituencies, neither has yet produced a *general* theoretical model of pornography which works as well for heteroporn as for gay men's or lesbian's porn, and vice versa. Why waste time developing, of all things, a theory of pornography in the midst of a global pandemic, when millions are dying? Simply because sexualized representations are at the social epicentre of AIDS.

The need for 'good' porn?

It would be a foolish person indeed who argued that HIV spreads quite independently of socially constructed vectors of power; such is demonstrably not the case. Poverty, stigma and oppression have always been implicated in excess morbidity and mortality (Hart, 1985; Abel-Smith, 1994; Doyal, 1995), and it would be extraordinary if the human immuno-deficiency virus were somehow able to set aside these powerful influences on health and well-being. The economic exploitation of the so-called Third World by the overdeveloped West, the subordination of women to men, growing material inequalities within capitalist states, institutional racism and the exploitation of children and young people by adults are at least as important as homophobia in shaping the epidemiology of HIV infection.[10]

Power is not biologically assigned, it does not *naturally* inhere in bodies which are white-skinned, adult and have penises. Power grows out of, is assigned/expressed within and reproduced by *social* relations. And social relations are organized, interpreted, constructed and reproduced by *representational practices*. From mediaeval European paintings which depict kings, gods or heroes as twice the size of ordinary people to the post-modern iconographic fallout which constantly drizzles sexualized images of women across our retinas, representation determines (and is determined by) relations of power.

> The political chances of different groups in society – powerful or weak, central or marginal – are crucially affected by how they are represented, whether in legal and parliamentary discourse, in educational practices, or in the arts . . . How a particular group is represented determines in a very real sense what it can do in society. (Dyer, 1982: 43)

There has been a long-standing and fruitful feminist critique of the representation of gender, and of the implications of this for gendered relations of power. There has been a similar anti-racist critique of the representations of race, and a vigorous queer critique of homophobic representational practices. Becuase hegemony depends on continually reasserting control of the machinery of representation, these critiques have largely been marginalized, belittled as 'political correctness', and muted. They have undoubtedly been influential nevertheless. In response to AIDS, and because of the immediate and tenacious association of AIDS with homosex, there has been a vociferous and insistent queer critique of AIDS representational practices *as homophobic*. Surprisingly, where it might have been reasonable to expect an equally vigorous feminist critique of such practices as sexist, relatively few feminist voices have been heard (Treichler, 1988a; Zita Grover, 1988; McGrath, 1990; Wilton, 1992a; 1994a; 1995a), and most of these have been writing within the immediate context of queer, rather than within the established feminist context.

This epidemic confronts us all with the urgent necessity to speak about sex. Evasion, secrecy, pretence and inaccuracy – the common hallmarks of sex speech – are today potentially lethal. Since education is the *only* means we have to slow the spread of HIV, educational materials must be detailed and explicit in their representation of sex acts. Yet the actions of both the US and British governments, together with the vitriolic frothings of moral entrepreneurs and religious bigots, have demonstrated a determination that people are better off dead than well informed about sex. What we are witnessing at this stage in the history of the epidemic is not so much a plague as a holocaust-by-negligence. There is a life-or-death responsibility to overturn the arrogant self-interest which mandates such genocidal stupidity. Yet implicit in this responsibility is the imperative to eradicate, not to reproduce, the various oppressions which enable the virus to spread unchecked. AIDS educational materials, however sexually explicit, collude with the already dominant genocidal mandate of capitalist heteropatriarchy if they are racist, sexist or heterosexist.

Queer solutions?

The queer pornutopian paradigm is probably an effective matrix for AIDS education/resistance within a specific and limited social context. Because its acolytes are among the most privileged voices in radical AIDS com-mentary, and because their address is unreflexively narrow, there is a danger that the very real problems with this approach to AIDS education will be ignored. Among gay male writers and activists are many who have drawn attention to its problems, seeing it as unhelpful to gay men and the gay community. One of the most reductive presentations of the queer pornutopian position is Bronski's. He writes:

> Between sex and death gay people have dealt very well with sexual pleasure.[11]
> We have liberated sex from the confines of the state and religion, from the proscriptions of gender and have legitimized unadulterated sexual pleasure – purely creative, not procreative – as an end unto itself. (Bronski, 1989: 226)

Setting aside the dubious accuracy of these somewhat naively ahistorical claims to liberation, this position sets up a monolithic dualism which cannot be anything other than inadequate to the complexity of gay men's lives, let alone lesbians'. There is no place here from which religious gays, lesbian or gay parents or lesbian feminists may read 'gay people' as including themselves. In addition, the queer = life versus straight = death binary does nothing to disrupt the hegemony of reproductive hetero-polarity, it merely claims a position eccentric to that polarity and hence reinforces the definitional, normative status of that which it seeks to challenge. '[Q]ueer power at its most outrageous . . . has enshrined a familiar reading of sexuality: queer against straight, perversion over normality, life as opposed to lingering death' (Mort, 1994: 210).

Foundational to Queer as a political position/reverse discourse/identity is the notion of transgression. As Elizabeth Wilson points out, transgression is inevitably counterproductive, in that it always acts to reproduce the hegemony of that which it seeks to transgress:

> The concepts of transgression, dissidence, subversion, and resistance – which have become familiar in radical discourse since the mid 1980s – are oppositional, negative. They are the politics of being *against*, they are the politics of rebellion. Yet since they are cast in the terms set by that which is being rebelled against, they are the politics, ultimately, of weakness. (Wilson, 1993: 109)

It is important to develop a reflexive critique of the transgressive stance which is currently so significant a component of certain strands of political radicalism if we are to develop an effective strategy of resistance to AIDS (both as epidemic and oppressive cultural construct). Transgressivity has traditionally followed an Oedipal trajectory whereby successive generations react against the radicalism of the previous generation in what seems to be a cultural/political rite of passage (Stacey, 1994). Thus, simplistically, 'gay' superseded 'homosexual' and was in turn superseded by 'queer' as the rallying cry of anti-homophobic activism. This Oedipal imperative is problematic on two counts. Firstly, it risks throwing armfuls of useful babies out with a spoonful of bathwater, and necessitates a never-ending reinvention of the political wheel. Exemplary of this tendency is the current reaction against feminism: 'For some lesbians and gay men feminism seems to have become the wicked stepmother, originator of the hated political correctness against which it's become so important to rebel' (Wilson, 1993: 114),[12] and in the context of safer sex promotion, this is problematic indeed.

The second problem with this generational process is that it gives rise to a politics whose content is drastically compromised by the imperative to behave badly, and which is weakened by elitism. '[T]he transgressive impulse is ultimately elitist in so far as once a transgression becomes merely a widespread habit it has lost its magical aura of initiation and privileged experience' (ibid.: 111), and this gives rise to the need to up the ante, constantly devising newly disobedient behaviours.

Whether generational/Oedipal or not, transgression *per se* – exemplified in the queer-political context by a polymorphous-perverse self-conscious deviance – is inadequate as the basis for a radical political strategy. Reaffirming rather than displacing the hegemony of what it sets out to disobey, it utterly fails on a structural-political level to live up to the excitement it sometimes delivers on the individual-political level. This is something which has been dogging feminism for decades, and although AIDS activist groups such as ACTUP show signs of having moved beyond transgression for transgression's sake, the queer pornutopian position appears to be stubbornly replaying this familiar scenario.

Even for gay men, then, a merely transgressive celebration of porn/ homosex/life is inadequate to the demands of the epidemic. Such inadequacy may be directly harmful, as indicated by Norwegian research (Prieur, 1990) which found that some gay men experienced safe sex as not only emo- tionally cold and distant but also – ironically – as carrying associations of disease and death. If safer sex becomes positioned on the 'wrong side' of the porn/homosex/life versus repression/heterosex/death binary (and it is easy to imagine how this might happen), the implications for continued HIV trans- mission among gay men are grave. For other constituencies the notion of 'pornographic healing' is still more unhelpful. For women, whether lesbian or not, the disciplinary regime of reproductive heteropolarity tends to structure erotic possibilities (including the possibility of practising safer sex) and gender/sexual identities. This structuration is not amenable to dispersal through the dissemination of pornography – not least because pornography is implicated in the discursive constitution of the reproductive heteropolar paradigm/regime. In order to develop representational practices which will be effective in promoting safer sex among women, we first have to distinguish the pornographic from the erotic or sexually explicit (they are not coterminous), and to identify the harms done by pornography.

Harmless pleasures

Despite misrepresentation by (among others) socialist feminists (Segal, 1994; McIntosh and Segal, 1993) and gay men (Watney, 1987), feminists who have problematized pornography (and they have been radical feminists for the most part) have *not* identified either sexual explicitness or sexual arousal *per se* as damaging to women. For feminists the harm done by pornography lies in the discursive construction and reproduction of gendered relations of power, a process in which pornography is neither more nor less instrumental than other genres of representation (advertising, 'high' art, health education, etc.). The disproportionate attention which feminists have paid to pornography relative to other sets of texts is due to three intersecting factors. Firstly, although it is difficult to identify a discrete set of texts called 'pornography' which is in any meaningful way distinct from representational practices more generally, some feminists have identified what Susanne Kappeler terms a 'pornography of representation' (Kappeler, 1986); namely a saturation of the wider field of representation with semiotic codes which may or may not *originate* in pornography but which are certainly most unambiguously discernible in pornographic texts. Secondly, in a culture where the pornographic takes the burden of speaking about sex, the sexualized representational practices of pornography are accorded unreasonably high status *qua* sex speech. Feminists are therefore obliged to pay respectful attention to this representational corpus.

Because the pornographic is a privileged arena for speaking about sex, the issue of distinguishing between fantasy and reality presents an acute imperative. Establishing the distinction between fantasy and reality is easy with other sets of texts – warrior myths, fairy stories, horror films, science fiction novels – because 'reality testing' is relatively straightforward. It is abundantly clear that, for example, creatures do not commonly emerge from black lagoons to begin romantic cross-species liaisons with lovely young female explorers. However, the speaking about sex which provides the relentless soundtrack to postmodern industrial culture is almost exclusively fantastic. It is not from our elders, parents or teachers, nor from 'factual' texts, that we hear most about sex. It is from fictive discourse – feature films, porn magazines, pop music videos, fan magazines, grand opera, advertisements, women's magazines, novels, video games, postcards, paintings, T-shirts and rock concerts. Reality testing is inevitably compromised when sex is located in such a peculiar (and still inadequately theorized) cultural matrix, and this has very real implications for the consumption of pornography, in particular for the pornographic construction of sex/gender and its reproduction of heteropolar norms.

Finally, feminists have been concerned with pornography because of the proposition that it is instrumental in the socio-cultural constitution of erotic and gender subjectivity of both women and men. Although some gay men have taken a particularly hostile position towards the radical feminist critique of pornography, those same gay men have quite explicitly celebrated gay pornography for reasons very similar to the three outlined here. Gay porn is good, according to the queer pornutopian position, *because* it offers information about sex, it is instrumental in constituting a gay sexual subjectivity, and it both reflects and suggests sexual codes to saturate gay 'culture' and sexualize that culture. Clearly, since the social position of women and queer people (especially queer men) is – however ideologically interwoven – very different, the resistance movements originating in both political communities have developed quite different theoretical and political positions on porn. Yet neither position can be adequate without engaging with the other.

If a critique of pornography is to be meaningful, it needs to distinguish quite clearly between pornography and sexualized imagery. This is particularly important when sexualized imagery is such a crucial tool in the struggle against AIDS. For Watney (1987) the distinction between pornography and reality lies in the fact that porn is clearly to be read as fantasy. This lies behind his anxious insistence that pornography is *the* key to HIV infection control, for fantasy offers the *only* way to manipulate sexuality:

> such materials[13] remain the *only means* by which recalcitrant desire can be worked upon, at the level of fantasy itself, in order to encourage changes in sexual behaviour which are our only defence against the virus. (Watney, 1987: 76; emphasis added)

The notion of 'recalcitrant desire' here (ironically) returns to what Jeffrey Weeks calls the 'hydraulic model' of male sexuality; a sexuality constructed in obedience to the heteropolar paradigm as uncontrollable, susceptible not to rationality or responsibility but only to covert manipulation. It is only too easy to see this discourse as yet another example of the general failure throughout this epidemic to treat men like responsible adults. The emphasis on sexual fantasy as the privileged site of behaviour modification also reproduces a disturbingly naive construct of sex as the last refuge of the irrational:

> Changes in sexual behaviour cannot be forced, they can only be achieved through consent, consent which incorporates change into the very structure of sexual fantasy. (ibid.: 129)

Fantasy cannot be segregated so straightforwardly from the materialities which structure and are structured by the erotic. Commenting that the masculinization of gay culture, 'whether . . . constructed as an instrumental or sexual reification of masculinity . . . is still a reification of the masculine', Tim Edwards questions 'whether such a convincing psychic split or separation of sexual fantasy from more structural reality is . . . practical or possible' (Edwards, 1994: 97). In other words even gay porn, which restricts itself to representations of sex between men, produced by men for consumption by men, cannot be detached from the wider socio-cultural matrix, a matrix which is structured by *gendered* relations of power. As Richard Dyer suggests (1989: 199), 'One central question . . . remains whether gay erotica/pornography necessarily *exploits* women, or reproduces the *conditions* for their exploitation' (emphasis in original).

In what way may *any* pornography be said to reproduce the conditions for the exploitation of women? Certainly it would be difficult to argue that sexually explicit or arousing images harm women. To argue this is to collude with the oppressive reproductive heteropolar construct of sexual desire and agency as intrinsically masculine. Colin Richardson comes close to a useful definition of pornography by taking the word back to its Greek root *porne*, meaning prostitute. He suggests that:

> From the start, the meaning of the word was loaded. Because of the connection with prostitutes, pornography means more than just the graphic depiction in words or pictures of sexual activity. The sex in porn is a particular kind of sex, that which the prostitute symbolises: sex outside marriage or the bounds of romantic love: sex as a transaction: sex with no other context than desire or reward. (Richardson, 1991: 234)

This is a peculiarly male view of the 'kind of sex . . . which the prostitute symbolises', the view from the perspective of potential john rather than sex worker, a sexual consumer rather than sexual commodity. Although I think Richardson is quite right to go back to the etymological root, and right to insist on the significance of the association with prostitution, my own feminist approach results in something significantly different from his emphasis on irresponsibility. Prostitution is, after all, primarily an economic relation, and one in which responsibility (for the survival of self and possibly family) is generally a *key* issue for the prostitutes themselves. It is not simply because men are constructed as sexual actors that they are able to buy sex on the open market. The ideology which assigns sexual agency to men simultaneously stigmatizes extra-marital sexual activity and does so with particular vehemence in the case of women. Prostitution is not a free choice for women in the way that using prostitutes is a free choice for men; rather it is the way in which many women are obliged to fulfil their responsibilities to their dependants, given that they have severely restricted access to formal paid labour.

It is, above all, women's *economic dependency* which is expressed by prostitution, a dependency which both reflects and contributes to the general subordination of women to men. The economically independent woman is a rare and recent phenomenon even in the developed West, and the economically independent woman who *chooses* to be a prostitute is as rare as hen's teeth. Relations of sex work, then, express the *material* as well as the ideological inequalities of gender. The harm done by 'pornography' is that it reflects, naturalizes and eroticizes this very specific set of relations. What constitutes the pornographic then is not sex, but *gender*. My definition of pornography is 'any text which represents gendered relations of power in the sexual arena as natural, normal or desirable'. To indicate that this specific meaning is intended, and to reference the semantic root of the word as I deploy it, I employ a slash: porno/graphy. Given this highly specific meaning, it is inappropriate to use the word 'porno/graphy' to refer to the *content* of gay men's sexualized imagery, although (importantly) the existence of gay men's 'porn' as a body of texts constitutes, *in the absence of an equivalent body of texts by and for women*, part of the porno/graphic structure of the heteropatriarchy.

Such texts, by reflecting, reproducing, naturalizing and eroticizing the relations of power within which and by which women are deprived of civil liberties, citizenship, human rights and (crucially) bodily integrity, are instrumental in *preventing* the practice of safer sex – by men as well as women. Yet, as we have seen from existing safer sex educational materials, the porno/graphic vernacular saturates AIDS discourse. In the next chapter I want to suggest how we might develop representational practices in AIDS education which will move beyond both reproductive heteropolarity and queer pornutopian naivety to offer an effective catalyst to the adoption of safer sex.

Notes

1. Among which 'establishments' he includes, somewhat strangely, liberal and radical feminists.

2. Indeed, it is a position I share. See my earlier book *Antibody Politic: AIDS and Society* (1992a).

3. Since the phrase appears in quotes in the text, it may not be Watney's own. However, he does not directly reference it, although the context suggests that it might come from a Canadian safer sex video.

4. The Women's Liberation Movement and Black Power were both characterized by radical 'reverse discourse' strategies which were truly shocking at the time. The same strategy is currently an important part of the Disability Rights Movement.

5. I hesitate to use the word 'community' here, since each city – let alone each country – has a number of intersecting gay communities, and all of these may stand in distinct relation to the 'scene'. It has always been and continues to be the case that many gay men are profoundly critical of the excesses of the scene, and it is misleading to write as if one particular gay lifestyle were common to all, or even to the majority.

6. It should be noted that Watney is one of the most rabidly anti-feminist of gay writers. His influential book *Policing Desire* contains references to 'the lunatic fringe of the women's movement' (1987: 56) – by which he means feminists who have adopted a social constructionist position on heterosexuality – and he characterizes 'many of today's feminists' as having a 'monolithic moralism organised around the family unit' (p. 62), together with many such misrepresentations of feminism. Although extreme, Watney's position on feminism is not untypical of many gay (and some lesbian) writers.

7. And, I have to admit, by some lesbians and some feminists, whether lesbian or not.

8. What we now know to be a viral infection with a very long dormancy/latency period did not, of course, 'come' in the early 1980s in the USA. People had been sickening and dying of mysterious conditions since the early 1970s, conditions which we can retrospectively diagnose as AIDS related. There was, for example, a phenomenon known as 'junkie pneumonia' which spread among some populations of injecting street drug users in the 1970s, and which is now believed to have been caused by HIV infection. When I say that 'AIDS came', I am referring to the moment when the medical profession was forced to recognize that something new and unexpected had arrived and was killing people. This happened in the USA in the first years of the 1980s.

9. Of course at this point in the epidemic the need was much more urgent for gay men. Nevertheless, it is important to point out that the homophobic moralism which informed the British and US governments' AIDS prevention strategies was in nobody's interests.

10. It is tempting to state that these factors are *more* significant than homophobia on a global level, but to do so is to fall victim to the homophobic construct of homosexuality as a white Western problem. There is certainly growing evidence to suggest that homosexuality is more present (though, perforce, hidden) in Third World cultures than hegemonic racist/ homophobia constructs of those cultures allow. However, it is abundantly clear that heterosex is by far the commonest route of HIV transmission worldwide.

11. He means gay men here. Bronski's tendency to appear lesbian-inclusive is transparently tokenistic.

12. Unfortunately, rather than challenging this rebellion, Elizabeth Wilson is more concerned to rescue *socialist* feminism, insisting that socialist feminism 'opposed the political thought police of separatist feminism' and hence, by implication, leaving the entire body of non-socialist feminist thought properly contained within the wicked stepmother model. Such sectarianism is neither intellectually defensible nor politically useful.

13. This refers to *Chance of a Lifetime*, a video produced by Gay Men's Health Crisis which used pornographic vernacular to promote a safe sex message. My criticism of queer pornutopianism should not be read as an attack on such materials, which I would defend with some vigour as imaginative and effective interventions in gay men's struggle against AIDS.

7

Action = Life

Reproductive heteropolar regimes of gender have always made sex dangerous for women. The discursive package 'gender' constitutes femininity as inherently passive, responsive, responsible, nurturative and innocent of sexual desire/agency and masculinity as inherently active, initiating, irresponsible, unattached and potent with sexual desire/agency. In the context of sexually transmitted diseases this gives rise to and intersects with a specific discursive package 'sex', whereby 'womansex' coalesces around notions of disease, contamination, death, treachery, excess, liquidity and entropy, all representing danger to men. Within this paradigm, 'man' is assigned attributes of cleanliness, health, patriotism, life, discipline, order and control, attributes which may be summed up in the word 'virility'. The fact that we have no female equivalent of 'virility', no word for sexual potency which locates positive sexual energy at the heart of femininity as 'virility' does for masculinity, is, I suggest, profoundly significant.

Virility is constructed as an active creative force which may be discharged, leak or drain away. Since heteropolar discourse assigns no such active force to women but, rather, constructs woman-as-receptacle, the paradigmatic sexual behaviour associated with femininity is *seduction*, against which virility may be powerless. Moreover, because woman = sex = disease = death, this seduction is the embodiment of *thanatos*, an eroticized desire for death. In addition to the straightforward polarity of gender, whereby one sex is seen as the 'opposite' of the other in terms of biological functionalism, this discourse sets up a polarization within the field of the erotic, whereby virility is positioned as the positive pole of life and health while womansex is positioned as the negative pole of entropy and death.

This discursive package resonates throughout the modern period in the representation of female sexuality and especially of the sexually transmitted diseases. I have suggested that AIDS discourse, far from disrupting this paradigm, has powerfully reproduced and reasserted its dominance. Although, as Cindy Patton comments (see above p. 65) the paradigmatic body affected by AIDS is, in the West, a *male* body, this does not detract from my critique. Rather, it reinforces my argument, for Patton's paradigmatic body is a *gay* male body. It is a defining characteristic of reproductive heteropolarity that heterosexuality is understood to structure proper relations of gender/sex, such that that which is *other than* male (and maleness is both a function of and expressed through heterosex) is female. Thus gay men, together with all women, whether lesbian or not, constitute the feminine,[1] and this has been particularly overt within AIDS discourse.

The hegemony of reproductive heteropolarity has profound consequences for the epidemiology of HIV infection and for the fight against AIDS. As execrated feminized 'other', gay men are not generally regarded as of consequence. They are, as Simon Watney often remarks, an entirely 'disposable' population. It has become a truism that the epidemiological accident which resulted in HIV disease first manifesting to the medical profession in the bodies of young gay men was crucial to the rapid growth of the epidemic in the developed West. In telling contrast to the frantic media and political response to those other (much smaller-scale) medical emergencies legionnaire's disease, toxic shock syndrome, bovine spongiform encephalitis or the Tylenol scare, Western governments and the straight media maintained *for years* an indifference to HIV/AIDS which was undoubtedly instrumental in the spread of infection. AIDS is, in the now familiar words of former Centres for Disease Control director Mathilde Krim, 'an epidemic that was allowed to happen'.

For many AIDS activists and commentators, the social factors which contribute to the continuing growth of the epidemic appear clear. The first, familiar as a contributory factor in all ill-health, is poverty. The second, which is especially significant in the context of a virus which may be transmitted via sexual contact and injecting drug use, is the newly reascendant moralism of the New Right and religious fundamentalism. As long as governments, religious leaders and moral entrepreneurs continue to prioritize the attempt to control sexual behaviour over the attempt to control the spread of HIV infection, it will not be possible to make any impact on the rate of growth of the epidemic. The cynicism with which those in power capitalize on sickness and suffering to reinforce their ideological/political credibility is not unique to AIDS. It is a depressingly familiar phenomenon:

> [In the nineteenth century] venereal disease came to be seen as an affliction of those who wilfully violated the moral code, a punishment for sexual irresponsibility. *These infections were employed to argue for a more restricted sexuality.* So long as these social *uses* of the diseases have dominated medical and public approaches, therapeutic approaches to the problem have necessarily remained secondary. (Brandt, 1985: 5; first emphasis added, second in original)

Sexually transmissible diseases have a history of exploitation in the interests of the social control of sexuality. They have therefore been allocated a perverse socio-political *function* by powerful groups with an investment in the disciplinary organization of the erotic. Disturbingly, this social function has taken priority over attempts to cure disease or relieve suffering, a profoundly unethical (indeed, immoral) tendency only too familiar in the sociology and social history of AIDS.

Few health educators would disagree that the cynical opportunism which mandates the co-option of AIDS to justify anachronistic moralizing (see, we told you, the wages of sin *is* death!) seriously impedes the global community in its fight to survive AIDS. In the light of this grotesque and genocidal foolishness it is not hard to understand that the gay pornutopian paradigm for promoting safer sex appears both urgently necessary and uniquely valid. Indeed, for the communities of gay men decimated by both the virus and the homophobic negligence of those responsible for ensuring their well-being, this has been the case. It would be offensive and inaccurate to suggest otherwise. However, while not denying the appropriateness of this response for the urban gay male communities of the industrialized West, what we now need is a more general account of the implications of the gay pornutopian paradigm for safer sex promotion generally.

One man's porn?

In what ways does the hegemony of reproductive heteropolarity tend to impede the adoption of safer sex? It is clear that a woman socialized to passivity and sexual responsibility and a man socialized to agency and sexual irresponsibility would have great difficulty transcending their proper gender relation – whereby his needs, pleasure and wishes are privileged and hers go unrecognized – long enough to agree to non-penetrative sex (in defiance of the cultural script identifying penetration as *the* act with the capacity to bestow proper sex/gender identity on both of them) or condom use. It is perhaps also unsurprising that, since gender/sexual maturity is intimately bound up with disobedience to authority figures (parents) and to the general social prohibition on sexual activity, a health education campaign which seems to prohibit certain sexual acts is unlikely to succeed. When the act prohibited is precisely that which confers sexual adulthood *and* proper sex/gender identity, the outlook is pretty bleak. This is why it has been such a gift for gay men that their community of resistance was able to represent safer homosex as *itself* disobedient to homophobic authority. No such strategy is as readily available to heterosexuals.

The powerlessness of women – which accrues to their continued economic dependency on men – is both expressed through and reproduced by the heteropolar construct of gender/sex. Although everywhere subject to challenge and resistance, contingent on social and cultural location and inflected by class, 'race', dis/ability, age and sexual preference, women's powerlessness *as a class* remains the context in which *all* erotic relations – between men, between women, between women and men – take place. It is evident in the social phenomena which characterize and (to a degree) structure the institution of gender: rape, the sexual abuse of children, prostitution, sex tourism, the sexualization of the workplace, sexual harassment, the struggle over abortion rights, female genital mutilation, access to contraception (Seager and Olson, 1986; Doyal, 1995; Adkins, 1995). Indeed it might be suggested that artificial contraception is inevitable only within reproductive heteropolar relations of power – if penetration were not totemized and if women had complete bodily integrity as of right, an unintended pregnancy would be a relatively rare occurrence.

The consequence of women's specifically sexual (and sexualized)[2] powerlessness is that sex carries a high degree of risk for women. In the context of HIV/AIDS, this becomes true for men as well, since unprotected penetration has the potential to transmit HIV from the penetratee to the penetrator. A more general risk is engendered by the ideological imperatives of heteropolarity. Ideologically, this results in the positioning of 'men' (manly by virtue of an achieved heterosexuality) as un-gazed-upon producers/subjects of discourse in diametric opposition to 'women' as objects of discourse and of the gaze. Thus, in the context of HIV/AIDS, 'women' (read, biological females of whatever sexual preference plus gay men) are problematized as source and natural location of HIV infection while the possible association between men and HIV remains extra-textual/ extra-discursive/inconceivable. As masters of the machinery of representation, men do not subject themselves to scrutiny.

I have suggested that porno/graphy is integral to the heteropolar project. By naturalizing and sexualizing the gendered relations of power which subjugate women, porno/graphy partakes in the discursive constitution of subjectivity in such a way as to perpetuate the hegemony of reproductive heteropolarity. The pornographic vernacular, which locates sexual desire and agency in the male and constitutes the female body as the object of the desiring male gaze, is complicit in the discursive structuration of precisely those gendered relations of power which impede the adoption of safer heterosex.

Some argue (Dyer, 1989; Richardson, 1991; Watney, 1987) that gay men's porn avoids this complicity in the subordination of women because it represents only men:

> Pornography tells the story of our lives . . . We have had to rethink sex, and our porn – however imperfectly – reflects this. Our sex is sex between people of the same gender, which automatically removes the actual or symbolic inequalities deriving from gender difference. (Richardson, 1991: 240–1)

Some gay male writers seem to suggest that sex between men is not only located outside the institution of gender, but that gay men are profoundly different from non-gay men in the ways they choose to express their sexuality. This difference, significantly, is often seen as the result of oppression. The need to struggle, individually and collectively, against homophobia has, it is suggested, enabled gay men to develop a fluid, free and reflexive sexual practice which is less docile to the dictates of heteropolarity.

> the gay man is truly polymorphous: he may fuck and be fucked, and is as much at home in the one-fantasy position as the other. He does not need the defensive refuge of an identity rooted in exclusive models of domination and submission, which can never make sense of his psychic and physical mobility. To the extent, however, that these models constitute the major available iconography for sexual

fantasy in our culture, the gay man or lesbian is endlessly able to play off such roles against one another. (Watney, 1987: 28)

There is a latent essentialism here which I find disturbing. It is, perhaps, unsurprising that gay writers reveal a stereotypical set of assumptions about heterosex which is at least equalled by straight writers' obvious ignorance about homosex, but to conclude that gay men are so easily able to escape the ideological strai(gh)tjacket which Watney assumes straight men cannot resist is surely naive. It is a far from well-kept secret that many straight men love to be dominated, to dress in women's clothes or to be fucked with dildo or fingers by their female partners (Garber, 1991; Hite, 1981; Comfort, 1972). Moreover, the queer subculture which allows and supports this pick-and-mix fluidity among gay men is culturally extremely specific (Shepherd and Wallis, 1989), and extensive research has demonstrated a wide range of attitudes to fucking among relatively discrete cohorts of gay men (Davies et al., 1993).

To argue that gay men's porn sidesteps the issues of gendered power relations is to adopt a peculiarly hermetic model of discourse. The hermeneutic cycle between gay porn and gay consumers of porn does constitute a privileged site for the negotiation of gay sexual identity and for resistance to the homophobic/erotophobic discourses of execration which mandate the policing of homosex. However, neither homosex nor the representation of homosex can accomplish an absolute rupture of gay men's gender or sexuality from reproductive heteropolarity. There is a (limited) sense in which being gay *problematizes* the masculinity of gay men. Within the heteropolar paradigm there is little doubt that being queer *compromises* gender identity, and we have seen that the reverse discourse engendered in response to this *reasserts* masculinity as entirely proper to gay men. However much it may be protested that the construct of masculinity circulating in gay men's subcultural discourse is camp, parodic, ironic, this does not in and of itself disrupt or subvert hegemonic constructs of gender. Taking as it does the reproductive heteropolar construct of masculinity as the *raison d'être* of its counter-hegemonic energies, this reverse discourse ends up by reinforcing precisely what it seeks to displace. It is, after all, in the nature of hegemony that it co-opts resistance into reaffirmation.

There is an increasingly sophisticated critique of the 'new machismo' of urban gay culture among some politically astute gay writers, a critique which has become more urgent in response to HIV/AIDS.

> Living in a social space with considerable numbers of us who are HIV-positive or who have AIDS is, in itself, a major challenge to our ability to relate to each other in an emotionally supportive as well as a sexual way . . . The sexual 'big bang' which accompanied homosexuality emerging out of the shadows is just one stage along the way. (Shiers, 1988: 246)

The intersections among the epidemic, gay men's identity, sexual practices and community norms and mores are clearly more complex than gay pornutopianism would suggest. The single-gender content of gay men's porn is in no sense an indicator of its 'escape' from the traditional infrastructure of gender. Moreover, as a body of texts, it cannot be 'read' in isolation from other bodies of texts in the same discursive field, in particular sexualized heterotexts. Such a general reading of sexualized textual production can alert us to the cumulative effect of variously targeted sets of texts.

It becomes highly significant in this context that gay men's 'porn' is focused on *sex*, abundant, highly sexualized, specifically addressed to *gay* men and celebratory. In contrast, women's 'porn' is slippery in focus, meagre in quantity, only vaguely sexualized, carries a protean address inclusive of almost all sexual constituencies and celebrates *femininity* rather than the erotic (see above pp. 85–92). Non-gay men's 'porn', while super-abundant in quantity, is repetitive, anxious, and generally obedient to a very narrow sexual script. The straight male audience addressed appears to respond with boredom, guilt and an uneasy sense of being exploited (Hite, 1981).

Taken together, these three sets of texts act to reinforce, rather than challenging in any way, dominant constructs of sex/gender. They collude with and (however tangentially) re/produce the wider social subordination of women to men and hence comprise a porno/graphic discourse. It may be argued that the notion of men as sexual objects for other men constitutes a radical departure from heteropolar norms, but I do not believe that this is so. The social status of adult masculinity symbolically inheres in and is expressed and reinforced by sexual agency. Masculine sexual agency is located in the male desiring gaze, the privilege of evaluating and choosing sexual partners, the obligation to initiate sexual contact and the act of penetration. Since the address of gay men's porn is to men, this construct is thereby reproduced rather than disrupted. The masculinity of the reader, reasserted by consuming images of desirable sex objects, is more significant here than the gender of the sex objects represented. Indeed, intrinsic to this gendered semiotics is the feminization of the object of the male desiring gaze (and the concomitant masculinization of the subject of that gaze), whatever their biological sex.

What of lesbian 'porn' in this discursive package? The phallocentric patriarchal response to the threat of lesbian desire has traditionally been to deny or erase the possibility of lesbian existence (Wilton, 1995b; Donoghue, 1993). The anxiety engendered by women whose desire is for other women rather than for the phallus has been assuaged by co-opting lesbian sexuality into the porno/graphic imaginary. Thus, lesbian sex is represented either as pathetically inadequate because lacking access to a penis (e.g. Scruton, 1986) or as extended foreplay to the authentic act of heteropenetration, staged for the voyeuristic pleasure of the male.[3] Lesbian-produced porn breaks away from this silencing and co-option. Moreover, since discourses of reproductive heteropolarity deny sexual agency or subjectivity to women, and since an erotic address *to female readers* is oxymoronic within the heteropolar paradigm, lesbian porn may well constitute a radically transformative representational practice. In the current absence of porn independently produced by and for non-lesbian women (all straight women's porn that I know of is produced by and within the mainstream of the male-dominated publishing industry), lesbian porn is probably the *only* gender-transcendent representational practice around.

Health educators in dirty macs?

If porno/graphy impedes the adoption of safer heterosex,[4] to what extent may current HIV/AIDS health education be said to break away from the porno/graphic paradigm? It is clear from the previous chapter that the bulk of materials produced by HIV/AIDS educators in the West are directly and unreflexively informed by porno/graphy. Health educational materials which aim to promote safer sex both adhere to and reproduce the dominant taxonomic categories of gay man, lesbian, heterosexual man and hetero-sexual woman, and they do so in ways which reinforce reproductive heteropolar constructs of gender and the erotic. Thus, gay men's AIDS educational materials construct 'gay man' as pre-eminently *sexual*, as sexually inventive and open whilst remaining *exclusively* gay, and as par-taking of gay pornutopian notions of gay/queer identity. Material for lesbians is rare, non-erotic and permeated with the discourse of traditional femininity – including a concern with the responsibilities of mothering and of caring – and as such reproduces the erasure of lesbian sexuality and the refusal of female sexual agency/desire. This refusal is still more overt where the address is to 'women', who are constructed by/within AIDS health education materials as *offended by* the erotic, as defined by responsibility to others and as object rather than subject of sexual desire. The absence of materials explicitly addressed to non-gay men is instrumental in reasserting the privilege of masculinity as sexual subject – owner of the desiring gaze – rather than sexual object, and in constructing masculine desire (hetero by definition) as unproblematic and *at risk* from sexual contact with women (and this 'women' includes gay men).

Thus a health educational initiative such as the leaflet which carries the warning 'Advice in this leaflet is explicit. Please do not read it if you are easily offended' *is porno/graphic*, in that it reflects and reproduces *as natural* the sexualized relations of power which permeate and structure the ideological/material institution of gender. No body of AIDS educational texts can be deconstructed in isolation: all such texts are always already located in relation to hegemonic constructs of gender/sex. Thus, if the advice in the THT leaflet *Hot Sex Now* (see above, p. 82) were to be simultaneously addressed to heterosexual women (who might be – startlingly – assumed to harbour similarly positive feelings towards their male partners' bodies), and, suitably modified, to heterosexual men and to lesbians, none of the resultant texts could be said to be porno/graphic. In isolation, the leaflet *is* unavoidably porno/graphic. Similarly, if careful and sensitive advice of a less lecherous tone were available to gay men, lesbians and heterosexual women and men rather than solely to 'women', such advice would responsibly meet the needs of many people currently 'written off' by many safer sex educators. The (offensive) assumptions, that *all* gay men are best served by the gay pornutopian approach and that *all* women are likely to be motivated by erotophobia/responsibility, together comprise the porno/graphic. Since the subordination of women is such a key social factor in the continued rapid growth of the epidemic (Panos Institute, 1990a; Berer with Ray, 1993; Doyal et al., 1994), the unexaminedly porno/ graphic nature of almost all HIV/AIDS health educational materials is instrumental in *impeding* rather than facilitating the struggle against HIV infection and AIDS.

One final but important point. People with HIV infection or AIDS are seldom explicitly addressed in safer sex education (although some materials produced within/by the gay community comprise an honourable exception to this). As such, HIV positive people are discursively 'feminized' within/by the health educational paradigm. Their desires are invisible, their need for information denied; although (depressingly), the position of the non-infected individual who may wish to have sex with someone who has HIV is acknowledged more frequently.[5]

A clear example of this tendency is the (in)famous British press campaign initiated in 1988–89 by the Health Education Authority (and critiqued in McGrath, 1990) showing a beautiful white woman. The ad is in two parts. The first warns, 'If this woman had the virus which leads to AIDS, in a few years she could look like the person over the page.' The reader turns the page anxiously, expecting to see the beautiful woman reduced to the intubated, skeletal terminal patient already familiar in media AIDS iconography. What we see instead is an unchanged face, still beautiful, the woman still wearing the same clothes (no fashion victim, she!), with the caption, 'Worrying, isn't it.' Far from worrying, as McGrath points out, if you have just been diagnosed HIV positive. Hugely reassuring, in fact, to think that 'a few years' with the virus may leave you unchanged, still desirable. But, of course, the person addressed is masculinized by the address on two counts. Firstly, as male and 'at risk' from the archaic woman/sex/disease/chaos/death monster (who is, of course, far more likely to be at risk herself from sex with a potentially infected man). Secondly, as male *because uninfected*. The woman's continued beauty is *only* 'worrying' because she gives no sign of danger to a potential sexual partner, and that 'worrying' assumes an uninfected status for any potential partners. Because the discursive structuration of AIDS has with such docility replicated the (nationalistic) reproductive heteropolar scripting of sexually transmitted disease, the infected *become women*. Their needs become irrelevant, their social status is reduced to that of 'dangerous object', their continued good health something not to be celebrated but to be abhorred on behalf of the not-yet-infected. As Treichler so perceptively notes (1988a), disease and woman do, indeed, have something in common.

Beyond transgression, towards transformation

I hope it is by now clear that health educators have an urgent and abiding responsibility to subvert reproductive heteropolarity in the interests of people with HIV infection or AIDS and in the interests of effective prevention of HIV transmission to the not-yet-infected. I must at this point insist that this responsibility does not lie primarily with the urban gay men's communities, which have done so much (in the face of official negligence) to slow the sexual transmission of HIV among gay men. Such communities do have the (urgent) responsibility to produce and disseminate safer sex promotional materials which move beyond the gay pornutopian paradigm and which engage respectfully with the needs of those gay men who do not identify with the 'scene'. However, this responsibility is not theirs alone. Health education bodies in the statutory sector, at national and local level, have for too long evaded their responsibilities to their gay clients, and must develop materials to meet the needs of a wide range of gay men, not just the promiscuous, cruising gay man of both gay pornutopian and homophobic porno/graphic fantasy (although clearly individuals whose behaviour makes them repeatedly vulnerable require a great deal of support).

The greatest challenge and most urgent task is to engage with the needs of women (lesbian and heterosexual) and of non-gay men for education about safer sex which is as accurate, explicit and useful as that developed by gay men. This is something which is, by definition, extraordinarily difficult, because to do so is to set aside the semiotic codes and discursive conventions which structure the subjectivity and social relations of every individual in the industrialized West. In a very real sense, we have to invent a new *language* for talking about sex and about gender, and we have to do so without falling into the trap of setting up a reverse discourse which reproduces the hegemony of that which it seeks to displace. This requires nothing less than a radical paradigm shift, and one which will disturb the deepest roots of social life – gender relations and sexual relations. It is one of the most frightening aspects of this epidemic that, despite the urgency, such tectonic social/cultural change cannot be revolutionary, cannot be sudden. Writing about the impact of AIDS on lesbians, Tessa Boffin suggested that, despite the slowness of the process of change, the epidemic offers an opportunity for transformation in the way we speak about sex:

> So what can a girl do? It takes some women years to come out. It takes some women years to become sexual. It takes some women years to talk about sex, let alone talk 'dirty' . . . Maybe then we should see AIDS as an ironic opportunity to further engage in discussions about sexual identities, practices, fantasies and fears, and why or how we might want to adopt safer sex practices. (Boffin, 1990: 57–8)

But it is not only on the practical level of talking about sex that transformation must take place. On the ideological level the difficulties are, if
anything, greater, since female sexual autonomy – essential if the sexual
transmission of HIV is to be slowed – is literally inconceivable in the terms
of hegemonic ideology and discourse. As Teresa de Lauretis warns,
engaging with the practice of representation will not be enough *per se* to
redefine female sexuality:

> The difficulty of defining an autonomous form of female sexuality and desire in
> the wake of a cultural tradition still Platonic, still grounded in sexual (in)differ-
> ence, still caught in the tropism of hommo-sexuality, is not to be overlooked or
> wilfully bypassed. It is perhaps even greater than the difficulty in devising
> strategies of representation which will, in turn, alter the standard of vision, the
> frame of reference of visibility, of *what can be seen*. (de Lauretis, 1993: 152;
> emphasis in original)

Using (in)difference here to indicate that the notion of sexual 'difference' is
in fact phallocentric/androcentric androgenerated (and andro*generative*, in
that it is instrumental in the construction of masculinity across discursive
and cultural boundaries), de Lauretis proposes that female sexuality be
represented and defined *outside* hegemonic discursive conventions/doctrines.
For reproductive heteropolarity is a discourse of masculinity (in the sense
both of a discourse arising from masculinity and a discourse about
masculinity). And this discourse is most precisely expressed/reproduced in
the field of the erotic.

> The construction and appropriation of femininity in Western erotic ethos has . . .
> had the effect of securing the heterosexual social contract by which all sexualities,
> all bodies and all 'others' are bonded to an ideal/ideological hierarchy of males.
> (ibid.: 144)

Herein lies a cogent set of contradictions, since any health educators who
attempt to define and meet the 'real' needs of 'women' must (as must
feminists) come to terms with the recognition that femininity is intrinsic to/
implicit in reproductive heteropolar ideology (as, of course, is masculinity).
In the words of Luce Irigaray (1975: 86), '*the feminine occurs only within
models and laws defined by male subjects*. Which implies that there are not
really two sexes but only one. A single practice and representation of the
sexual.' However, although Irigaray's 'hommosexual' discourse constitutes
men as subjects and subjectivity as masculine, male 'subjects' are subject *to*
that discourse as much as subjects *of* and *by reason of* it.

All this is highly theoretical, and appears to offer little to the health
educator anxious to develop a radical and effective practice. However,
what it does offer is the recognition that, inasmuch as the constitution of
subject/object, male/female within the reproductive heteropolar paradigm is
a function of discourse (albeit a discourse which originates in and is
instrumental in maintaining male supremacy) then it is neither useful nor
necessary to agonize over the nature of 'real' or 'authentic' female (or male)
sexuality/identity that pre-exists discourse. Additionally, since gender/erotic

subjects are in part constituted through representational practices, such practices may, by assuming certain characteristics in the reader, *give rise to* (or at least increase the likelihood of) such characteristics. Susan Sontag recognized this in her long essay *On Photography* (1977), where she identifies the role of photographic representation, with its apparently unmediated reflection of 'reality', in the development of twentieth-century subjectivity.

For the health educator the problem of producing AIDS educational materials which rupture, rather than reproducing, currently hegemonic constructs/scriptings of gender and sexuality does not depend on any prior transformation in such constructs. Rather, health educational representational practices *may themselves* set the agenda for radical transformation, initiating the necessary paradigm shift rather than depending on some other social or cultural instrument to do so. This is certainly to ask much of health educators, but it is a not unprecedented enterprise. After all, we have seen that gay identity and gay community have both been significantly informed and structured by a conscious set of discursive/representational practices, strategically deployed in the struggle against homophobia. Since the institutionalization of gendered power relations compromises women's access to the machinery of representation to an even greater degree than it does gay men's, it is still more significant that feminism has catalysed a radical transformation in lesbian textual/representational practice:

> the women's movement has proved capable of producing lesbian texts in a context of total rupture with masculine culture, texts written by women exclusively for women, careless of male approval. (Wittig, cited in de Lauretis, 1993: 149)

Such an achievement would not have been possible without the partial shift in the *economic* relations of gender which enabled the women's movement to establish independent publishing houses, distribution outlets, etc. More significant in the context of health education is the existence both of a women's *movement*, and of a lesbian and gay *movement*. Such radical transformations in social relations, and in the representational practices which inform, reflect and reproduce those transformations, are successful only because of political will and collective struggle. The rich variety of gay men's safer sex promotional materials is due to the political will and collective struggle of an already politically astute community; likewise the limitations of such materials is rooted in the narrowness of the gay pornutopianism which currently motivates much gay/queer political activism in the urban centres of the industrialized West.

Come back feminism, all is forgiven?

It is noticeable that feminist activists and writers have not engaged with the question of HIV/AIDS representational practices to the extent that the queer communities have. This is perhaps strange, given the robust and theoretically coherent feminist critique of representational practices generally which developed in the 1970s and 1980s. My own suspicion is that critiquing sexualized or sexually explicit texts has become very difficult for feminists because of the unresolved conflicts (and extraordinary hostility) generated by the pornography debate and the so-called 'sex wars'. It is particularly hard for feminists to enter the representational debates engendered by AIDS because a feminist response has been pre-empted by those who claim that the radical feminist critique of porno/graphy is as much the enemy of safer sex promotion as is the moral agenda of the right wing (e.g. Manchester City Council, 1990; Watney, 1987). The feminist critique is presented as motivated by nothing more sophisticated than prudery and erotophobia (see Watney, 1987 for the most overt presentation of this position) or as an unthinking knee-jerk reaction: 'Sexual images *can* be about liberation, which is why the moral Right wants to ban them. But it is almost impossible to produce such images without someone raising the cry "pornography"' (Richardson, 1991: 239).

Collective political activism in the time of AIDS urgently needs an informed and sophisticated critique of relations of gender and the sexualization of gender. The traditional liberal critique of the repression of sexual minorities and the sexual libertarian concern for the rights of the individual to sexual expression are simply not adequate to deal with the complexities of the oppressions which have coalesced around and been compounded by this epidemic. Nor indeed are they adequate in the long term to eradicate homophobia, implicated as it is in the larger hegemonic project of reproductive heteropolarity.

Among lesbian and gay writers and activists the most theoretically and politically sophisticated are those informed by feminism. It is tempting to interpret the vocal anti-feminist stance of so many queer people as part of a 'backlash' against feminism, or as an Oedipal/generational function of the need to assert mature adult status in reaction to the radicalism of an earlier generation. But this is oversimplistic and, moreover, ignores the continuing engagement with feminist ideas among gay writers such as Richard Dyer, Tim Edwards and others.

Outside the queer milieu, meeting the HIV/AIDS educational needs of heterosexual people (whether women or men) requires a fundamental rupture of the reproductive heteropolar paradigm, a rupture which has traditionally been sited within feminist discourse. However, if feminist activism/theory is to support rather than impede the struggle against AIDS, it is important that feminists recognize the distinction between sexually explicit/erotic representational practices and the porno/graphic. Since the construction of women as innocent of desire/sexual agency is intrinsic to reproductive heteropolar ideology and discourse, the production and consumption of explicit sexualized images and texts *by* and *in the interests of* women (rather than by and in the interests of the male-owned porno/graphy industry) is equally intrinsic to an oppositional feminist discourse (Wilton, 1996a).

Of course, such an oppositional discourse is already established. Books of erotic fiction for both lesbian and non-lesbian women have been produced by feminist publishing houses, and lesbian-authored erotic photography is a growing (if beleaguered) enterprise. There is also a well-established commercial trend which exploits a female heterosexuality clearly perceived as active and desiring; a trend exemplified by the half-nude photographs of male popular icons from the Chippendales to Take That, from Marky Mark to Prince, which, despite a somewhat anxious attempt at recapture by the desiring gay male (e.g. Simpson, 1994), are consumed with some gusto by straight women.

In my job as lecturer in Health Studies I have often had cause to discuss HIV/AIDS health educational materials with my students – mostly nurses, social workers, health educators and youth workers. The nature of the jobs done by the trainee professionals I work with means that most of them are women. Without exception, they respond extremely positively to those explicit and erotic materials addressed to gay men whose address does not overtly exclude them (by, for example, depicting sexual activity taking place between two men). Faced with luscious colour images of half-naked, lone men, they cheer, clap and whistle. Faced with the kind of material typically addressed to women they groan, hiss and become very angry. Why should *men*, they want to know, *still* have all the fun? And what kind of idiot still believes all that offensive rubbish about women being prudes and uninterested in sex?

The point of my argument is that for health educators to offer these women what they want would constitute nothing but good professional practice on three counts. Firstly, good and effective health education is rooted in consultation, in *identifying* the needs and wants of specific groups, *not* in making ill-informed assumptions about those needs. Secondly, if erotic and sexually explicit materials have worked for (some) gay men, it should at least be grounds for research into whether they work for (some) women. Finally, and most significantly, offering women a readership position which invests *them* with the desiring gaze, whether the object of that gaze is male or female but *especially* when it is male, transgresses/transcends the regime of reproductive heteropolarity and offers the possibility for transforming gendered subjectivity and gendered relations of power. This is a transformation which is already taking place, in the marketplace and in some political contexts (the women's movement, among some groups of lesbians), and it is ridiculous as well as counterproductive for health education not to exploit and further the transformative process.

Somewhere man . . . ?

Central to this counter-hegemonic process must be the radical repositioning of heterosexual men. The very act of addressing heterosexual men *as* heterosexual ruptures the reproductive heteropolar paradigm whereby masculinity is the property of those who sexually penetrate women and 'man' *means* heterosexual man. It simultaneously challenges the association of AIDS with the 'women' of the epidemic – biological women and queers of all genders. Texts which *overtly* construct and address a specifically heterosexual male reading position (rather than doing so by default, as is the case for so many addressed to a supposedly gender-neutral 'general public') would constitute a radical departure from current practice. This address is not, however, enough *per se*; such texts must avoid colluding with porno/graphic conventions and must refuse to reproduce the sex = woman = disease = chaos construct.

Texts addressed to heterosexual men face a particular problem in negotiating their semiotic codes in relation to porno/graphy. There is a strong case for asserting that *any* sexualized representation of women intended for consumption by men partakes of and reproduces the institution of the porno/graphic, simply because such representations replicate the construction of the desiring gaze as male and the proper object of that gaze as female. Heterosexual men (as a class and as individuals) have an over-determined response to sexualized representations of women, a response which, for many, incorporates feelings of unease, resentment, shame or an awareness of being exploited (Hite, 1981). It would be facile to suggest here strategies for engaging with this deeply problematic situation, but good health educational practice mandates at the very least consulting with a wide range of heterosexual men's groups in order to develop anti-porno/graphic, sexually explicit and sex-positive materials.

There is a marked tendency within gay pornutopian commentary on AIDS to elide 'sex-positive' and 'erotic'. The argument that sexual fantasy is so unruly, so various and so urgent that safer sex promotion can only work if it turns people on is demonstrably hoist on its own petard. For if fantasy is so protean and unpredictable (and the committed student of erotic literature and art is in fact more likely to remark on the *limitations* of the erotic imagination), then any particular text will be experienced as erotic by only a relatively small number of individuals. A realistically cost-effective strategy – and in the increasingly market-orientated world of health care this is likely to be ever more important – cannot afford to put resources into the production of materials whose effectiveness is limited to the particular group of individuals who have the good fortune to find it arousing. Moreover, it is quite straightforward to represent safer sex in ways which are explicit, sex positive and accessible without being intentionally arousing. Two examples of good practice spring to mind. The first is a set of six cards produced by the Terrence Higgins Trust, each focusing on a specific piece of information. Each card carries a brightly coloured new-psychedelic image overlaid with a single word in upper case: FUCK, SUCK, KISS, LICK, WANK and FACT, and on the reverse gives a brief summary of essential information. Thus the 'LICK' card has a list of street terms: clit licking, eating pussy, muff diving, etc., and the advice 'Low risk of getting HIV. More risk of getting HIV if your mouth's a mess (bleeding gums or sores). More risk during her period. No risk to you if you're licked. No HIV risk from arse licking. No risk if you use a barrier.'[6] All the cards carry an invitation to call the THT helpline for further information. The images on the front of the cards contain puns on street terms which are so tenuous (and so dreadful when you do get the joke) that figuring them out adds a unique element of pleasure. Thus a flight of steps represents 'going down', a scuba diver's legs disappearing out of sight suggest 'muff diving', white froth speaks of 'hand shandy', etc. The cards manage to be fun, sex positive and redolent of a specific cultural idiom while making no attempt to be erotic.

The second is a quite substantial booklet produced by a British charity, the Haemophilia Foundation, in 1990. Called *Haemophilia, HIV and Safer Sex – The Choice is Here*, the booklet represents sex in both text and illustrations as enjoyable, intimate and worthy of imaginative experimentation. Because the illustrations are highly stylized drawings (by Luis Cook) rather than photographic or 'realistic', they manage to convey a sense of pleasure and robust physicality without falling into the porno/graphic vernacular.

Promoting health: some wider policy implications

It is generally accepted (see above pp. 42–3) that health education is, on its own, inadequate to initiate substantial or sustained behavioural change. Indeed the successful adoption of safer sexual practices by large numbers of gay men has followed on, not simply from well-designed leaflets and posters, but from a unique saturation of urban gay subcultures in safer sex initiatives in a variety of forms. Gay men's telephone sex line ads frequently carry safe sex reminders, the winner of the annual 'Mr Leather' contest in the US spends his year engaged in safer sex education, the Sisters of Perpetual Indulgence promote their gospel 'get the rubber habit' (Doran, 1994), and a hunk drawn by Tom of Finland proclaims 'I use rubber'. The urban gay scene has been (in the context of HIV infection at least) transformed into an exemplary health-promoting environment.

If the stated aim of health promotion is to make the healthy choice the easy choice, the complexities are daunting when the healthy choice involves such specific changes in sexual behaviour. To promote sexual health in the age of AIDS demands massive and wide-ranging shifts in public policy in many areas, ranging from education to sexual offences legislation. Such broad-based policy shifts are not unique to the demands of the HIV epidemic: World Health Organization targets established as part of the *Health for All* programme in 1984 recognize that the promotion of health inevitably requires nothing less than a radical reshaping of national and global infrastructures (see Table 1).

Table 1   *WHO Targets for 'Health for All', 1984*

I	Prerequisites for health: – Equity, minimum income, nutrition, peace, water, sanitation, housing, education, work, political will and public support
II	Lifestyle: – opportunity – health promotion
III	Environment: – hazardous conditions
IV	Appropriate care: – priorities – primary health care
V	Research: – health knowledge
VI	Health development support: – policy – management – education and training – technology assessment

Source: WHO, 1984, *Targets for Health for All*, WHO, Copenhagen

This set of requirements holds as true for HIV/AIDS health promotion as it does for any other health concern. There can be no doubt, for example, that warfare is likely to exacerbate HIV transmission in the areas affected and reduce the survival time and quality of life of people with HIV or AIDS. But there are specific and detailed policy changes needed in the industrialized West if the sexual transmission of HIV is to be effectively prevented.

It is painfully ironic that a 'new' sexually transmissible infection should have come to public attention at the very time when the New Right in Britain and the US was consolidating a political position predicated on the avowed intention of 'saving' the (heterosexual, nuclear, biological) family from the perceived threat of a sexual permissiveness proclaimed as the damaging legacy of the 1960s. The ideological association of national strength with proper masculinity, sexual restraint and discipline (both fiscal and social) which was the familiar foundation of the policies of the Third Reich, re-emerged with new vigour under Thatcher and Reagan.[7] 'A nation of free people,' declared Prime Minister Margaret Thatcher in 1987, 'will only continue to be great if family life continues and the structure of that nation is a family one' (cited in Watney, 1987: 24). Integral to the expressed project of protecting the family were legislative measures designed to protect children from the horrors of school sex education. The far Right Conservative Family Campaign stated their intention to:

> save a generation from the immoral propaganda for promiscuity, homosexuality, anti-marriage views, fornication, and encouragement of children to experiment with sex, which has passed in far too many schools during the last two decades as sex education. (*The Times*, 23 September 1986)

The Conservative administration responded by putting sex education in the hands of school governors, allowing parents to withdraw their children from sex education lessons, and instructing schools to teach about sex in a context which promoted abstinence, marriage and monogamy. This position is clearly unacceptable in the context of HIV/AIDS, and shifts in government policy around sex education in schools are urgently needed. It is simply not tolerable to prioritize the promotion of monogamous marital sexuality over the promotion of health.

Similarly, the censorship legislation which has had such a dire effect on the distribution of safer sex materials must be overturned, prostitution should be decriminalized,[8] an equal age of consent must apply to all – lesbian, gay or straight – and legislation which discriminates against lesbian or gay citizens (such as Section 28 of the 1988 Local Government Act in Britain) must be repealed. Such initiatives are of direct relevance to the promotion of sexual health.

Yet, as I hope this book has demonstrated, matters of sexuality cannot be separated from matters of gender. Transforming the reproductive heteropolar paradigm which structures subjectivity and social life (through relations of disobedience and resistance as well as through capitulation or compliance) requires that gender and the erotic be integrated, both theoretically and politically. Thus, measures to eradicate the material and social subordination of women (appropriate income maintenance and welfare policies, equality of opportunity in education/training and in the labour market, adequate provision for dependent children and adults, etc.) are, as Jonathan Mann recognizes, extremely important in HIV/AIDS health promotion (Mann, 1993).

Above all, the *bodily integrity of women* is a *sine qua non* of AIDS health promotion. The criminalization of rape within marriage, free and general access to safe contraception and abortion, the criminalization of sexual harassment, equal rights and protections for lesbians and the right to give (or withhold) informed consent to all medical procedures have long been the focus of feminist struggle. Because such measures would establish women's rightful 'ownership' of their bodies, and because that notion is ideologically intolerable within reproductive heteropolarity, effective HIV/AIDS health promotion cannot occur in their absence – and this is as true of the so-called Third World as it is of the industrialized West (Panos Institute, 1990a).

Reproductive heteropolarity, and the oppression which it engenders, is probably the most significant stumbling block to preventing the sexual transmission of HIV in the West. It is also, of course, radically implicated in the philosophy, ideology, political and social structures of all nations (Morgan, 1984). It is embodied and reproduced in the doctrine of the world's most powerful religions: Christianity, Islam, Judaism, Sikhism and Hinduism; and is foundational to the nation state and to capitalism. No paradigm, however, is monolithic or constant, and the hegemony of reproductive heteropolarity is everywhere negotiated, challenged and compromised. It is not only the urban queer communities of the West which have developed radical and transgressive interventions in response to AIDS. It is not merely wishful thinking, masochism or romanticism to see AIDS as bringing opportunity in the wake of tragedy. As Susan Ardill and Sue O'Sullivan suggest, the epidemic offers a very real opportunity to transform dominant relations of gender/sex, simply by giving women (and, by implication, men) permission to speak about sex in new ways:

> AIDS has opened up space and legitimized a feminist discussion on sexuality. AIDS gave us all permission, to talk sex, talk desire, talk 'dirty', talk fear, talk confusion, talk fantasy. It gives us the chance to talk about how we feel about men, how we feel about feelings, pressures to be sexual, pressures not to be sexual. It gives us a chance to talk about lesbianism, heterosexuality, bisexuality; about the links between sex and sexuality, class, gender, race, age, and what is really 'normal' or 'natural' about any of it. (Ardill and O'Sullivan, cited in Boffin, 1990: 161)

The chance AIDS gives us is the chance to move in a new direction, away from the offensive and oppressive frameworks in which we have spoken about sex and gender. It is a chance which we dare not refuse to take, for the body – desiring, enmeshed in meanings, threatened by disease and death – is made vulnerable to HIV not primarily by mere biology but by its location in the web of social forces which Foucault described as 'a political field':

> The body is directly involved in a political field; power relations have an immediate hold upon it; they invest it, train it, torture it, force it to carry out tasks, to perform ceremonies and to emit signs. (Foucault, 1979: 25)

Perhaps AIDS offers the opportunity to initiate a radical transformation in the political field in which bodies are located. Perhaps, unexpectedly, the business of health promotion has itself been transformed into the (potential) site for the most radical shift in social relations we may imagine. This is in no sense to suggest that the millions who have died and will die with HIV infection and unpleasant opportunistic infections are martyrs to a glorious cause, nor that their suffering is somehow magically made 'worthwhile' by the possibilities engendered by the epidemic. Dying of the miserable results of an HIV-engendered collapsed immune system is probably few people's chosen way to end their life, and the waste of lives caused by the negligence of governments, the profit motive and the legacy of colonialism remains cause for deep and bitter anger. The potential for social transformation which AIDS represents does not erase or diminish the tragedy of the epidemic. Rather, AIDS *impels* us towards social transformation in the interests of those already infected and of preventing transmission of the virus to the as yet uninfected. While social transformation does not confer martyrdom on the suffering and the dead, to refuse to instigate that transformation is to betray them. AIDS offers not so much an opportunity, more an obligation.

Notes

1. There is an argument, which space does not allow me to enter into properly here, that the white racist imaginary positions the black man alongside this 'feminine', and that relations between white and black tend to be structured around the struggle between white and black *men* over the status and privileges of virility. This gendered polarity also nuances struggles between owning- and working-class men; poverty, dependency on other men and unemployment all being seen as 'emasculating' and shameful.

2. Anyone who doubts that feminine powerlessness is eroticized in hegemonic discourse should cast an eye over cultural artefacts such as Alex Comfort's best-selling *The Joy of Sex* or Pauline Reage's *L'Histoire d'O*, or the Japanese *manga* comic genre.

3. A special 'lesbian' issue of British soft porn magazine *For Men* (1995) depicts women in pseudo lesbian scenarios, reassuring the viewer that: 'it's done wonders for my relationship with Jake. He gets unbelievably rampant when I get home after a session with Lisa and tell him all about what I've been up to' (p. 24), or 'Dawn and I are both such horny little bitches. We love girl to girl sex but we do need cock as well. Our very favourite scene is us two together, plus a couple of well hung guys . . . Of course the guys are watching us and we're watching the enormous dicks waiting for us' (p. 36)

4. It may well impede the adoption of safer homosex between men as well. Much has been made of the successes of erotic safer sex material for gay men, but I suspect that there are men for whom it is not as successful. Judging by the ambiguity which some gay men express towards porn (and some gay men have said to me in the past that they find explicit safer sex materials offensive), this is an area which urgently needs further research. It may be the case that the needs of many gay men are not being met adequately by the pornutopian approach to safer sex education.

5. Thus continuing the 'feminization' of the person with HIV or AIDS, since the desiring gaze is located in the non-infected individual, and the sex/disease/death package which signifies female sexuality remains the property of the already infected *object* of desire.

6. Although I suspect that some young people may need help in working out what a 'barrier' is . . .

7. Both the US and Britain are currently struggling to avoid the consequences of the post-colonial (now post-communist) era and of international capitalism – namely, the dwindling power of once-imperial Britain and one-time 'leader of the free world' America. It appears that Fascist politics tends to become dominant during periods of national decline (as in Germany before the rise of the Third Reich).

8. Decriminalization is not the same as regulation. Most sex workers oppose state regulation of prostitution, which simply replaces the role of the pimp or organized crime syndicate with institutional pimping.

References

Abel-Smith, Brian (1994) *An Introduction to Health: Policy, Planning and Financing*. London, Longman.

Abelove, Henry (1994) 'The Politics of the "Gay Plague": AIDS as a US Ideology', in Michael Ryan and Ann Gordon (eds) *Body Politics: Disease, Desire and the Family*. Boulder, CO, Westview Press.

Acevedo, Cynthia (1990) 'Too Much Denial', in ACT UP/New York Women & AIDS Book Group (eds) *Women, AIDS and Activism*. Boston, South End Press.

ACT UP/New York Women & AIDS Book Group (eds) (1990) *Women, AIDS and Activism*. Boston, South End Press.

Adams, Mary L. (1988) 'All That Rubber, All That Talk: Lesbians and Safer Sex', in Ines Reider and Patricia Ruppelt (eds) *AIDS: The Women*. San Francisco, Cleis Press.

Adkins, Lisa (1995) *Gendered Work: Sexuality, Family and the Labour Market*. Buckingham, Open University Press.

Aggleton, Peter (1990) *Health*. London, Routledge.

Aggleton, Peter, Horsley, Chrissie, Warwick, Ian and Wilton, Tamsin (1990) *AIDS: Working with Young People*. Horsham, AVERT.

Allison, Dorothy (1995) *Skin: Talking about Sex, Class and Literature*. London, Pandora.

Altman, Dennis (1986) *AIDS and the New Puritanism*. London, Pluto Press.

Armitage, Gary, Dickey, Julienne and Sharples, Sue (1987) *Out of the Gutter: A Survey of the Treatment of Homosexuality by the Press*. London, Campaign for Press and Broadcasting Freedom.

Baaden, James (1991) 'Sells Papers, Ruins Lives: Homophobia and the Media', in Tara Kaufmann and Paul Lincoln (eds) *High Risk Lives: Lesbian and Gay Politics after THE CLAUSE*. Bridport, Prism Press.

Baynes, Ken (1972) *Art and Society: Sex*. (Arts Council of Great Britain). London, Lund Humphries.

Beardshaw, Virginia, Hunter, David and Taylor, Rosemary (1990) *Local AIDS Policies: Planning and Policy Development for Health Promotion*. London, Health Education Authority/The King's Fund.

Berer, Marge with Ray, Sunanda (eds) (1993) *Women and HIV/AIDS: An International Resource Book*. London, Pandora.

Black HIV/AIDS Network (1991) *AIDS and the Black Communities*. London, BHAN.

Bly, Robert (1992) *Iron John: A Book about Men*. Shaftesbury, Dorset, Element.

Boffin, Teresa (1990) 'Angelic Rebels: Lesbians and Safer Sex', in Teresa Boffin and Sunil Gupta (eds) *Ecstatic Antibodies: Resisting the AIDS Mythology*. London, Rivers Oram.

Brandt, Allan M. (1985) *No Magic Bullet: A Social History of Venereal Disease in the United States since 1880*. Oxford, Oxford University Press.

Brandt, Allan M. (1988) 'AIDS: From Social History to Social Policy', in Elizabeth Fee and Daniel M. Fox (eds) *AIDS: The Burdens of History*. Cambridge, MA, MIT Press.

Breitman, Patti, Knutson, Kim and Read, Paul (1987) *How to Persuade Your Lover to Wear a Condom: And Why You Should*. San Francisco, Prima.

British Broadcasting Corporation (1995) *AIDS: Behind Closed Doors*. (Text adapted from *Horizon* programme transmitted 4 December). London, Broadcasting Support Services.

Bronski, Michael (1984) *Culture Clash: The Making of a Gay Sensibility*. Boston, South End Press.

Bronski, Michael (1989) 'Death and the Erotic Imagination', in Erica Carter and Simon Watney (eds) *Taking Liberties: AIDS and Cultural Politics*. London, Serpent's Tail.

Brown, Jennifer (1988) 'Life and Death with Joan: A Lesbian Discusses Her Lover's Suicide', in Ines Reider and Patricia Ruppelt (eds) *AIDS: The Women*. San Francisco, Cleis Press.

Brown, Judith C. (1989) 'Lesbian Sexuality in Medieval and Early Modern Europe', in Martin Bauml Duberman, Martha Vicinus and George Chauncey Jnr. (eds) *Hidden from History: Reclaiming the Gay and Lesbian Past*. Harmondsworth, Penguin.

Brownmiller, Susan (1975) *Against Our Will: Men, Women and Rape*. London, Secker and Warburg.

Bury, Judy (1994) 'Women and HIV/AIDS: Medical Issues', in Lesley Doyal, Jennie Naidoo and Tamsin Wilton (eds) *AIDS: Setting a Feminist Agenda*. London, Taylor and Francis.

Butcher, Kate (1994) 'Feminists, Prostitutes and HIV', in Lesley Doyal, Jennie Naidoo and Tamsin Wilton (eds) *AIDS: Setting a Feminist Agenda*. London, Taylor and Francis.

Butler, Judith (1990) *Gender Trouble: Feminism and the Subversion of Identity*. London, Routledge.

Butler, Judith (1994) 'Critically Queer', *GLQ: A Journal of Lesbian and Gay Studies*, 1 (1): 17–32.

Califia, Pat (1988) *Sapphistry: The Book of Lesbian Sexuality*, 3rd edn. Tallahassee, FL, Naiad Press.

Califia, Pat (1995) 'Slipping', in Randy Turoff (ed.) *Lesbian Words: State of the Art*. New York, Richard Kasak.

Campbell, Bea (1987) 'Bealine', *Marxism Today*, (December): 9.

Clift, Stephen and Kanabus, Annabel (1993) *AIDS and Young People* (booklet). Horsham, AVERT.

Cockburn, Cynthia (1991) *Brothers: Male Dominance and Technological Change*, 3rd edn. London, Pluto Press.

Comfort, Alex (1972) *The Joy of Sex*. London, Quartet.

Comstock, Gary David (1991) *Violence against Lesbians and Gay Men*. New York, Columbia University Press.

Cooper, Emmanuel (1994) *The Sexual Perspective: Homosexuality and Art in the Last 100 Years in the West*, 2nd edn. London, Routledge.

Coote, Anna and Campbell, Beatrix (1987) *Sweet Freedom: The Struggle for Women's Liberation*, 2nd edn. Oxford, Basil Blackwell.

Cousins-Mills, Jane (1988) *Make It Happy, Make It Safe: What Sex Is All About*. Harmondsworth, Penguin.

Coxon, Anthony P.M. (1985) *The 'Gay Lifestyle' and the Impact of AIDS* (Project Sigma Working Paper No. 1). Cardiff, University of Cardiff Social Research Unit.

Crimp, Douglas (1988) 'How to Have Promiscuity in an Epidemic' in Douglas Crimp (ed.) *AIDS: Cultural Analysis, Cultural Activism*. Cambridge, MA, MIT Press.

Crimp, Douglas, with Rolston, Adam (1990) *AIDS DemoGraphics*. Seattle, Bay Press.

Cvetkovich, Ann and Gordon, Avery (1994) 'Not in Our Name: Women, War, AIDS', in Michael Ryan and Avery Gordon (eds) *Body Politics: Disease, Desire and the Family*. San Francisco, Westview Press.

Davidson, Neil (1990) *Boys Will Be? Sex Education and Young Men*. London, Bedford Square Press.

Davies, Peter et al. (1990) *Longitudinal Study of the Sexual Behaviour of Homosexual Males under the Impact of AIDS: A Final Report to the Department of Health* (Project SIGMA Working Papers). London, DoH.

Davies, Peter, Hickson, Ford, Weatherburn, Peter and Hunt, Andrew (1993) *Sex, Gay Men and AIDS*. London, Falmer Press.

Day, Sophie and Ward, Helen (1990) 'The Praed Street Project: A Cohort of Prostitute Women', in Martin Plant (ed.) *AIDS, Drugs and Prostitution*. London, Routledge.

de Groot, Wayne and Nicholls, Francis (1992) 'AIDS in Asia', *Knave*, 24 (9): 12–15.

de Lauretis, Teresa (1993) 'Sexual Indifference and Lesbian Representation', in Henry

Abelove, Michele Aina Barale and David M. Halperin (eds) *The Lesbian and Gay Studies Reader*. London, Routledge.

D'Emilio, John and Freedman, Estelle (1988) *Intimate Matters: A History of Sexuality in America*. New York, Harper and Row.

DiClemente, Ralph J. (ed.) (1992) *Adolescents and AIDS: A Generation in Jeopardy*. London, Sage.

Doane, Mary Ann (1985) 'The Clinical Eye: Medical Discourse in the "Women's Film" of the 1940s', in Susan Rubin Suleiman (ed.) *The Female Body in Western Culture: Contemporary Perspectives*. Cambridge, MA, Harvard University Press.

DoH (Department of Health) (1992) *Health of the Nation*. London, Her Majesty's Stationery Office.

Donoghue, Emma (1993) *Passions between Women: British Lesbian Culture 1668–1801*. London, Scarlet Press.

Doran, Denis (1994) *Get the Rubber Habit! The Sisters of Perpetual Indulgence* (postcard book). London, Blase.

Doud, Kat (1990) 'Demanding a Condom', in ACT UP/NY Women and AIDS Book Group (eds) *Women, AIDS and Activism*. Boston, South End Press.

Doyal, Lesley (1994) 'HIV and AIDS: Putting Women on the Global Agenda', in Lesley Doyal, Jennie Naidoo and Tamsin Wilton (eds) *AIDS: Setting a Feminist Agenda*. London, Taylor and Francis.

Doyal, Lesley (1995) *What Makes Women Sick? Gender and the Political Economy of Health*. London, Macmillan.

Doyal, Lesley, Naidoo, Jennie and Wilton, Tamsin (eds) (1994) *AIDS: Setting a Feminist Agenda*. London, Taylor and Francis.

Dyer, Richard (1982) 'The Celluloid Closet', *Birmingham Arts Lab Bulletin*, April–June: 6–9.

Dyer, Richard (1989) 'A Conversation about Pornography', in Simon Shepherd and Mick Wallis (eds) *Coming on Strong: Gay Politics and Culture*. London, Unwin Hyman.

East Midlands Men's Health Network (1994) *National Men's Health Resource Catalogue*. Scarsdale, North Derbyshire Health.

Edwards, Tim (1994) *Erotics and Politics: Gay Male Sexuality, Masculinity and Feminism*. London, Routledge.

Ehrenreich, Barbara and English, Deirdre (1979) *For Her Own Good: 150 Years of the Experts' Advice to Women*. London, Pluto.

Ewles, Linda and Simnett, Ina (1985) *Promoting Health: A Practical Guide to Health Education*. Chichester, John Wiley.

Fee, Elizabeth (1988) 'Sin versus Science: Venereal Disease in Twentieth-Century Baltimore', in Elizabeth Fee and Daniel Fox (eds) *AIDS: The Burdens of History*. Berkeley, University of California Press.

Firestone, Shulamith (1979) *The Dialectic of Sex: The Case for Feminist Revolution*. London, The Women's Press.

Fitzpatrick, Ray, McLean, John, Boulton, Mary, Hart, Graham and Dawson, Jill (1990) 'Variation in Sexual Behaviour in Gay Men', in Peter Aggleton, Peter Davies and Graham Hart (eds) *AIDS: Individual, Cultural and Policy Dimensions*. London, Falmer Press.

Formani, Heather (1991) *Men: The Darker Continent*. London, Macmillan.

Foucault, Michel (1976) *A History of Sexuality, Vol. 1: An Introduction*. Harmondsworth, Penguin.

Foucault, Michel (1979) *Discipline and Punish*. Harmondsworth, Penguin.

Francatelli, Charles Elme (1861/1993) *A Plain Cookery Book for the Working Classes*. Whitstable, Pryor Publications.

French, Marilyn (1992) *The War against Women*. London, Hamish Hamilton.

Frye, Marilyn (1990) 'Lesbian "Sex"', in J. Allen (ed.) *Lesbian Philosophies and Cultures*. New York, State University of New York Press.

Garber, Marjorie (1991) *Vested Interests: Cross-Dressing and Cultural Anxiety*. Harmondsworth, Penguin.

Gavey, Nicola (1993) 'Technologies and Effects of Heterosexual Coercion', in Sue Wilkinson and Celia Kitzinger (eds) *Heterosexuality: A Feminism and Psychology Reader*. London, Sage.

Giddens, Anthony (1992) *The Transformation of Intimacy: Sexuality, Love and Eroticism in Modern Societies*. Cambridge, Polity.

Gillies, Pamela and O'Sullivan, Anna (n.d.) *Streetwize UK*, 1, AIDS issue: Nottingham, Nottingham Health Authority and the Department of Community Medicine and Epidemiology, University of Nottingham.

Gilman, Sander L. (1988) 'AIDS and Syphilis: The Iconography of Disease', in Douglas Crimp (ed.) *AIDS: Cultural Analysis, Cultural Activism*. Cambridge, MA, MIT Press.

Glanz, Alan (1991) 'Gay Bars: Positive Changes, But No Room for Complacency', in *AIDS Dialogue*, 9 (February): 6. London, Health Education Authority.

Gordon, Peter and Mitchell, Louise (1988) *Safer Sex: A New Look at Sexual Pleasure*. London, Faber and Faber.

Gorna, Robin (1992) 'Delightful Visions: From Anti-porn to Eroticising Safer Sex', in Lynne Segal and Mary McIntosh (eds) *Sex Exposed: Sexuality and the Pornography Debate*. London, Virago.

Graham, Hilary (1993) *Hardship and Health in Women's Lives*. Hemel Hempstead, Harvester Wheatsheaf.

Grau, Gunter (1995) *Hidden Holocaust? Gay and Lesbian Persecution in Germany 1933–45*. London, Cassell.

Green, Gill (1994) 'Sex, Love and HIV: The Impact of an HIV-positive Diagnosis upon the Sexual Relationships of Men and Women with HIV'. Paper given at the British Sociological Association conference, Sexualities in Social Context, University of Central Lancashire, March.

Haddon, Celia and Prentice, Thomson (1989) *Stronger Love, Safer Sex*. London, Macmillan.

Haeberle, Erwin J. (1989) 'Swastika, Pink Triangle and Yellow Star: The Destruction of Sexology and the Persecution of Homosexuals in Nazi Germany', in Martin Bauml Duberman, Martha Vicinus and George Chancey (eds) *Hidden from History: Reclaiming the Gay and Lesbian Past*, Harmondsworth, Penguin.

Hague, Gill and Malos, Ellen (1993) *Domestic Violence: Action for Change*. Cheltenham, New Clarion Press.

Hart, Nicky (1985) *The Sociology of Health and Medicine*. Ormskirk, Causeway Press.

HEA (Health Education Authority) (1988) *AIDS Programme Information Pack*. London, HEA.

Hite, Shere (1981) *The Hite Report on Male Sexuality*. London, Macdonald.

Hobbs, Andrew (1992) 'The Invisible Man', *Versus the Virus*, 3 (Spring/Summer): 10–12.

Holland, Janet, Ramazanoglu, Caroline, Scott, Sue, Sharpe, Sue and Thompson, Rachel (1991) 'Between Embarrassment and Trust: Young Women and the Diversity of Condom Use', in Peter Aggleton, Graham Hart and Peter Davies (eds) *AIDS: Responses, Interventions and Care*. London, Falmer Press.

Holland, Janet, Ramazanoglu, Caroline, Scott, Sue, Sharpe, Sue and Thompson, Rachel (1994a) 'Desire, Risk and Control: The Body as a Site of Contestation', in Lesley Doyal, Jennie Naidoo and Tamsin Wilton (eds) *AIDS: Setting a Feminist Agenda*. London, Taylor and Francis.

Holland, Janet, Ramazanoglu, Caroline, Scott, Sue, Sharpe, Sue and Thompson, Rachel (1994b) 'Achieving Masculine Sexuality: Young Men's Strategies for Managing Vulnerability', in Lesley Doyal, Jennie Naidoo and Tamsin Wilton (eds) *AIDS: Setting a Feminist Agenda*. London, Taylor and Francis.

Homans, Hilary (ed.) (1985) *The Sexual Politics of Reproduction*. Aldershot, Gower.

Homans, Hilary and Aggleton, Peter (1988) 'Health Education, HIV Infection and AIDS', in Peter Aggleton and Hilary Homans (eds) *Social Aspects of AIDS*. London, Falmer Press.

Hoogland, Renee C. (1994) 'Perverted Knowledge: Lesbian Sexuality and Theoretical Practice', *Journal of Gender Studies*, 3 (1): 15–29.

hooks, bell (1994) 'Women's Studies: Beyond Western Cultural Imperialism'. Plenary address to Women's Studies Network (UK) annual conference, University of Portsmouth, 9 July.

Hooven III, Valentine (1992) *Tom of Finland: Introduction*. Cologne, Benedikt Taschen.

Hort, Vada (1986) 'Lesbians and A.I.D.S', *Gossip: A Journal of Lesbian Feminist Ethics*, (2): 90–6.

Humphreys, Land (1970) *The Tearoom Trade*. London, Duckworth.

Huston, Nancy (1985) 'The Matrix of War: Mothers and Heroes', in Susan Rubin Suleiman (ed.) *The Female Body in Western Culture: Contemporary Perspectives*. Cambridge, MA, Harvard University Press.

Institute of Medicine (National Academy of Sciences) (1986) *Mobilizing against AIDS: The Unfinished Story of a Virus*. Cambridge, MA, Harvard University Press.

Irigaray, Luce (1975) 'Cosi fan tutti', in *This Sex Which is Not One*, trans. Catherine Porter. Ithaca, NY, Cornell University Press, 1985.

Jackson, Gail (1988) 'Promotion of Safer Sex: Or, the Patriarchy, Misogyny and the Condom'. Unpublished paper, Terrence Higgins Trust, London.

Jarman, Derek (1991) *Queer Edward II*. London, British Film Institute.

Jeffreys, Sheila (1990) *Anticlimax: A Feminist Perspective on the Sexual Revolution*. London, The Women's Press.

Jones, Carol and Mahony, Pat (1989) *Learning Our Lines: Sexuality and Social Control in Education*. London, The Women's Press.

Juhasz, Alexandra (1993) 'Knowing AIDS through the Televised Science Documentary', in Corinne Squire (ed.) *Women and AIDS: Psychological Perspectives*. London, Sage.

Kappeler, Susanne (1986) *The Pornography of Representation*. Cambridge, Polity.

Katz, Jonathan Ned (1983) *Gay/Lesbian Almanac: A New Documentary*. New York, Harper Colophon.

Kayal, Philip M. (1993) *Bearing Witness: Gay Men's Health Crisis and the Politics of AIDS*. Boulder, CO, Westview Press.

King, Edward (1993) *Safety in Numbers: Safer Sex and Gay Men*. London, Cassell.

Kippax, Susan, Noble, Jason, Prestage, Garrett, Crawford, June, Campbell, Danielle, Baxter, Don and Cooper, David (1990) 'The Importance of Gay Community in the Prevention of HIV Transmission' (paper). Sydney, University of Macquarie School of Behavioural Sciences.

Kippax, Susan, Noble, Jason, Prestage, Garrett, Crawford, June, Campbell, Danielle, Baxter, Don and Cooper, David (1995) 'Sexual Negotiation: Negotiated Safety Revisited'. Paper presented at HIV, AIDS and Society conference, Macquarie University, Sydney, July.

Kirkpatrick, Alison and Kirkpatrick, David (1987) *AIDS*. Edinburgh, Chambers.

Kiss and Tell (1991) *Drawing the Line: Lesbian Sexual Politics on the Wall*. Vancouver, Press Gang.

Kiss and Tell (1994) *Her Tongue on My Theory: Images, Essays and Fantasies*. Vancouver, Press Gang.

Kitzinger, Celia and Wilkinson, Sue (1993) 'The Precariousness of Heterosexual Feminist Ideologies', in Mary Kennedy, Cathy Lubelska and Val Walsh (eds) *Making Connections: Women's Studies, Women's Movements, Women's Lives*. London, Taylor and Francis.

Kleinberg, Seymour (1987) 'The New Masculinity and Gay Men', in Michael Kaufman (ed.) *Beyond Patriarchy: Essays by Men on Pleasure, Power and Change*. Toronto, Oxford University Press.

Kramer, Larry (1990) *Reports from the Holocaust: The Making of an AIDS Activist*. Harmondsworth, Penguin.

Lees, Sue (1993) *Sugar and Spice: Sexuality and Adolescent Girls*. Harmondsworth, Penguin.

Leonard, Zoe (1990) 'Lesbians in the AIDS Crisis', in ACT UP/NY Women and AIDS Book Group (eds) *Women, AIDS and Activism*. Boston, South End Press.

Lerro, Marc (1989) 'Safer Sex Behaviour Reinforcement in Public Parks'. Unpublished report produced for AIDS Prevention Project, Dallas County Health Department, Texas.

Llewellyn-Jones, Derek (1985) *Herpes, AIDS and Other Sexually Transmitted Diseases*. London, Faber and Faber.

Lowy, Ilana (1993) 'Testing for a Sexually Transmissible Disease 1907–1970: The History of the Wassermann Reaction', in Virginia Berridge and Philip Strong (eds) *AIDS and Contemporary History*. Cambridge, Cambridge University Press.

Lucia-Hoagland, Sarah and Penelope, Julia (eds) (1988) *For Lesbians Only: A Separatist Anthology*. London, Onlywomen Press.

Lupton, Deborah (1994) *Moral Threats and Dangerous Desires: AIDS in the News Media*. London, Taylor and Francis.

McCarthy, Tony (ed.) (1972) *Bawdy British Folk Songs*. London, Wolfe.

Macciocchi, Maria-Antonietta (1979) 'Female Sexuality in Fascist Ideology', *Feminist Review*, 1: 76–9.

McClintock, Anne (1995) *Imperial Leather: Race, Gender and Sexuality in the Colonial Contest*. London, Routledge.

McGrath, Roberta (1990) 'Dangerous Liaisons: Health, Disease and Representation', in Tessa Boffin and Sunil Gupta (eds) *Ecstatic Antibodies: Resisting the AIDS Mythology*. London, Rivers Oram.

McIntosh, Mary and Segal, Lynne (eds) (1993) *Sex Exposed: Sexuality and the Pornography Debate*. London, Virago.

Manchester City Council HIV/AIDS Policy Group (1990) *AIDS, HIV and Civil Liberties*. Report of conference, 22–3 March.

Mann, Jonathan (1993) 'AIDS, Health and Human Rights', *Terrence Higgins Trust Newsletter*, 29 (December): 3.

Mellor, Phillip A. and Shilling, Chris (1993) 'Modernity, Self-Identity and the Sequestration of Death', *Sociology*, 27 (3): 411–32.

Metcalf, Andy (1985) 'Introduction', in Andy Metcalf and Martin Humphries (eds) *The Sexuality of Men*. London, Pluto.

Miles, Agnes (1991) *Women, Health and Medicine*. Buckingham: Open University Press.

Millett, Kate (1977) *Sexual Politics*. London, Virago.

Misha (1993) 'Witness', in Marge Berer with Sunanda Ray (eds) *Women and HIV/AIDS: An International Resource Book*. London, Pandora.

Moeti, Matshidiso R. (1995) 'Gender, Sexual Health and Reproductive Health Promotion', in *AIDS/STD Health Promotion Exchange*. Royal Tropical Institute/Southern Africa AIDS Information Dissemination Service, No. 3.

Morgan, Robin (ed.) (1984) *Sisterhood is Global*. Harmondsworth, Penguin.

Mort, Frank (1994) 'Essentialism Revisited? Identity Politics and Late Twentieth-Century Discourses of Homosexuality', in Jeffrey Weeks (ed.) *The Lesser Evil and the Greater Good: The Theory and Politics of Social Diversity*. London, Rivers Oram.

Naidoo, Jennie and Wills, Jane (1994) *Health Promotion: Foundations for Practice*. London, Baillière, Tindall.

Oakley, Ann (1976) 'Wisewoman and Medicine Man: Changes in the Management of Childbirth', in Juliet Mitchell and Ann Oakley (eds) *The Rights and Wrongs of Women*. Harmondsworth, Penguin.

Paalman, Maria (ed.) (1990) *Promoting Safer Sex*. Amsterdam, Swets and Zeitlinger.

Panos Institute (1989) *AIDS and Children: A Family Disease*. London, Panos Publications and Save the Children.

Panos Institute (1990a) *Triple Jeopardy: Women and AIDS*. London, Panos Publications.

Panos Institute (1990b) *The Third Epidemic: Repercussions of the Fear of AIDS* (in association with the Norwegian Red Cross). London, Panos Publications.

Panos Institute (1992) *The Hidden Cost of AIDS: The Challenge of HIV to Development*. London, Panos Publications.

Pateman, Carole (1992) 'Equality, Difference and Subordination: The Politics of Motherhood and Women's Citizenship', in Gisela Bock and Susan James (eds) *Beyond Equality and Difference: Citizenship, Feminist Politics and Female Subjectivity*. London, Routledge.

Patton, Cindy (1985) *Sex and Germs: The Politics of AIDS*. Boston, South End Press.

Patton, Cindy (1989) 'Resistance and the Erotic', in Peter Aggleton, Graham Hart and Peter Davies (eds) *AIDS: Social Representations, Social Practices*. London, Falmer Press.

Patton, Cindy (1990) *Inventing AIDS*. London, Routledge.

Patton, Cindy (1994) *Last Served? Gendering the HIV Pandemic.* London, Taylor and Francis.

Patton, Cindy and Kelly, Janis (1987) *Making It: A Woman's Guide to Sex in the Age of AIDS.* New York, Firebrand.

Phillips, Keith (1993) 'Primary Prevention of AIDS', in Marion Pitts and K. Phillips (eds) *The Psychology of Health: An Introduction.* London, Routledge.

Pitts, Marion, Magunse, Noleen and McMaster, John (1994) 'Students' Knowledge of the Use of Herbs and Other Agents as Preparation for Intercourse', *Health Care for Women International*, 15 (2): 91–9.

Porter, Dorothy and Porter, Roy (1988) 'The Enforcement of Health: The British Debate', in Elizabeth Fee and Daniel Fox (eds) *AIDS:The Burdens of History.* Berkeley, University of California Press.

Prestage, Garrett, Kippax, Sue and Noble, Jason (1995) 'Positive Men and Sexuality'. Paper given at third annual HIV, AIDS and Society conference, Macquarie University, Sydney, July.

Prieur, A. (1990) 'Gay Men: Reasons for Continued Practice of Unsafe Sex', *AIDS Education and Prevention*, 2 (2): 110–17.

Raymond, Janice (1996) 'A Vision of Lesbian Sexuality', in Lynne Harne and Elaine Miller (eds) *All the Rage: Reasserting Radical Lesbian Feminism.* London, The Women's Press.

Rich, Adrienne (1981) 'Compulsory Heterosexuality and Lesbian Existence', in (1987) *Blood, Bread and Poetry: Selected Prose 1979–1985.* London, Virago.

Richardson, Colin (1991) 'Porn Again', in Tara Kaufmann and Paul Lincoln (eds) *High Risk Lives: Lesbian and Gay Politics after THE CLAUSE.* Bridport, Prism Press.

Richardson, Diane (1989) *Women and the AIDS Crisis.* London, Pandora.

Richardson, Diane (1990) 'AIDS Education and Women: Sexual and Reproductive Issues', in Peter Aggleton, Peter Davies and Graham Hart (eds) *AIDS: Individual, Cultural and Policy Dimensions.* London, Falmer Press.

Richardson, Diane (1992) 'Constructing Lesbian Sexualities', in Ken Plumer (ed.) *Modern Homosexualities: Fragments of Lesbian and Gay Experience.* London, Routledge.

Richardson, Diane (1993) 'Sexuality and Male Dominance', in Diane Richardson and Virginia Berridge (eds) *Introducing Women's Studies.* London, Macmillan.

Richardson, Diane (1994) 'Inclusions and Exclusions: Lesbians, HIV and AIDS', in Lesley Doyal, Jennie Naidoo and Tamsin Wilton (eds) *AIDS: Setting a Feminist Agenda.* London, Taylor and Francis.

Rieder, Ines and Ruppelt, Patricia (eds) (1988) *AIDS: The Women.* San Francisco, Cleis Press.

Rooney, Michael (1991) 'Gay Men and HIV: Health Promotion Still Needed', *AIDS Matters*, 5 (June): 4–5. London, National AIDS Trust.

Ryan, Barbara (1992) *Feminism and the Women's Movement.* London, Routledge.

Schmidt, Gunter (1990) 'The Influence of AIDS on Sexuality', in Maria Paalman (ed.) *Promoting Safer Sex.* Amsterdam, Swets and Zeitlinger.

Schoppmann, Claudia (1995) 'The Position of Lesbian Women in the Nazi Period', in Gunter Grau, *Hidden Holocaust? Gay and Lesbian Persecution in Germany 1933–45.* London, Cassell.

Scriven, Angela and Orme, Judy (eds) (1996) *Health Promotion: Professional Perspectives.* London, Macmillan/The Open University.

Scruton, Roger (1986) *Sexual Desire: A Philosophical Investigation.* London, Weidenfeld and Nicolson.

Seager, Joni and Olson, Ann (1986) *Women in the World: An International Atlas.* London, Pan Books.

Segal, Lynne (1994) *Straight Sex: The Politics of Pleasure.* London, Virago.

Shepherd, Simon and Wallis, Mick (eds) (1989) *Coming on Strong: Gay Politics and Culture.* London, Unwin Hyman.

Shiers, John (1988) 'One Step to Heaven?', in Bob Cant and Susan Hemmings (eds) *Radical Records: 30 Years of Lesbian and Gay History.* London, Routledge.

Shilts, Randy (1987) *And the Band Played On: Politics, People and the AIDS Epidemic.* New York, St Martin's Press.

Simpson, Mark (1994) *Male Impersonators: Men Performing Masculinity*. London, Cassell.

Smith, Anna Marie (1992) 'Resisting the Erasure of Lesbian Sexuality: A Challenge for Queer Activism', in Ken Plummer (ed.) *Modern Homosexualities: Fragments of Lesbian and Gay Experience*. London, Routledge.

Smith, Francis B. (1979) *The People's Health 1830–1910*. New York, Holmes and Meier.

Smyke, Patricia (1991) *Women and Health*. London, Zed Books.

Smyth, Cherry (1990) *Lesbians Talk Queer Notions*. London, Scarlet Press.

Sontag, Susan (1977) *On Photography*. Harmondsworth, Penguin.

Spence, Christopher (1986) *AIDS: Time to Reclaim our Power*. London, Lifestory.

Squire, Corinne (ed.) (1993) *Women and AIDS: Psychological Perspectives*. London, Sage.

Stacey, Jackie (1994) 'Lesbian Thinking Today'. Paper given at round-table colloquium, British Sociological Association annual conference, Sexualities in Social Context, Preston, March.

Staub, Roger (1991) 'The Swiss Hot Rubber Campaign: Self-proclaimed Group Take Responsibility for Informing their Community', in *AIDS Prevention through Health Promotion: Facing Sensitive Issues*. Geneva, World Health Organization and Royal Tropical Institute, Amsterdam.

Stewart, Fiona (1991) 'Why It's Not On to Tell Him', *Youth Issues Forum* (journal of the Youth Affairs Council of Victoria, Australia), Summer: 11–14.

Stewart, Fiona (1992) 'Young Women and Condoms: On Whose Terms is Safe Sex?' Paper presented to biennial conference of the Australian Association of Adolescent Health, University of Melbourne, November.

Stimpson, Catharine R. (1988) *Where the Meanings Are: Feminism and Cultural Spaces*. London, Routledge.

Stoddard, Tom (1989) 'Paradox and Paralysis: An Overview of the American Response to AIDS', in Erica Carter and Simon Watney (eds) *Taking Liberties: AIDS and Cultural Politics*. London, Serpent's Tail.

Stoltenberg, John (1989) *Refusing to Be a Man*. Glasgow, Collins.

Te Puni Kokiri (1994) *Mate Ketoketo/Arai Kore: A Report about HIV/AIDS and Maori*. Wellington, NZ, Te Puni Kokiri.

Terrence Higgins Trust (1991) *Hot Sex Now* (booklet). London, THT.

Townsend, Peter, Davidson, Nick and Whitehead, Margaret (1988) *Inequalities in Health: The Black Report and The Health Divide*. Harmondsworth, Penguin.

Treichler, Paula (1988a) 'AIDS, Gender and Biomedical Discourse: Current Contests for Meaning', in Elizabeth Fee and Daniel M. Fox (eds) *AIDS: The Burdens of History*. Berkeley, University of California Press.

Treichler, Paula (1988b) 'AIDS, Homophobia and Biomedical Discourse: An Epidemic of Signification', in Douglas Crimp (ed.) *AIDS: Cultural Analysis, Cultural Activism*. Cambridge, Mass, MIT Press.

Ussher, Jane (1991) *Women's Madness: Misogyny or Mental Illness?* London, Harvester Wheatsheaf.

Warwick, Ian, Aggleton, Peter and Homans, Hilary (1988) 'Young People's Health Beliefs and AIDS', in Peter Aggleton and Hilary Homans (eds) *Social Aspects of AIDS*. London, Falmer Press.

Watney, Simon (1987) *Policing Desire: Pornography, AIDS and the Media*. London, Methuen.

Watney, Simon (1990) 'Safe Sex as Community Practice', in Peter Aggleton, Peter Davies and Graham Hart (eds) *AIDS: Individual, Cultural and Policy Dimensions*. London, Falmer Press.

Watney, Simon (1994) 'How We May Mourn Them', *Gay Times*, June: 38.

Weeks, Jeffrey (1986) *Sexuality*. London, Routledge.

Weeks, Jeffrey (1990) *Coming Out: Homosexual Politics in Britain from the Nineteenth Century to the Present*, revised edn. London, Quartet.

Weeks, Jeffrey (1991) *Against Nature: Essays on History, Sexuality and Identity*. London, Rivers Oram.

Weindling, Paul (1993) 'The Politics of International Co-ordination to Combat Sexually

Transmitted Diseases, 1900–1980s', in Virginia Berridge and Philip Strong (eds) *AIDS and Contemporary History*. Cambridge, Cambridge University Press.

Wellings, Kaye (1983) 'Sickness and Sin: The Case of Genital Herpes'. Paper presented to the Medical Sociology Group of the British Sociological Association, York, September.

Whitehead, Tony (1989) 'The Voluntary Sector: Five Years On', in Erica Carter and Simon Watney (eds) *Taking Liberties: AIDS and Cultural Politics*. London, Serpent's Tail.

WHO (World Health Organization) (1991) *Aids Health Promotion Exchange* (newsletter of the WHO Global Programme on AIDS), (4): 1.

WHO (World Health Organization) (1994) *AIDS: Images of the Epidemic*. Geneva, WHO.

Wilson, Elizabeth (1993) 'Is Transgression Transgressive?' in Joseph Bristow and Angelia Wilson (eds) *Activating Theory: Lesbian, Gay and Bisexual Politics*. London, Lawrence and Wishart.

Wilton, Tamsin (1992a) *Antibody Politic: AIDS and Society*. Cheltenham, New Clarion Press.

Wilton, Tamsin (1992b) 'Desire and the Politics of Representation: Issues for Lesbians and Heterosexual Women', in Hilary Hinds, Ann Phoenix and Jacky Stacey (eds) *Working Out: New Directions for Women's Studies*. London, Falmer Press.

Wilton, Tamsin (1994a) 'Feminism and the Erotics of Health Promotion', in Lesley Doyal, Jennie Naidoo and Tamsin Wilton (eds) *AIDS: Setting a Feminist Agenda*. London: Taylor and Francis.

Wilton, Tamsin (1994b) 'Silences, Absences and Fragmentation', in Lesley Doyal, Jennie Naidoo and Tamsin Wilton (eds) *AIDS: Setting a Feminist Agenda*. London, Taylor and Francis.

Wilton, Tamsin (1995a) *Lesbian Studies: Setting an Agenda*. London, Routledge.

Wilton, Tamsin (1995b) 'On Not Being Lady Macbeth: Some (Troubled) Thoughts on Lesbian Spectatorship', in Tamsin Wilton (ed.) *Immortal, Invisible: Lesbians and the Moving Image*. London, Routledge.

Wilton, Tamsin (1996a) 'Genital Identities: An Idiosyncratic Foray into the Gendering of Sexualities', in Lisa Adkins and Vicki Merchant (eds) *Power and the Organization of Sexuality*. London, Macmillan.

Wilton, Tamsin (1996b) *Finger-Licking Good: The Ins and Outs of Lesbian Sex*. London, Cassell.

Wilton, Tamsin and Aggleton, Peter (1991) 'Condoms, Coercion and Control: Heterosexuality and the Limits to HIV/AIDS Education', in Peter Aggleton, Graham Hart and Peter Davies (eds) *AIDS: Responses, Interventions and Care*. London, Falmer Press.

Wise, Sue and Stanley, Liz (1987) *Georgie Porgie: Sexual Harassment in Everyday Life*. London, Pandora.

Zita Grover, Jan (1988) 'AIDS: Keywords', in Douglas Crimp (ed.) *AIDS: Cultural Analysis, Cultural Activism*. Massachusetts, MIT Press.

Index

ETRUSCAN
Myths